Routledge Revivals

Dakota War-Whoop:

or
Indian Massacres and War in Minnesota, of 1862-'3

Dakota War-Whoop:

or
Indian Massacres and War in Minnesota, of 1862-'3

by
Harriet E. Bishop McConkey

First published in 1970 by Ross & Haines, Inc.

This edition first published in 2018 by Routledge
2 Park Square, Milton Park, Abingdon, Oxon, OX14 4RN
and by Routledge
52 Vanderbilt Avenue, New York, NY 10017, USA

Routledge is an imprint of the Taylor & Francis Group, an informa business

© 1970 Taylor & Francis

All rights reserved. No part of this book may be reprinted or reproduced or utilised in any form or by any electronic, mechanical, or other means, now known or hereafter invented, including photocopying and recording, or in any information storage or retrieval system, without permission in writing from the publishers.

Publisher's Note
The publisher has gone to great lengths to ensure the quality of this reprint but points out that some imperfections in the original copies may be apparent.

Disclaimer
The publisher has made every effort to trace copyright holders and welcomes correspondence from those they have been unable to contact.
A Library of Congress record exists under ISBN:

ISBN 13: 978-0-367-02358-4 (hbk)
ISBN 13: 978-0-367-02361-4 (pbk)
ISBN 13: 978-0-429-39996-1 (ebk)

DAKOTA WAR WHOOP:

DAKOTA WAR WHOOP:

OR,

INDIAN MASSACRES

AND

WAR IN MINNESOTA,

OF 1862–'3.

BY

HARRIET E. BISHOP McCONKEY,

Author of "Floral Homes," &c.

REVISED EDITION.

ROSS & HAINES, INC.
Minneapolis — 1970

Entered according to Act of Congress, in the year one thousand eight hundred
and sixty-three, by
HARRIET E. B. M'CONKEY,
In the Clerk's Office of the District Court of the District of Minnesota.

Ross & Haines, Inc.
Reprint 1,500 copies
November 1970

TO BRIGADIER GENERAL
𝔥𝔢𝔫𝔯𝔶 𝔥. 𝔖𝔦𝔟𝔩𝔢𝔶,
ON WHOM HONORS WERE NEVER UNFITTINGLY
OR UNWORTHILY BESTOWED,
THIS BOOK
IS VERY RESPECTFULLY INSCRIBED.
THAT THE LAUREL WREATH
WHICH ENCIRCLES HIS BROW, MAY
NOT FADE
TILL EXCHANGED BY THE DIVINE HAND
FOR A CROWN OF IMMORTAL GLORY,
IS THE EARNEST PRAYER OF
THE AUTHOR.

PREFACE.

This edition of the DAKOTA WAR WHOOP, is a careful revision of the first, with additional items of interest, and is a reliable historical work, detailing facts in their time and order, so far as possible, and endorsed by the most conspicuous actors in the great drama. Gen. Sibley, a prominent actor, as will be seen, said to the writer, after a close perusal of the first edition, that it seemed quite a mystery, "how one, not an eye witness of the events, could detail them so graphically and minutely correct." So, also, another: "It is a truthful and vivid picture of the scenes represented." But we know the vast arena and scores of the sufferers, and have lost no opportunity in collecting personal experiences, and yet, horrid as it seems, heart-sickening as is the detail, there are unwritten facts, still more horrid, which would seem but the emanation of a distorted brain, or too vivid imagination.

We take pleasure in crediting the photographs from which the engravings and cuts were made, to Whitney's celebrated gallery, in St. Paul, to whom was awarded the first prize medal, at the Chicago National Fair.

ST. PAUL, November 9th, 1864.

MRS. HARRIET BISHOP MCCONKEY.

Dear Madam:

I have been very much gratified with the perusal of the "DAKOTA WAR WHOOP." Although previously impressed with the conviction that no one was better qualified than yourself, to give to the public a graphic and impartial account of the unprecedented massacres and outrages perpetrated by the savages on our frontier in 1862 and 1863, yet I must acknowledge my surprise at the general accuracy of the book, and the intimate acquaintance displayed by you with details and occurrences, new to me, although I was present and engaged in the military operations against the Indians, most of the period referred to.

The work is intensely interesting, and I take pleasure in commending it to the public, as a faithful and authentic history of the terrible events connected with the outbreak of the Sioux Indians, which involved so many of our border settlers in desolation and ruin.

With kind regard, I am

Very respectfully Yours,

S. MILLER,

Gov'r Minn.

FOREWORD

MINNESOTANS SUFFERED through what may well have been their most prolonged and intense season of terror in history during six weeks of late summer and early autumn, 1862. Between August 17, when four Sioux from the Rice Creek band near the Minnesota River killed five settlers at Acton, Meeker County, and September 26, when 269 white and half-breed captives of the Indians were freed at Camp Release near present-day Montevideo, the Sioux Uprising of 1862 cost more in lives and property damage than most Indian outbreaks in American history.

Estimates vary, but at least 450 settlers and soldiers were killed, and the loss of life may have reached as high as 800. Large areas were all but depopulated as panic-stricken fugitives dashed to Fort Ridgely, or to towns like St. Peter or St. Paul, or out of the state entirely. Many months passed before Minnesota citizens, already busy supporting the Northern effort in the Civil War, could overcome Indian difficulties sufficiently to get on again with the business of settlement. Meanwhile, the Sioux and Winnebago Indians who had lived in the state were banished to the west.

As might be expected from such a dramatic occurrence, the Sioux Uprising has inspired an extensive literature. This history of the outbreak by a pioneer schoolteacher of St. Paul was part of what might be called the first wave of contemporaneous accounts. Although Harriet E. Bishop McConkey was not actually an eyewitness to the harrowing events she recorded, she was on the fringe of the action in St. Paul and got some of her material firsthand from participants themselves. This prompted her to become emotionally involved in her story and enabled her to give it a feeling of immediacy.

In several respects Mrs. McConkey's book deserves to be grouped with two other well-known contemporary versions of the uprising—*History of the Sioux War and Massacres of 1862 and 1863,* by Isaac V. D. Heard (a lawyer who served as recorder at the Sioux trials), and *A History of the Great Massacre by the Sioux Indians in Minnesota,* by Charles S. Bryant and Abel B. Murch. Although both of these works went through several editions, *Dakota War Whoop,* first published in 1863, came out only in one revised edition in 1864 and then had to wait slightly over a hundred years for another edition. In 1965 R. R. Donnelley & Sons Company of Chicago, which operates the Lakeside Press, included Mrs. McConkey's book in its "Lakeside Classics" series in a somewhat cut version edited by Dale L. Morgan. Now *Dakota War Whoop* is available once more in this reprint of the 1864 revision.

Like the works of Heard and of Bryant and Murch,

this one is not only a frequently fascinating narrative but also a significant source of information on the uprising. Perhaps Mrs. McConkey's chief contribution is the extensive report she got from George H. Spencer, a fellow member of St. Paul's First Baptist Church. He apparently was the only white man to survive several weeks of Indian captivity before his rescue along with many women and children at Camp Release. Wounded early in the outbreak at the Lower Sioux Agency near present-day Morton, Spencer escaped death because he was sheltered by an Indian friend. Spencer provided important information for several of Mrs. McConkey's chapters.

Another asset of *Dakota War Whoop* is that it at least touches upon practically all phases of the uprising story. It follows the sordid business through to the hanging of thirty-eight Sioux at Mankato on December 26, 1862, and on through Henry H. Sibley's punitive expedition against the Sioux in Dakota Territory during the summer of 1863.

But also like its competitors already mentioned, *Dakota War Whoop* needs to be read and used with caution. Mrs. McConkey told many atrocity stories in the interest, partly at least, of readership and sales. The Indians did get out of hand in their age-old way of fighting, but some of the atrocity tales are doubtless overdrawn. Also, Mrs. McConkey failed to quote verbatim from the military reports she used to cover various battles and skirmishes. Although she in no way violated the substance of the reports, she did tamper with the language, and the reader should be aware of this. She also was careless with spelling. Burton Eastlick should be Merton Eastlick, for example, and Lake Shetak should be Shetek.

Also there are errors in interpretation. She hinted that Indians were spurred on by Confederate agents, for instance, but nothing has been found to substantiate this. Then, too, although Mrs. McConkey was a religious woman, she showed none of the sympathy that Episcopal Bishop Henry B. Whipple did for the Indians' plight. She was as bitter against the Indians as practically all whites. One looks in vain for any understanding that the Sioux had considerable provocation for the outbreak, that they resented white encroachments on their small reservations along the Minnesota River, and that they could not understand why money (annuity payments were late) and food were denied them in the face of poor crops and the specter of hunger. Traders were calloused in their treatment of the Sioux and were among the first targets after the uprising began under the leadership of Little Crow.

According to a biographical sketch by Zylpha S. Morton in the June, 1947, issue of *Minnesota History,* Harriet Bishop was born in Panton, Addison County, Vermont, on January 1, 1818. She took teacher training under Catherine Beecher, a member of the famous Boston family, at New York State Normal School in Albany. In answer to an appeal for a female teacher by Dr. Thomas S. Williamson, who had organized an

FOREWORD

Indian mission at the Sioux village of Kaposia (near present-day South St. Paul) in 1846, Miss Bishop left her native New England for the Minnesota wilderness. She arrived by steamboat at St. Paul in July, 1847, and proceeded to establish the first permanent school there. As she described later in her first book, *Floral Home* (1857), she opened her school in a "mud-walled log hovel" that was once a blacksmith's shop. Her first student body numbered only seven, two of whom were white, but eventually it grew to about forty, moving to a better building at what is now the foot of Jackson Street. She taught until 1850. Miss Bishop also is credited with opening the first Sunday school in St. Paul as well as a "female seminary" to train teachers.

Miss Bishop married John McConkey in 1858 and used her married name in publishing *Dakota War Whoop*. She later was divorced, however, and used her maiden name, which was restored to her by the Minnesota legislature in 1867, when she published a volume of poetry in 1869. Then Miss Bishop suffered a protracted illness and died on August 8, 1883.

Three years later T. M. Newson included a candid sketch of Miss Bishop in his *Pen Pictures of St. Paul, Minnesota, and Biographical Sketches of Old Settlers*. "Whatever else may be said of her," Newson observed, "she was sincere and earnest. She taught, she wrote, she worked — all for the cause of God. She was ambitious; she sought fame, and hence she wrote several works — some poetry, and a history of the Sioux outbreak." Then Newson turned literary critic: "These works were not marked by any particularly brilliant characteristics, but they read well and showed a vast amount of labor and research, which give the reader a faint conception of the ever busy pen and busier brain of the dead authoress."

Returning to comments about Miss Bishop herself, Newson added that "She was angular, positive, determined — such a woman as is necessary for frontier life. She knew no policy. She attacked evils upon their merits; never conciliated or compromised; hence she often antagonized some of her best friends working with her in the same good cause." Newson balanced this by describing Miss Bishop as "a woman of comely appearance; tall, with a good figure; a bright, expressive face; earnest and decided in manners, and quick in speech. She . . . seemed always in a hurry. Until within a few years she wore curls, and looked much younger than she really was . . . Old settlers remember her kindly, and future historians will give her a pleasant niche among the golden days of the past."

That niche doubtless will be more solid if the reader of *Dakota War Whoop* chooses to overlook her moralizing and her errors and remembers that she performed a service in putting down, however imperfectly, a record of an Indian outbreak that really started a succession of wars of thirty years duration. They did not end until that so-called battle — it was actually a massacre of Indians — at Wounded Knee in South Dakota in 1890.

— Kenneth Carley
Author of *The Sioux Uprising of 1862*

CONTENTS.

CHAPTER I.
INTRODUCTION. — News of the outbreak.................................... 17

CHAPTER II.
THE BREAD RAID. — Troops called to Yellow Medicine — Threatening aspects — Heroic conduct of Lieut. Sheehan — Quiet restored............... 20

CHAPTER III.
THE FIRST BLOW. — Commencement of hostilities — Burial of the dead — Evacuation of the settlement... 30

CHAPTER IV.
THE COUNCIL FIRE. — Little Crow and his intent — Indian wrongs (!) — Preparations for attacking the inhabitants — Annuity Indians — Upper and Lower Agency... 37

CHAPTER V.
THE OUTBREAK AT RED WOOD. — James W. Lynde, the first victim — Fall of Andrew Myrick, and horrid treatment of his body — Wm. Bourat's fall and escape — Death of Doct. Humphrey and family — Surprise of the whites.. 41

CHAPTER VI.
THE SLAUGHTER. — The fury — Miraculous escape from a burning mill — Torture of women and children — Bloody work of Cut Nose — Slaughter of a family — The daughter made captive — Murder of George H. Gleason..... 46

CHAPTER VII.
GEORGE H. SPENCER. — Early manhood — Home among the Indians and its object — Attempts on his property and life — Was wounded at first fire, and made captive — Saved by an Indian friend.............................. 50

CHAPTER VIII.
CAPTIVITY AND RELEASE OF GEORGE SPENCER, AS TOLD BY HIMSELF. — Dissatisfaction of the Indians — The people's security — The first note of alarm on the morning of 18th Aug. — Knew it to be a war party — Four comrades shot — Spencer receives three balls, and rushes up stairs — Position of danger there — Intense suffering — rescued by Chaska, his Indian friend — Little Crow's treatment of him... 55

CHAPTER IX.
U. S. TROOPS CUT TO PIECES. — Alarm at Fort Ridgley — Death of Capt. Marsh — Lieut. Sheehan going North — Double quick return — Assumes command — Maj. Galbraith.. 61

CONTENTS.

CHAPTER X.
PAGE.
YELLOW MEDICINE. — Mission stations — Dakota council fire — John Otherday — News of the outbreak at Red Wood, its effect — The anxious night — Sixty-two persons saved by Other Day — Mr. Garvie...................... 65

CHAPTER XI.
THE FAMILY OF AN OLD SETTLER TAKEN CAPTIVES. — Their first alarm — Start for the Fort — are captured by Indians — Dead bodies — At the house of Little Crow — Escape of Charles Blair 72

CHAPTER XII.
THE PANIC. — Flight of women and children — Depopulated country — Sad condition of refugees — 30,000 involved in the massacre, directly or indirectly.. 75

CHAPTER XIII.
ATTACK ON NEW ULM. — Its situation and character of citizens — Their sacrilegious work on Sabbath, August 17, and what followed — Assault of the town — Arrival of Judge Flandrau in command...................... 81

CHAPTER XIV.
ATTACK ON FORT RIDGLEY.—Return of Lieut. Sheehan — His efforts to meet the expected attack — Isolated position — The attack — Excitement in the Fort — The spirit of the leader diffused through the ranks — condition of the Fort — Fire arrows — The life struggle — Re-enforcements sent — Anxiety for their arrival — Minnesota Third — Promotion of Lieut. Sheehan...... 85

CHAPTER XV.
SECOND AND FINAL ATTACK ON NEW ULM.— Preparations for renewal of hostilities — Destructive work of the Indians — Courage of Commandant Flandrau — The turning point in the struggle — The savages repulsed — Evacuation of New Ulm — Mournful cortege.................................. 97

CHAPTER XVI.
OFFICIAL REPORT OF JUDGE FLANDRAU.— Destruction of New Ulm.......... 101

CHAPTER XVII.
THE MISSION PARTY.— Rev. Dr. Williamson — Peril of Rev. S. R. Riggs — Peril of Dr. Williamson — Prairie Wanderings — Joy and disappointment on nearing the Fort — Dangers of the way — Norwegian grove — housed with friends... 111

CHAPTER XVIII.
MASSACRE AT BIG STONE LAKE.— Government plans — Surprise and capture of Government hands — Escape of Manderfield — Ruins visited some months afterwards — Dead bodies then found..................................... 117

CHAPTER XIX.
MURDER OF AMOS W. HUGGINS.— Early settlement of Missionaries — Amos Huggins and his work — His home — Miss La Frambois — Strange conduct of the Indians — they shoot Mr. Huggins — The excitement, etc.......... 120

CHAPTER XX.
CAUSE OF THE WAR — WHAT IS AN INDIAN !— Mr. Spencer's statement — Cause of complaint — The Indian defined — Their language — Half-breed interpreters — The Agent volunteers into the service of his country — Impression of the Indians in regard to it — British flag in their possession — Desire of Little Crow for British protection — Little Priest assisting in the fights — Expectations of assistance from other tribes, &c. — Demand of Standing Buffalo.. 124

CONTENTS.

CHAPTER XXI.

LAKE SHETAK MASSACRE.—The community — The memorable 20th Aug. — Mr. Phineas P. Hurd — Mrs. H.'s unwelcome morning visitors — The raid on her house — Fall of the hired man — Driven from home — her wanderings and sufferings of her two children — Willie sick — Her mother heroism to get on with both, after Willie became unable to walk — Arrival at a cabin — Disappointment in finding nothing to eat — She finds some decaying meat, and her boy is saved from starvation — Joined by other refugees..... 133

CHAPTER XXII.

THE GENERAL ONSLAUGHT — Starting for the other settlements — Attack by Indians — Twelve killed — Women made captives — Mrs. Eastlick left for dead — Mrs. Errett and two children killed — Mrs. Eastlick revives and returns to the battle-field — Mr. Myres and family overtaken by the wounded fugitives — Their sad condition — Perils by the way — Fears, &c. — Mr. Myres goes to New Ulm and finds the battle raging — The others to Mankato — Protection of U. S. troops — Care for their wounds................. 139

CHAPTER XXIII.

OUTBREAK AT THE NORTH. — Attack on the Breckenridge House — Old Mrs. Scott, her perils, sufferings and escape — Little Jimmy Scott — Life adventurers 145

CHAPTER XXIV.

SIEGE OF FORT ABERCROMBIE. — The first alarm — Rush to the Fort — First battle — Return of Messengers — A friend of the writer in peril — Birth of three children — Edgar Wright — his body exhumed and mutilated.... 150

CHAPTER XXV.

INDIANS AT SIOUX FALLS CITY. — Murder of J. B. Amidon and son — Departure of the populace — The place burnt.............................. 157

CHAPTER XXVI.

THE HEROIC BOY. — Mr. Ireland — his captive daughters — sufferings, mental and physical — Burton Eastlick starts on a tour of 90 miles with his baby brother in his arms — Mrs. Eastlick, wounded and suffering, follows — Meets her children — August Garzene — Mrs. Hurd and Mrs. Truland — Ten days at "Brown's" — Relief sent — Burial of the Shetak dead........ 160

CHAPTER XXVII.

SIEGE OF HUTCHINSON — Capt. Stuart's report — Mrs. Adams — Murder of her child... 168

CHAPTER XXVIII.

BATTLE OF BIRCH COOLIE. — The dead on the prairies — the detachment sent to bury them — 85 bodies found — Encampment — Morn of Sept. 2 — Desperate fighting — Extreme peril — Benjamin S. Terry — his life given from love to his friend Spencer — Corporal Wm. M. Cobb — Sergeant Wm. Irvine — Continued fighting — Relief sent — Joy of the men in the trenches — Burial of the dead and removal of the wounded — Robert Gibbons — Mr. J. W. Decamp fought to retaliate the supposed death of his wife and children, who lived to weep at his grave — Other refugee women.............. 171

CHAPTER XXIX.

BATTLE OF BIRCH COOLIE.— OFFICIAL REPORT OF MAJ. J. R. BROWN........ 182

At

CONTENTS.

CHAPTER XXX.

WANDERING REFUGEES. — Escape and rescue of Almira Harrington — Mrs. Caruthers claimed by two Indians — escapes by the aid of a squaw — paddles her own canoe — safe in the fort — An Indian playing priest, which enables his fair captive to escape — Peril of a young man and his escape..... 190

CHAPTER XXXI.

THE MANIAC.— A poem.. 194

CHAPTER XXXII.

TALES OF SUFFERING. — A woman and four children found after three weeks of prairie wandering and suffering — Shocking mutilation of children — Escape of the parents — Further search reveals further horrors — Mrs. Boetler's eight weeks of prairie life — Dead bodies found and buried...... 196

CHAPTER XXXIII.

THE ATHENÆUM. — Succor given to the refugees — Changes of a day in their circumstances — the fair-eyed babe saved as by miracle — Heart-thrilling tales told by the sufferers.. 201

CHAPTER XXXIV.

THE CAPTIVE'S EXPERIENCE AS FURTHER RELATED BY HIMSELF. — The Indians break camp for removal to Yellow Medicine — Spencer recognizes the body of Gleason — Soldier's Lodge — Firing of buildings 206

CHAPTER XXXV.

EFFORTS TO REGAIN THE PRISONERS. — Correspondence between Gen. Sibley and Little Crow... 209

CHAPTER XXXVI.

CORRESPONDENCE OF GEN. S. AND LITTLE CROW CONTINUED — Letter from Wabashaw and Taopee — Forward the troops — Body of Philander Prescott —A brief history of the good man.. 212

CHAPTER XXXVII.

BATTLE OF WOOD LAKE — Burial of George Gleason — Preparations for battle — The Indians driven — Fidelity of Other Day — Wisdom of the General commanding 217

CHAPTER XXXVIII.

OFFICIAL REPORT OF COL. SIBLEY TO GOV. RAMSEY........................ 224

CHAPTER XXXIX.

THE CHIPPEWAS. — Proclamation of Hole-in-the-day — Threatening aspect at the North — Efforts for treaty unsuccessful — Accomplished by Gov. Ramsey — Novelty of the Indian dance — They become a terror — An embassy of Chippewas visit the capital — The "talk," the feast, and ride on the "fire wagon".. 229

CHAPTER LX.

THE CAPTIVE'S PERIL.. 235

CHAPTER LXI.

THE FRIENDLY CAMP. — Efforts to form it — Final success — Release........ 239

CONTENTS.   11

CHAPTER XLII.

CAMP RELEASE. — Two hundred and twenty captives rescued — Strategy of Mrs. Reynolds — Terrible sufferings of Miss Mattie Williams while a captive — Joy on release — Approach of Col. Sibley's troops — Joy at camp Release — Glory of the achievement.. 242

CHAPTER LXIII.

TRIAL OF THE PRISONERS.— Heavy criminal calendar — Various subterfugees 247

CHAPTER LXIV.

MRS. HUGGINS IN CAPTIVITY. — Trials and heart-aches — Mr. Manderfield receives kindness at her hands — Julia takes leave of Mrs. H., and goes with her brother — She goes to De Cota's — Unwelcome reception — Kind reception at the lodge of Walking Spirit — De Cota's fears for his scalp......... 252

CHAPTER LXV.

MRS. HUGGINS in care of Walking Spirit — Kindness of her host — Redeeming traits — Effects of their new mode of life — Her employment — Perplexities of various kinds — The children — Insulting proposal — Day of the week lost.. 257

CHAPTER LXVI.

THE ALARMS. — Train of Northerners — Fears for her children — Return of a detachment of Northerners — Feast with the chief — A letter — A bad man — Explanation of his conduct.. 262

CHAPTER LXVII.

LEAVING FOR THE PLAINS.—Mrs. H. decides to go — Mode of travelling — Incidents of the way — Fears — Trust... 267

CHAPTER LXVIII.

RELEASE AND RETURN. — Last outward bound night — Increase of the caravan — Darkest hour before dawn — Preparations for company — Joy in the arrival — Release of two little girls — Steps retraced — Perils — Visits the grave of her husband, &c. — At Camp Release............................. 270

CHAPTER LXIX.

REMOVAL TO CAMP SIBLEY. — Trial resumed — The criminal calendar at last cleared — The sufferers of New Ulm... 274

CHAPTER L.

REMOVAL OF THE "GOOD INDIANS" TO FORT SNELLING.— Winter quarters — Old Betsey — Ta-o-pee — First note of freedom to the captives — Chaska.. 277

CHAPTER LI.

PROTEST ON SENATOR WILKINSON. — Thrilling rehearsals, &c............... 280

CHAPTER LII.

CAUSE OF THE DAKOTA UPRISING. — The normal savage state — The desolation — The hidden harm — Secession the main-spring of action — Indian councils — Discussion of the war theme — The rebel Col.'s plan — Where rests the guilt — Its enormity deduced from the data...................... 287

CONTENTS.

CHAPTER LIII.

PREPARATIONS FOR THE EXECUTION OF THE CONDEMNED INDIANS. — Its announcement to the prisoners — Col. Miller's remarks — Confession of their guilt — Death-song — General appearance — Ascent of the gallows — Intense interest of the throng — Fall of the platform — 38 souls launched into eternity.. 292

CHAPTER LIV.

THE EXECUTION.. 300

CHAPTER LV.

THE CONDEMNED. — Spiritual advice given them — Apparent spiritual change — Removal to Davenport, Iowa — Improved condition..................... 304

CHAPTER LVI.

THE WINNEBAGOES DECLARE WAR WITH THE SIOUX. — Former alliance — Awful scene in Mankato — Removal to new Reservation................... 306

CHAPTER LVII.

AN ALARM. — Troubles at Medalia — Col. Marshall sent in pursuit of the foe 309

CHAPTER LVIII.

REMOVAL OF THE GOOD INDIANS. — Families of the scouts remaining — Costume — Blameworthy treatment of the Indians — Work of progress in their new homes, &c... 312

CHAPTER LIX.

HORSE STEALING. — Gangs prowling through the country — Murders frequent — Bounty for scalps... 317

CHAPTER LX.

MURDER OF THE DUSTIN FAMILY. — Appearance of hostile Indians in Hennapin Co. — Horrid state of the bodies — One little girl alive................. 320

CHAPTER LXI.

LITTLE CROW'S WHEREABOUTS.. 323

CHAPTER LXII.

THE RANSOMED. — Months of torture — Horrid boasts of the savage — Saved by Maj. Galpin — Meeting of Mr. Everett with his little daughter Tilla... 326

CHAPTER LXIII.

THE INDIAN EXPEDITION. — Camp Pope — Arrival of Gen. Sibley — His bereavement — Departure for the plains — Organization of the expedition — Drouth and drawbacks — Resting on the Sabbath......................... 330

CHAPTER LXIV.

DEATH OF GEN. LITTLE CROW. — The boy Lampson shoots an Indian — Excitement in town — Striking resemblance to Little Crow — Gen. Sibley and others declare it the veritable Chief himself — confirmed................. 339

CONTENTS.

CHAPTER LXV.

CAPTURE OF WO-WI-NAP-A. — His wanderings after his father's death — condition when taken — His own statement — The boy chief when an infant — Kissed by the writer...... 344

CHAPTER LXVI.

THE CAPTIVE BOYS. — George Ingalls — Little Jimmy Scott...... 349

CHAPTER LXVII.

THRILLING ADVENTURE OF MR. BRACKETT, AND DEATH OF LIEUT. FREEMAN. — Mr. Brackett's story — Eulogy of Lieut. Freeman...... 352

CHAPTER LXVIII.

THE CAPTIVE, JOHN JULIEN. — Ten months in captivity — Sad experience with the Indians — Deliverance 359

CHAPTER LXIX.

PROGRESS OF THE EXPEDITION. — Above calumny — Delay of tidings — Col. Marshall's adventurous return — He brings reports of their engagements with the Indians — Rehearsed...... 364

CHAPTER LXX.

CAPTURE OF A TETON. — When found — His motive in coming out — Kindly treated and discharged — A boat-load of returning miners killed — brave fighting and slaughter by them...... 379

CHAPTER LXXI.

DEATH OF LIEUT. BEEVER. — Col. Crooks with his men scour the woods and drink of the Missouri waters — the body found — Sadness in camp...... 382

CHAPTER LXXII.

TERMINUS OF THE CAMPAIGN. — Return order...... 385

CHAPTER LXXIII.

OFFICIAL REPORT OF MAJ. GEN. HENRY H. SIBLEY...... 389

CHAPTER LXXIV.

OFFICIAL REPORT OF BRIGADIER GENERAL ALFRED SULLY...... 406

CHAPTER LXXV.

TIE OF COMRADESHIP — Death of Chaska — Attachment to Geo. H. Spencer — Brave and faithful — Sudden death — Poison the probable cause...... 420

CHAPTER LXXVI.

HOME AGAIN...... 426
CONCLUSION...... 428

BRIG. GEN. HENRY H. SIBLEY.

DAKOTA WAR WHOOP.

CHAPTER I.

INTRODUCTION.

"THREE HUNDRED THOUSAND MORE!" The nation's rallying cry had electrified every telegraph wire and intensified the great heart of the Northwest. Women, with the spirit of the Revolutionary mothers, had bidden their loved ones GO, glad that they had husbands or sons to give in the crushing of a rebel foe. Minnesota was thoroughly aroused. Though as a State she had yet scarcely seen her first decade, she had already sent her Fifth Regiment into the field. Fired with the spirit of the immortal "First," which won laurels even in defeat,* her quota was again being filled. Young men, the flower, vigor, and hope of the State, with musket in firm grasp, stood ready, impatiently awaiting "orders!"

"Home work enough to engage our troops for the present," said the "other half" of myself, excitedly, as he entered from a spirited war meeting. "It is well that they had not received 'marching orders.'"

"Another Indian 'scare,'" I interrogatively replied.

---
* At the memorable battles of Bull Run and Ball's Bluff.

"It is no 'scare,' I assure you, but an earnest and terrible reality."

"To frighten the credulous and the 'new comer'— nonsense!"

"'TRUTH is stranger than fiction.' Facts need no further confirmation. An army of savages are even now sweeping down the Minnesota River valley, swearing destruction to all in their course, and death to every white man!"

"It is not the first time our nerves have been set vibrating by such unpleasant rumors, and I have long since ceased to give credence to these crazy reports, which have had their birth in some wild brain. If the Indians would have made us trouble, it would have been when we were only a handful, and they strong as now, and in close proximity. It is all nonsense to think of it!" And thereupon I proceeded to dash off the remaining stanza of a patriotic song, which was pulsating in every nerve and quivering on my pen's nib, when he entered.

Alas! the visions of the night troubled me, despite my unbelief. To fancy's ear came the fearful wail and the groans of the dying, and to fancy's eye came only one blood-blinding scene—the dead, in tall prairie grass, or at their own hearth-stones; and above the shrieks and groans of their victims rose the terrible war whoop of the government-pampered Dakotas, furious from a taste of blood, and panting for more.

With the celerity of execution for which Gov. Ramsey is noted, he had, on the following morning, four companies armed and equipped, and moving towards the murder scenes, where hands were already stained with the blood of more than one thousand victims. The demand for energetic action was met by prompt effort, otherwise the savage hordes might have carried out their design; swept through the land, killed or driven off the inhabitants, and re-possessed the soil for which they were receiving annually the interest on its equivalent, in gold and goods, thereafter to revel amid their blood-gained spoils.

It is a dreadful tale — one from which the heart recoils and the pen shrinks; but I have girded me for the effort, and what though every hair of the head is erect, and every nerve a vibrating medium, making me, for the time being, as a living, actual witness of all I rehearse; the reading world shall hear, if they cannot see, what young Minnesota has experienced, how her adopted sons and daughters have suffered from the savage bullet and bloody tomahawk, while yet is undulating the clear, prairie air, in brutal fierceness, never to die from the ear of the sufferers, the terrible Dakota war-whoop.

CHAPTER II.

THE BREAD RAID.

The Dakota or Sioux Indians number about thirty thousand. These are divided into Bands, and each Band has its own Chief. They ignore the name of Sioux, by which they are known in the civilized world, and answer only to the name of Dakota. The purchase of the late Reservation secured to the small number of the Bands interested in the sale, the interest annually in gold on $2,000,000 for the ensuing fifty years, together with blankets, provisions, etc., which, with any provident foresight, would place ordinary economists quite above want. On their new Reservation, Government had established two Agencies, the lower at the mouth of the Red Wood, the Upper Agency at the mouth of the Yellow Medicine rivers, both tributaries of the Minnesota. The lower bands, residing mostly at or near the Lower Agency, went there for their pay, while the upper bands, living mostly on the plains, came to the Upper Agency.

Choosing their own time to assemble, or instigated to it by a secret foe, the upper bands, numbering nearly 7,000 men, women and children, had come to their Agency, demanding annuities, the arrival of which was delayed, and in regard to which, the Agent, Thomas J. Galbraith, was not advised. They had brought little or no provisions with them, and the small amount of game, with the fish they caught, hardly served to satisfy so many hungry stomachs. They demanded flour, for which orders of distribution had not yet been given — shot an ox belonging to the Agent, which was scarcely a mouthful, among so many. The begging dance would furnish them food for a day or two, and so with the buffalo dance; but they had no idea of seeking any laudable or remunerative employment, even though some of their children had died, they said, from starvation. But it was a formidable work — knowing the character of the Indians, as they did, that once giving them, you must continue to give — to think of feeding so many, for a period quite indefinite; besides, Government had not provided boarding accommodations at this point, on so grand a scale. But the spirit of unrest became more and more apparent, and indicative of hostilities. The tents of their encampment were struck, and hurriedly removed two miles to the rear. Dark, portentous clouds were evidently gathering in the political heavens, Siouxward. A consultation of the few Government officials resulted in sending to Fort Ridgley for an armed force.

In 1856, the frontier settlers were thrown into panic by the murder of forty persons, at Spirit Lake Settlement, in Iowa and the southern extreme of Minnesota. The leader of the desperado gang was Ink-pa-du-ta, the basest among the base, who, ever since, had roamed at large, the vilest wretch unhung. It had been feared that his going unpunished and unpursued would embolden the evil inclined, — that the leniency would be a precedent on which they might base their future deeds. Still, dangers slept; the settlers were unmolested, and those who had known him longest, became quite stupid in relation to the red man, so that when the clarion notes rang with such vibrating thrill through the State, one company of volunteers of the Minnesota 5th, at each of the three military posts, was all deemed essential for the protection of Government stores and frontier defense. Capt. Marsh was in command at Fort Ridgley, on the Minnesota, Capt. Hall at Fort Ripley, on the Crow Wing, and Capt. Vanderhock at Abercrombie, on the Red river of the north, and the least expectation of these men was, that they were to bear the brunt in the outset, of a home outbreak, and so check the savage onset as to save the State from general desolation, while relief forces were mustering, hurriedly, for the conflict. Well that we may not lift the curtain and peep into futurity. Experience, as it falls in life's pathway, is quite enough for our finite view, while, if the scope of mental vision enabled us to comprehend the whole in one, the effect would be overwhelming. The Divine Ruler has his marked men for the emergency, though they know it not; and rich in the fact is that man whose God is the Lord, and who can so await the disposal of His will, as to say in the results, "my life has been to a purpose."

The 18th of June, 1862, Lieut. Thomas J. Sheehan, Co. C., Fifth Regiment Minnesota volunteers, a young man, full of patriotic fire, and burning with intense desire to combat a rebel foe, had orders to report with a detachment of fifty men, to Capt. Marsh, and ten days after, loud cheers for their arrival rang through Fort Ridgley. The following morning, June 29, Capt. Marsh issued orders that Lieut. Sheehan, with his detachment from Co. C., and fifty men from Co. B., Fifth Minnesota, with Lieut. Gere, report forthwith to Agent Galbraith, at Yellow Medicine, "for the purpose of preserving order, and protecting United States property, during the time of annuity payment."

The Indians would listen to no advice to return home, secure their crops, and await the Agent's call, when their annuities should arrive. Assuming no military dictation, but regarding "discretion the better part of valor" in warding the impending blow, Commandant Sheehan waited upon the Agent, with the earnest desire that provisions, to the extent of his ability, be issued, to satisfy the constant demand for "something to eat."

As if to add intensity to kindling fire of desperation, two of their tribe were killed by the Chippewas, a few miles from camp. At early morn, the following day, an imposing array of mounted and armed Indians, 1500 strong, clad only in moccasins and the breechlet, started on the "war path," but at night they returned, crest-fallen from disappointment, directing vicious glances at the soldier's camp, which augured no good. To avert their minds from pursuit of the foe, a feast is promised, with the stipulation that they submit to be counted when thus convened, an ordeal essential to payment. Citizens and soldiers, some of whom kept guard, enjoyed the rare fun of the scramble, each for his share, as barrel after barrel of crackers were emptied on the ground. It was a hilarious time, and one of apparent satisfaction to the participants. Some forty barrels of water were served to satisfy the demand of the clamorous crowd for "drink," after which, for an hour or two, the friendly pipe passed from hand to hand, and the counting process was the finale of the day.

On the 27th July, the following order was issued, giving little hope of rest for mind or body of our young hero:

"SIR: I have to request that you detail a small detachment of your command, and with it proceed forthwith in the direction of Yellow Medicine river, in search of Inkpaduta and his followers, who are said to be camped somewhere in the region, with stolen horses, &c.

"You will take said Inkpaduta and all Indian soldiers with him, prisoners, alive if possible, and deliver them to me at the Agency. If they resist, I advise that they be shot. Take all horses found in their possession, and deliver them to me.

"A party of reliable citizens will accompany you; they will report to you and be subject to your orders.

"Ten or twelve men will, in my opinion, be sufficient. They should, by all means, be mounted on horses or mules. You should take at least nine days' rations, and should start a sufficient time before daylight to get away without the knowledge of our Indians. While I recommend prompt and rigorous action to bring these murderers, thieves and villains to justice, dead or alive, yet I advise prudence and extreme caution.

"Very respectfully, your ob't servant,
THOS. J. GALBRAITH,
Sioux Agent.
"LIEUT. T. J. SHEEHAN,
"Commanding Camp at Sioux Agency."

Accompanying the expedition was a Christian Indian, who acted as guide. He seemed most eager of all the party to bring the scamp to justice, while he boasted of having before killed his son, and was one of the party who rescued Mrs. Nobles and Miss Gardner from their hands, after the Spirit Lake Massacre. After a chase of many a weary mile, finding the deserted camp, their eyes gratified only with the sight of a solitary Indian in the distance, supposed to be a spy of Inkpaduta, whom the best horse speed could not overtake, and after continuing the search till further pursuit seemed useless, their horses were headed campward, where they arrived on the evening of August 3d, most opportunely. Notwithstanding the drumming and pow wow at the Indian encampment, during the night, the adventurers rested well after the excitement and travel of the last five restless days and nights, a needed refreshing for the ordeal of the morrow.

Scarcely had the sun of August 4th gilded the bluffs, when, painted and stripped for the work, the entire body of male Indians, with axes, hatchets and clubs, made general onslaught on the warehouse, the doors of which soon yielded to the well wielded blows. Then followed an unceremonious seizure of goods, flour and bacon, which the squaws, with wide spread blankets, (the common receptacle of all things,) awaited to receive, and, so far as able, convey to their encampment. They had chosen this early hour, before the powers of resistance should be astir, but in quick time the alarm was beat, and the little band of stout hearts were ready for action. Leaving the rest to guard camp, Lieut. Sheehan, with twenty-five men, hastes to the scene of confusion. The resistance of the immortal one hundred, in Sumter's walls, to ten thousand rebels, was less daring, had less of cool and determined bravery than this. What power have twenty-five men to cope with fifteen hundred infuriated savages, armed to the teeth? But ah! there was a power in the courage of the bearing, in the determined flash of the eye, when he ordered them to "fall back," threatening with instant death any who disobeyed. See them quail beneath it — their withering glances change to awe, as they coweringly obey. The gun of private Foster was jerked from his hand, discharged, his scalp was seized, and about to pass from his head to savage hands, when arrested by the above order. Mr. Fadden and James Gormon, warehouse and trader's clerks, were the only citizens rendering any assistance during this emergency, and are deserving of much credit and the thanks of the State at least.

Now followed a grand stampede for camp, for though

awed, they were not subdued. Here they were rushing to and fro, insulting the soldiers, and evidently daring them to unequal contest; but when the howitzer, by order, was turned upon them, there was a "scattering in hot haste," for they had no power to cope with this, to them, most dreaded monster. The lull in the raging of human elements was seized by Lieut. Sheehan for an interview with the Agent, in the quiet of his own home. Permission was granted for convening a council with his "red children." The chief speaker shook hands in mock friendliness with the commanding officer, and made a speech as follows:

"We are the braves. We have sold our land to the great father, (the President,) and we think that he intends to give us what he has promised, but we can't get it, and we are starving; we want something to eat."

Commandant Sheenan replied: "You should have gone to the agent before breaking open the warehouse, and asked him for something to eat, which he was intending to give you to-day. If your great father heard that you had committed these depredations, breaking open the warehouse and attempting the life of his soldiers, he would not forgive you, for it would make him very mad."

"We have asked the Agent almost every day, but he will give us nothing; now we are starving, and we want you to ask him for us. We know if we kill the soldiers, it will make our great father mad. We held a council last night, and concluded we must have something to eat."

B

"If I get you a good issue of provisions this afternoon, will you all go back to your teepees, and not trouble my camp, nor come around the warehouse any more?"

"Yes, that is what we want."

The whole responsibility being thrown upon the shoulders of this young officer, with results which followed, may have had its parallel, but has been surpassed by few. The plunder being ordered returned to the warehouse, the execution of the order devolved on him, but it was hauled from the shoulders of the men, by the Indians, as often as raised thereto. Matters again seemed rife for a general massacre. Guards were set by the savage rebels, and the lowering war clouds again muttered their thunders. Still the determined courage of the man for the hour did not forsake him, and in every effort was nobly seconded and aided by his comrade, Lieut. Gere, and he again demanded an issue of provisions, for which "they were as eager," he says, "as wolves for blood." This being received, the aggressors retired to feast in their own encampment, regarding themselves, no doubt, victors of the day. Considering all things, this was a fortunate ending, even though but temporary. The following day, some of the ring-leaders were arrested and put in jail, when came a demand for their release, with a threat to kill every man, and blot out the Agency, if not complied with. Agent Galbraith ordered their release.

Capt. Marsh, in compliance with the request of Lieut. Sheehan, arrived in camp, August 6th, and gave immediate and peremptory orders for the issue of the goods and provisions on hand, when quiet returned, and seeming satisfaction was restored. The military force having other, and, as thought, more important posts of duty, withdrew. Alas, for limited human foresight! Little thought they that the startling events of these two weeks were the foreshadowings of the horrid tragedies so soon to make every heart faint with their recital, and pale every cheek with terror — the result, perhaps, of a long maturing plot.

CHAPTER III.

THE FIRST BLOW.

The first event in this great Sioux raid to confirm the fact that they had broken truce with the whites, was at Acton, Meeker county, on Sunday, the 17th of August, 1862. A party of six or seven reckless young warriors from the Lower Agency, forty miles south, had gone out the previous day on a Chippawa "scalp hunt," but meeting no success in that line, and imbibing largely of "fire water," they entered that isolated settlement, intent on carrying out whatever promptings their evil hearts might devise. The house of Mr. Jones, the postmaster of Acton, was first visited by them, where they were loud in their demand for whisky, but in lieu of which he gave them tobacco, to their apparent satisfaction, when they left with no unfriendly demonstrations. Still, Mr. Jones was suspicious that evil was lurking in their hearts, as he an hour after asserted at the house of his step-son, Mr. Howard Baker, where he and his wife had gone, leaving his niece, an adopted daughter, with a child a year old, alone in the house.

Three weeks previous to this, a "prairie schooner," a mere speck on the horizon, was seen approaching the settlement. It "cast anchor" before the door of Mr. Baker, and its crew was Mr. and Mrs. Webster, who had come to start life in that really inviting region. Here a temporary home was given them, while preparations for their own went forward.

A little before noon, these same Indians, in their usual unceremonious manner, entered the house of Mr. Baker, where the friends were still in social converse. Save the fact of their being drunk, there was nothing to incite suspicion. In such a state they are always to be feared. After much meaningless talk, they proposed to "go out and shoot at a mark."

Mr. Webster, who had never before seen an Indian, stood on the door step, a mere spectator of the game. The Indians, taking advantage of the discharged guns of the others, made him their first victim. His wife was in the covered wagon, unpacking some articles for use, and thus screened, escaped their bullets. Mr. Jones ran a short distance, when an unerring aim brought him down. Mr. Baker rushed into the house, where he and his mother, Mrs Jones, were soon prostrate in death. His wife, with her two children, of four and six years, had fled to the cellar, and so escaped. The sight of blood infuriated their demon thirst, and hastily they return to Mr. Jones', break down the door which the young girl had fastened, and killing her, spared the child, which the next day is found lying in the blood of the slain, which is in coagulated pools on the floor.

As soon as satisfied it was safe to do so, Mrs. Webster and Mrs. Baker come from their concealment and, almost paralyzed with horror, survey the dreadful scene. The life-blood of Mr. W. had not yet ceased its flow, and an hour afterwards he dies in the arms of his heart-stricken wife. It was no time for communion with grief, but prompt and decisive action. With feelings akin to joy, they call to a white man then passing. He stands in the doorway when, with speechless lips and bursting hearts, they point to their dead. With a demoniac smile he says, "O, they've got the nose bleed," and turned to go. "But you will not leave us alone with these dead bodies," agonizingly pleaded the women.

"They're doing well," was the reply of the heartless wretch, and then he followed in the wake of the Indians.

Various were the conjectures as to who this inhuman monster might be, some of the more charitable believing him insane. Not so in the neighborhood where the tragic scene transpired. By those, he was believed to be in league with the enactors, and inciting to the bloody deeds.

Three miles away was an intelligent Swede settlement, and thither these women and helpless children wend their lonely way. The sun had sank to rest, ere with sickned hearts and weary feet they are welcomed at a friendly abode — friendly, though the spoken language of each is not understood by the other. The Indians had been seen; yea, a fine span of horses had been mounted and rode off by two of them. Then the intelligent signs; the grief-marked faces, and the blood-bedabbled dresses told the awful tale. Before midnight, the whole settlement was aroused and their course determined.

On the following morning, some two hundred in all, every man armed, went out to bury their murdered friends. Mr. Jones, whom the women had supposed instantly killed, and was concealed from their view by an outbuilding, had evidently had a severe grapple with death, deep holes having been dug in his struggles by his hands and feet. Already the bodies had become very offensive, and pools of clotted blood were all over the floor of the house. The burial party was fired on by the Indians before the hasty rites were finished; a ball passing through the hat of one, which was returned with even less effect, save in causing them to mount their stolen steeds and fly to the covert of the woods.

That was an anxious, restless night, for those about to abandon their homes for safety. Guards were stationed around the house where the women and children were gathered, while the main body of men were preparing to depart on the morrow. In that vast train of sixty teams was one bright Swede girl, who was afterward employed as a domestic in the home of the writer. From her the minutiæ of these facts were obtained. All was smiling with plenty and homes were becoming attractive, when the rude touch of savage hands passed over them, and subsequently wrote desolation on all. Change, how sudden, had come over their earthly hopes! Blight how unexpected had fallen on their prospects! As they wind over the prairie, both ear and eye are alert, lest an ambushed or grass hidden foe lurks with deadly aim; but safely they are guided to a haven of rest, where present dangers are past. The smitten hearts find sympathizing friends; but no kindness can efface the memory of that Sabbath day, when, powerless to save, their loved ones lay dead before them. During that day's trial and those which followed, these women evinced rare good sense and genuine intelligence, impressing those who conversed with them, of their worth and virtues.

LITTLE CROW.
(The Bloody Chief.)

CHAPTER IV.

THE COUNCIL FIRE.

The purpose of Little Crow, chief of the Lower Annuity Indians, was to strike a strong, decisive blow at the Lower Agency as soon as "paid off," before the whites had scattered to their homes, and this to be followed up by extermination and a repossession of the entire State.

A premature and unbidden blow had been struck at Acton, and with lightning speed some of the fiendish perpetrators hastened on their stolen steeds to Red Wood, or Lower Agency, twelve miles above Fort Ridgley and at midnight, stand before their chief, exhibiting their blood-stained hands, and recounting in fiendish triumph, the deeds of the day, and urging an immediate onslaught on the whites. For well they knew the consequences if they were given up to receive justice at the hands of a proper tribunal — if withheld, war, they urged, was inevitable.

Little Crow had, in several trips to Washington, and otherwise, picked up some knowledge of the world, and the nation's power, and he knew well the element with which he had to contend. He had so far adopted the customs of the whites as to wear their apparel, live in a brick house, sleep in a bed, eat at table and drink all the whisky he could get. Being an adept in craft, he hesitates, though his heart thirsts for blood, and he covets the rewards of the white man's industry. But there is much at stake. "Wait till paid off," he said, and then the work should begin. Still, if his young men were going to fight, even now, he coveted the glory of leadership, — they could have their own way.

Here let us say that the name by which this bloody Chief is known, is only a nickname, which descended to him from his grandfather, who received it from wearing a crow's skin upon his breast. His true name is Tah-o-ah-ta-doo-ta, meaning "his scarlet people." The band he governed was known as the Lightfoot Band.

The longer that council fire burned, the higher and brighter rose the flame, and the more determined grew the spirit emitted by the lightning flashes of their eyes. They urged that the whites, all but the old men and boys, had "gone to the war," and that these, with the women and children, could be easily exterminated. Now was the time for the work of death to begin, — to avenge their wrongs.

Here let us pause and investigate those wrongs. Personal wrongs there may be, but national wrongs in relation to them we fail to see. Sloth is their own worst and most powerful enemy. Like the care of a provident parent for the children of his love, is the government provision to render them useful and happy. To encourage civilization among them, it has used every means that money or influence could induce. To every Indian who will lay aside his blanket, cut off his hair, and put on white man's apparel, is accorded, in addition to his annuities, a farm of eighty acres, prepared and stocked, and farming implements provided; on this a house is built and furnished, and medical attendance guaranteed. In addition to this, he receives a percentage on every rod of fence built, on every bushel of grain or potatoes raised, and for every acre of new land cultivated, with full ownership of the same, so long as he continues to occupy it, or follow industrial pursuits. How would the souls of poor white men expand with ambition, was the same kindly governmental care extended to them! There would be far less poverty and wretchedness in our large cities than now. But in the main, the Indians prefer their own mode of life, and despise the one who thus sells his tribal birthright (his blanket,) and goes to work like a white man. Some, however, have done it, in spite of the disgrace, as many small but comfortable brick houses at Red Wood and elsewhere will testify. This, however, is the exception, not the rule. More generally, you will find their chivalrous spirit manifested in lounging and smoking, while the women perform all the labor, except fighting and eating.

The decision was made. The remainder of the night, while the populace slept in security, was spent in preparations for action. Before dawn, the spirit was deeply imbibed by all, with few exceptions, and the murderous weapon was clutched with a desperation which even their blood-thirsty souls had never before known. They were eager for the onset.

The signal for general attack was to be the firing of a gun by the store where waved the American flag, when the assailants, previously divided into squads and stationed at every house, would each discharge a volley, and the people, rushing from their houses to learn the cause, would become an easy prey. Thus it was settled, and thus eating and drinking, they wait and watch for the first glimmerings of day.

It will be remembered that the Lower Annuity Indians all resided at or near the Lower Agency, and a day was sufficient to bring them all together to payment, whenever the gold and goods should arrive. These for all time, they were now willing to exchange for the booty they would obtain, and the glory of wearing a scalp feather.

CHAPTER V.

THE OUTBREAK AT RED WOOD.

That Monday morning of August 18th, 1862, dawned clear and mild, all nature seemed radiant with life and hope, and more like a festive bridal morn than the enacting of the dark plottings of the night.

Their plan was admirably carried out, and had blood alone been their intent, not one would have escaped to tell the tale. The people, as they had presumed, rushed to the doors to ascertain the cause of the strange alarm, with no apprehension of evil. Men were indiscriminately shot down, hatchets were buried in the heads of women and children, or they were dragged off into captivity, a fate far worse. Soon arose the smoke of burning buildings — and the shrieks and groans of the sufferers, as the tomahawk cleft their bones and chopped their flesh in pieces, was terrific, beyond the power of pen to describe. There were women and children imploring mercy at the hand where there was none, from those whom their own hands had fed, and their own houses, now in flames, had often sheltered from the pitiless rain and cold, now as reckless of all as the weapon which seeks the brain. O the horrors of that one first hour! One has very truthfully said, that these barbarities could "not have been exceeded, had all hell been turned loose, with no opposition or restraint."

So paralyzed were the people, that, strange to say, not a gun was fired, not a hand was raised in defense, and such unlooked for success seemed but to madden their rage into more violent fury.

The first victim was James W. Lynde, son of an eminent Baptist minister of Covington, Kentucky. He was a single man, thoroughly cultivated in all the physical, social, intellectual and refined elements of manhood. His soul-absorbing love of nature led him where he could revel amid her beauties, and worship amid her smiles. His passion for music and the muses he had highly and extensively cultivated. He had held the position of editor of the "HENDERSON DEMOCRAT," had served with acceptance as State Senator, and held many other offices of trust in his adopted State. As they had predicted, he with others stepped to the door to learn the cause of the tumult, when he was made a target for seven balls, and fell dead.

Andrew Myrick, formerly of Westport, N. Y., when the first gun was fired, ran up stairs, where for a long time he lay concealed under a dry goods box. The Indians, with all their daring, are arrant cowards, and no one dare to be the first one up for fear of being a victim to whatever death weapon he might have. To bring him down, they in a loud voice proposed to fire the store, when he climbed through the scuttle to the roof, let himself down by the lightning rod to the roof of a low addition, and from thence jumped to the ground and ran toward the brush, where, had he not been seen, he might have been safe. Unfortunately, it was otherwise, and a shower of arrows pierced him through. He was then dragged back to the store, and his face indignantly pelted with the gold coin they had found in his safe, while the vilest imprecations fell from their lips. The burying party of Birch Coolie notoriety, of whom more anon, found his body and buried it, so marking his grave that his brother had him afterward removed to St. Paul.

William Bourat was clerk in the store, and on being wounded, rushed up stairs with another, whose history demands a separate chapter, securely fastened the trap door and prepared for their fate. With a wild whoop of triumph, the Indians had rushed in and taken possession of the store, and while distributing the goods, were concocting their plans to dispatch these hapless victims, and then burn the building. Bourat hearing this, determined to make a bold dash for his life, wounded and bleeding as he was, rushed down stairs and through the crowd, clamorous in securing their plunder, and passed out in safety. When two hundred yards from the building, he received a heavy charge of duck shot in the side, and another in his leg, which brought him to the ground. Nor had this satisfied the savage thirst. His clothing was stripped from him, and then he was piled with logs to prevent escape, till they could return and "cut him up," as they talked among themselves. What a moment was that! To do or die, was the only alternative. None could look to a comrade for aid, and few knew the fate of their friends. He must save himself if saved, and by superhuman effort he removed the logs and went on the way rejoicing in his own escape.

Doct. Humphrey, Government physician, had fallen in death, at his own door, which he had turned to enter, when his house, in which his wife and children were fastened, was set on fire, and she and her three little girls were burned in it. Several weeks after, their charred and blackened remains were found in the cellar, and with the decayed and mutilated body of her husband, decently buried. A little boy of this family, eleven years old, escaped from the burning building to the woods, across the river, where he remained concealed till the arrival of troops, when he "fell in," and stood in the thickest of the fight, while the unequal contest raged, and was by them protected till conveyed to friends in St. Paul, — the sad-hearted lone remnant of an unbroken happy family of the previous day.

Such was the surprise of the whites, that they were as nearly paralyzed with wonder as alarm. Some mistake, thought they, and in some instances, actually gazed at the elevated rifle, threatening to send a bullet to the heart. But in less time than I am writing, the true intent was evinced by bloody reality. Many had come out with half made toilets, some of whom were shot down, and others barely escaped with their lives, having no time to return for more clothing. What a scene! burning dwellings, dead men strewing every yard, and forbidding entrance to every door, women butchered or dragged into captivity, children screaming, till their brains are dashed out against a tree, or the butt of a rifle, and all so sudden, so unlooked-for! My God, is there vengeance in heaven!

With demoniac yells, they seize upon every treasure. Goods are recklessly trodden down, money safes broken open and the contents divided, and a scene of such carnage and plunder, modern history does not record. When the sun arose, the smoke of burning buildings darkened its rays, and the earth was drinking the blood of the slain.

CHAPTER VI.

THE SLAUGHTER.

A few had escaped by the ferry, and, the Indians well knew, would carry the news of their dreadful work to the Fort, and that retributive justice was sure to follow. To retard this, they secure the ferry-boat, kill the ferryman, disembowel him, chop off his head, hands and feet, which they insert in the cavity, and then dance around him, in hellish triumph, at what their own hands had done, and their own savage hearts devised.

In some instances, after the first excitement of the onslaught, persons met their death by slow torture. A boy, in trying to escape, was overhauled, stripped to the skin, and then pierced with sticks and knives, as he was driven along, they in the meantime mimicking his agonies, hooting and laughing at him till death ended his sufferings.

One man leaped from the window of the mill, which they set on fire, to the river, not soon enough, however, to prevent their well-aimed balls from entering his breast. With more than mortal energy, he swam the river, and was scarcely alive when he reached the opposite shore. For four days, without food, he dragged himself round in swamps and grass more dead than alive, and was at last found by a party of refugees, sixty-five miles from his starting point, and by them taken to a place of security.

Women were tortured in every imaginable manner. Some, with infants in their arms, had their breasts cut off, others their toes, and some were hamstrung and dragged over the prairie till torn and mangled; from that alone they died. Those who escaped, spread the alarm. The people seemed paralyzed to all but personal safety, and fled precipitately, not knowing whither they went. In one instance, several families, not far away from home, had congregated in consultation as to their course, when they were overtaken by the Indians, at the head of whom was "Cut Nose," one of whom it might emphatically be said, "Ye are of your father, the devil, and his works ye do." The first volley killed the few men, which, the women and children seeing, in their defenseless state, huddled more closely together in the wagons, and bending low their heads, drew their shawls tightly over them. Two of the fiends held the horses while Cut Nose jumped into a wagon, containing eleven, and deliberately cleft the head of each, while, stupefied with horror, and powerless from fright, each awaited their turn, knowing the tomahawk would soon also tear through their flesh and bones, in like manner. Then kicking these butchered victims from the wagon, they filled it with plunder from the burning houses, leaving them a prey to vultures and ravenous wolves.

Forcing an infant from its mother's arms, with the bolt of a wagon they fastened it to a tree, and holding the mother before it, compelled her to witness its dying agonies. They then chopped off her legs and arms, and left her to bleed to death. And thus they butchered twenty-five, within an area of as many rods.

To serve their base passions, some of the younger women were saved alive, while perhaps the parents were cut down before their eyes.

One family, who lived a few miles out, consisting of the parents, son and daughter, fled from the back door, as the murderers appeared at the front door. The father fired the first gun that had been raised against them, but before he could re-load, with fiendish yells the savages sprang upon them. The father, mother and son fell dead, and the daughter, with genuine tact, fell to the ground, holding her breath and feigning death. The monsters, after hacking and mutilating the quivering flesh of the others, seized her feet to drag her off — unconsciously, she attempted to adjust her dress — which these barbarians seeing, stopped short, and sparing her life for viler purposes, sent her back to swell the company of hapless captives.

On the route between Yellow Medicine and Red Wood, George H. Gleason, Agency Clerk, having in charge Mrs. Wakefield and two children, was surprised by a party of these Red Wood murderers, who now were ravaging the country in every direction, and maddened by every fresh taste of blood, were still dealing death and captivity to all in their way. Gleason was a favorite with all, and they had never received aught but kindness from his hands. But that did not save him. A bullet quick went to his heart. His person was searched, valuable papers scattered to the four winds, and he left, stripped nearly to the skin, while Mrs. Wakefield and her children were carried into captivity, there to remain until the time of the great release had come.

CHAPTER VII.

GEORGE H. SPENCER.

The subject of this chapter, who has furnished much material for, and will play a conspicuous part in the tragedy announced, came to St. Paul in the early dawn of manhood, while yet the thriving young city was struggling in swaddling bands. West of the Mississippi river, the Sioux title was not yet extinct. Their villages and encampments were in close proximity to town, and numbers of them were daily parading the the streets, visiting the stores to trade, and the houses to beg.

Young Spencer, as clerk, found a knowledge of their language quite essential to success in business. Devoting half of the night to study, and being a persevering scholar and good linguist, he soon acquired a perfect knowledge of the Dakota language. This made him a favorite, and some strong personal friendships were formed with some of the most deserving of the tribe.

The study which our hero most loved was the starry heavens. Watching the planets as they rose, tracing the stars in constellation, and the comets, till they moved off in unknown space, he, in nature's observatory, would be lost to all else, save in adoration of Him who made them all, till his garments were drenched with the dews of night. To perfect himself in the glorious study of Astronomy, was the one absorbing desire of his life. And to facilitate this, was the main inducement for forming a co-partnership with Wm. H. Forbes, which would isolate him in the heart of the Indian country for the five succeeding years. The lumber which entered into the construction of his store, was drawn more than two hundred miles, and none could be obtained nearer.

Goods were readily converted into furs, and these into gold, which poured into the coffers of the firm like rain from full clouds. True, the life of Spencer was in jeopardy, or, to use his own words, he was obliged to "risk his scalp" in carrying out his designs; for though he had many professed friends among them, those who sought his advice, and offered to him their daughters for wives, which he rejected with a firmness they could but respect, yet he well knew there was many a secret lurking foe, who would not hesitate to do him any amount of evil.

Once his store was fired in the night time, when, but for timely notice by his Argus-eyed friends, he and all his goods would have been consumed.

Another time, his store had, all the evening, been filled with those who came for trade or gossip, when, at a late hour, he drank from a pail of water, to which all had had free access. An unusual taste excited his suspicion, in test of which he gave some to a cat, which died in violent convulsions, in less than a minute. Investigation proved the presence of strychnine. His heavy moustache had collected the poison, and thus saved his life. Those more honorable than their fellows, tried, in both of these instances, to find out the guilty, but investigation was a failure. He had learned thereby a lesson of caution, and that, as a race, the Sioux were worthy of little confidence.

Mr. Spencer was en route to visit his host of St. Paul friends, where he held membership in the First Baptist Church, and stopped to spend the Sabbath at the Agency. He was at the store of his partner when the attack was made, and thinking there must be some mistake in what he saw, was looking on in perfect wonder, till recalled by the power of three convincing bullets. But as Mr. Spencer still lives, after being forty days regarded as dead, we shall let him tell his own story, simply adding, that this Chapter was commenced as a biography when there was scarcely a hope of his being alive. That he was shot, and said he must die, was all that his escaped friend knew of him or his fate. But there was "joy in that city," when it was told that he lived, was safe with his Indian friend, who designed to restore him to his white friends, as soon as safe to do so.

The engraving represents him in the dress in which he was taken captive, the bullet holes being distinctly seen. While a captive, he was, as all others, obliged to wear the Indian costume, but his clothes, watch, diamond pin and ring, together with his money, were carefully kept, by his Indian friend, and returned to him on his release.

CHAPTER VIII.

CAPTIVITY AND RELEASE OF GEORGE H. SPENCER, AS GIVEN BY HIMSELF

"Upon Monday morning, August 18th, 1862, the dissatisfaction which had long been manifested by the Mile-na-kan-toan and Wah-pe-ku-te bands of the Sioux Indians, reached the culminating point, and inaugurated one of the most horrible massacres of which we have any record.

"About six o'clock in the morning, the inhabitants of the Agency were, as usual, pursuing their customary avocations, little dreaming that that bright and beautiful sun which was diffusing its genial rays over the earth, had risen for the last time upon them, and that when he should have performed his daily journey, and returned to his resting place at eve, their mutilated and mangled remains would be left food for the vultures, and their unprepared souls summoned into the presence of their Creator.

"I had arrived in the place on Saturday evening, the 16th. On Sunday evening, the 17th, I attended the Rev. Mr. Hinman's Church, where I heard a very fine and appropriate sermon. Had the Rev. gentleman known that the events which transpired on the following morning were to have taken place, he could not have preached a more appropriate sermon for the occasion.

"On Monday morning, about six o'clock, on going

to the door, I noticed an unusual number of Indians coming down the road into the village, all armed and naked, except the breech-cloth. I knew it was a war party, and upon arriving in the village, they divided into small parties, and stationed themselves around every building in the place, and upon inquiring of those around our building—(the store of Wm. H. Forbes)—what the matter was, I was told that some of the enemy were seen near by, and that they were going to attack them. Supposing they meant Chippewas, I thought no more about the matter. Presently, however, I heard the firing of guns, and hideous yelling outside, when I rushed to the door, with five or six others, and just had time to see that the trading house of Messrs. Myrick & Co., had been attacked by them, and that they were firing into it, when a volley was discharged at us. Four men fell dead, and I received three balls, one through my right arm, another struck me in the right breast and the third in the stomach. One white man, William Bourat, and a half-breed boy, were not hit. I did not fall, and with these two, rushed up stairs. Upon reaching the foot of the stairs, I turned to see if they were following, when I saw the store was filling with Indians, and one had followed me to the stairs, where, placing his double-barrel gun almost against my body, endeavored to shoot me, but, providentially, both barrels missed fire, and I succeeded in reaching the upper story, without further injury.*

"After being up stairs a short time, the half-breed, looking through the window, saw an Indian, to whom he called. The Indian told him to come down, and he should not be hurt; he thereupon opened the door and went down.

"It was a trap door, secured by two or three boxes of guns, making it quite impossible for the Indians to open from below.

"Bourat also gave himself into their hands, and after getting outside of the house, perceiving a good opportunity, started, and ran for life. The Indians fired upon him, and two charges of duck-shot struck him in the side and hips.

"He fell, and feigned death. Some of them then threw some sticks of wood upon him, but he never moved, and they, supposing him to be dead, left him, saying they would come back and cut him up, when their other work was done. After a while, seeing the coast clear, he succeeded in making his escape.

"The half-breed,* through fear, I am inclined to think, joined the Indians in some of their raids, and confessed to having killed a white woman. He was among those who surrendered themselves to Gen. Sibley's command, and was convicted and executed at Mankato, with the others.

"Being thus left alone up stairs, and my wounds becoming painful, I threw myself upon a bed, expecting, if I did not very soon die, that the Indians would come

---

* His name was Paulite Osier, once a pupil of the writer, and by her taught the first rudiments of education. He was now a clerk in Forbes' store.

up and dispatch me. While lying there, I could hear distinctly, all that was going on below.

"I soon learned, from their conversation, that they were afraid to follow me up stairs, as they had the impression that I was standing at the head of the stairs, with a gun. There were four cases of double barreled shot guns, and one case of rifles, in the upper story, of which they were aware. They proceeded to open the boxes and bales of goods and to carry them out. They appeared very anxious to get at the guns, but would not come up, each one fearing to be the first one up, as they supposed he would be shot. They talked of firing the building. Fearing this, I arose quietly, and took off my shoes, and took a bed-cord and attached one end to the bed-post, and carried the other end to one of the windows, which I raised. I thought if they did apply the torch, I would lower myself to the ground and take the chances of being shot again, rather than to be burnt to death. About this time, an Indian called out to me, from below, to come down, that I should not be hurt, or, as he expressed it, 'you shall live.' I went to the door, but not recognizing him, refused to go down. I had been in tight places before, among the Indians of the plains, but a kind providence had always watched over me, and delivered me safely, and I now put my trust in that same Power, to deliver me from this most dangerous situation.

"Thus matters stood, and things began to look desperate, when I heard a well known, and to me, most welcome voice, shouting my name from below. I recognized the voice at once, and hastened to the door, and called him up. I was saved for the present, at any rate. It was the voice of my Indian comrade, Wa-kin-yan-tu-wa, (Chaska.) We had been intimate friends and comrades for the past ten years, and he happened to hear that I was wounded, but still living, and hastened to where I was, to save me, if possible. When he came up, several others followed him, some of whom took me by the hand, and appeared to be very sorry that I had been hurt. My friend asked me 'if I was badly hurt, and if I thought I would die.' I replied, I did not know, but that my wounds were very painful. He then said that he would take me home with him, and cure me, if he could, and if I died, he would bury me like a white man.

"He then assisted me in getting down stairs, when several Indians cried out, 'kill him! kill him! show mercy to none! spare no American!' &c., when my friend, who was unarmed, seized a hatchet that was lying near by, and declared that he would cut down the first one who tried to do me any further injury. Wa-kin-yan-tu-wa had always been noted for his bravery on the war-path against the Chippewas, and they knew that he was not to be trifled with. Said he, 'this is my friend and comrade; we have been comrades for ten years, and if you had killed him before I got here, of course I could have said nothing, but now that I have seen him, I will protect him or die with him.

"They then suffered him to pass out. After getting out of the house, he gave me in charge of a couple of squaws, and told them to take care of me while he got a wagon to carry me home. His lodge was about four miles above, at Little Crow's village. After putting me in the wagon, he ordered the squaws to take me home, saying that he would be along in a few minutes. We were stopped on the way three or four times, by armed Indians, on horse-back, who would ride up to the wagon, and demand 'what that meant.* Upon being told, by the squaws, that 'this is Wa-kin-yan-tu-wa's friend, and he has saved his life,' we were allowed to pass on, and reached the lodge in safety.

"My friend soon came home with some roots, with which, after washing me, he dressed my wounds, which were, by this time, exceedingly painful. Several of the Indians came in to see me, and to talk over their wrongs, (?) &c., and the reasons why they had declared war.

"Little Crow, with whom I had been personally acquainted for many years, came in to see me frequently, and assured me that I need have no fears, that I should be well treated, and thought that I could be very useful to him as soon as I recovered from my wounds. This professed friendship, however, did not last long, for my friend utterly refused to join in the war against the whites — Little Crow attributed it to my influence over him — and they frequently quarreled in regard to the disposition that was to be made of me."

---

* This was the first adult male captive whose life was saved, and the only one.

CHAPTER IX.

U. S. TROOPS CUT TO PIECES.

At the time of the outbreak, only eighty men, all told, garrisoned Fort Ridgley, which was distant from Red Wood twelve miles. At nine o'clock, the first breathless refugee had told them of the awful slaughter, and one-half of the command, with Capt. Marsh, post commander, were hastily moving toward the scene of carnage.

At noon, they approach the ferry, but all is as quiet as death, with which they are surrounded. Not a red skin is to be seen. The ferry boat is on the other side, and the ferryman killed. There is no means of crossing the river, and they wait in consultation, and doubt how to proceed. The ambushed Indians, all stained with blood of the slain, see their dilemma, and lose no time in wily movements to surround them. Crawling through grass and bushes to a bend above, they get across the river in canoes, and by moving unperceived by the troops, till sending one forward with instructions to detain them in friendly conversation through Interpreter Quinn, whom they beckoned to their aid till the adroit manœuvre is successful. Then a galling, a terrible fire is poured upon them from both sides of the river. In panic they broke and run, but twenty-six of their number fell, to rise no more. Capt. Marsh, a brave man, but bewildered by the unexpected onslaught, rushed into the river, sword and pistol in hand, as his only means of escape. Whether his death was occasioned by an enemy's ball or by drowning, is not known. He was carried down by the current, and one month later was found among driftwood, one mile below, his body in a remarkable state of preservation. He had been stripped of his coat and sword, which had been worn and flourished by the defiant savage, as testified by Spencer.

The remnant of the command, fourteen in number, reached the Fort by different routes during the day, where the wildest alarm now reigned. Refugees, many of whom were wounded, and all torn, worn and weary had come in, to the number of five hundred. The stock of ammunition was small; their leader dead, and only thirty men capable of bearing arms. What was to be done in case of attack, which might come, any moment? It was a question to be tested! He who "is stronger than the strong man armed," taught them, most emphatically, in the lessons which followed — "that the race is not the swift nor the battle to the strong."

With the other events of the day to be chronicled, was the arrival of the long-delayed annuities, but for the delay of which, the trouble would have been postponed or prevented. It is but personal justice, however, to say, that the delay was unavoidable, "the powers that be" having had much trouble in purchasing the gold, for such was the treaty stipulation, and with no other funds would they be satisfied. This having been forfeited, their treaty, annulled by their own base hands, it is needless to say, never went to the Agency.

The reader will recollect, that some two weeks previous to the general outbreak, Lieut. Sheehan, with one hundred men, had been ordered to Yellow Medicine, that their armed presence might awe into quiet, the hordes of Indians awaiting "payment." From thence he had been ordered to attend Commissioner Dole, in efforts to make a treaty with the Red Lake Indians. So, when the blow was struck, the match ignited so soon to produce a conflagration, the glare of which would be seen all over the State, yea, and nation, he was forty miles away in rapid march northward.

Orders were dispatched for his return, and his men hurried through most of the way on "double quick," and providentially arrived at the Fort on Tuesday noon, Aug. 19th, having made the distance in 9 1-2 hours. The command now, by the death of Capt. Marsh, devolved on Lieut. Sheehan, and how nobly and how well he performed his duty, we shall soon see. The mantle of the lamented dead fell not on unworthy or unfitting shoulders.

The morning previous to the outbreak, Maj. Galbraith, government agent, who apprehended no more trouble, had left his family and post to raise the company of Renville Rangers, had reached the Fort, fifty strong. When tidings of the outbreak reached them, they were on the way to Fort Snelling, to be mustered into the volunteer service of the general government, in response to the first three hundred thousand call. Thus in one day was that little handful, unexpectedly when hope was well nigh sinking, re-enforced by one hundred men, ready for action. Without these, the Fort must have fallen, and an unparalleled massacre have ensued.

For days, Maj. Galbraith continued in the active discharge of duty, writhing with intense desire for the fate of his family, whom he had little doubt had shared in the general massacre. This gave intensity to his efforts to meet the foe, and vigor to his arm when the siege had commenced. He would avenge their death! He would mete to them the full reward of their doings. But, fortunately, these, after many days, were heard from. They had made their escape mid dangers thick around them, and now the husband and father hears of them in St. Paul.

CHAPTER X.

YELLOW MEDICINE.

The settlement at Yellow Medicine is emphatically a farming community, the country for miles being laid off in eighty acre farms, on which are comfortable houses and other buildings. The owners are "farmer Indians," and this is the encouragement which government gives to all who will adopt the customs and habits of the whites. Here at Hazelwood, was the Mission station of Rev. Mr. Riggs; and here, in their little chapel, on Sunday, while the Acton tragedy was being enacted, was celebrated the supper of our Lord and Savior, of which several Indians partook. We speak of this here, because these persons, thus remembering Him, were so soon to act an all-important part in the temporal salvation of their white neighbors.

One mile below this point was the Mission house of Rev. Dr. Williamson, of whom the writer has many pleasant and almost fraternal remembrances; and, three miles below this, the Agency, with all the government buildings and the dwellings of other citizens. Here, the "upper Indians" came, annually to payment, and here, in addition to those residing here, they were now gathered, to the number of several thousand, for this purpose.

Secure, as in months agone, the people had slept

that night, and the morning dawned as others, bright and beautiful, full of hope and promise, for there were no premonitions of danger. They knew not that all day long the council fire in the Dakota encampment, the same which, two weeks before, had withdrawn its threatening atittude, burned with fearful brilliancy; that their great captain, the Devil, had stirred the demoniac spirit in their hearts, till the war-spirit was sending its lightning flashes from their eyes, and maddening them for the onset. He had instigated them simultaneously to strike the blow of extermination, and duped them into the belief that they were fully adequate to the task. Then they should be a great and mighty people, like the "big knives" (Americans.) Other tribes would see and admit their greatness when the tree of prosperity should wave over them, and they would have no need of war, for their acknowledged power would forever keep their enemies in awe.

John Other-Day, the christian name of one seated in that council, was, four years before, a miserable drunken Indian; now his very presence seemed a terror to those inclined to evil. What had wrought the change? Hear what he saith: "It is the religion of Jesus Christ alone; but for this, I should have been the bloodiest of the murderers." Who shall gainsay the power of the living vital principle which can so tame the savage heart?

His dress was now the white man's, and by his side sat a white woman, whom he had brought from Washington to be "the Indian's bride" and the light of his home, which had been transformed from a bark lodge to a comfortable brick house. He urged them to heed no more the muttering war thunders, but listen to the good spirit rapping at their hearts, and patiently await their annuities, and then return peaceably to their homes, adopt the customs and industrious habits of the whites, and the religion which the missionaries preached, so would they be prosperous and happy. Though he could not prevent, he evidently delayed the decision.

Just as sunset's rosy tints were thrown athwart the sky, a horseman, with flashing eye, flowing hair and blood-stained blanket, rode up to the council circle. Intuitively they understand the message he brings. Every determined warrior springs to his feet and clutches his musket. The work of destruction has commenced. Red Wood is a heap of smouldering ruins. Other-Day waits to hear no more. Taking his wife by the arm, he moves in the direction of the Agency, and loses no time in warning all of their danger. In obedience to his directions, sixty two persons flee to the Agency warehouse, a strong brick building, for safety. Around this building, with four others, he keeps faithful watch all that anxious night.

Still outside of these, a hostile guard was set, with the supposed intent of dispatching them and attacking the building, at the moment when came the signal for general attack. But the Almighty Ruler thwarted their purposes, and permitted these sixty-two persons to escape, and saved the populace alive.

At the sombre gray of dawn, the sharp crack of musketry was heard, followed by loud and triumphant yells. The hostile guard yell in fiendish response, and run for their share of the booty. The attack was on the government stores, and richest spoils awaited those soonest on the ground. Their preconcerted signal had failed, through venal desire. By this bold dash, their own hands were greatly strengthened, the hand of resistance weakened. At the two Agencies, during these two days, they took some twenty tons of ammunition to aid in their deadly work.

Seeing the coast clear, Other-Day and his party hastily prepare for evacuation of their night's quarters. The sixty-two persons, with a small amount of provisions, were crowded into five wagons, and before the sun had arisen, they had looked their last on their pleasant homes and the scenes which association had rendered dear.

From Tuesday morn till Friday noon they wandered over the prairie, with little rest for man or beast, when they found themselves directly opposite the Lower Agency, only thirty eight miles in advance of their starting point. They had desired, on crossing the river, to take the main road to the Fort, to which Other-Day would not listen, and refused to act longer as their protector, unless they yielded to his wish. Events proved the wisdom of his choice, and the only course by which they could have escaped massacre.

We regard John Other-Day as one having this especial mission to fulfill, as one whose heart the Lord had

JOHN OTHER DAY.
(The Christian Indian.)

prepared to act this very part in the bloody drama. A full week had passed before all were safely housed with friends at various points at the lower settlements, truly grateful for their escape, and anxious for the future.

Mr. Garvie, a pioneer and for several years a trader at Yellow Medicine, inclined not to credence of the reports brought to him at an early hour, and at all events resolved to stay and defend his property to the last; but before many hours, he found reality in the alarm, and all night vigorously defended himself and his barricaded building. He listened not to their frequent calls to surrender, and was finally hit by a ball fired in at a window. He escaped from the rear of the building and reached the warehouse, about a half a mile distant, where Other-Day and his party were convened. His wounds aroused them to a keener sense of their danger. Before the terminus of their eventful journey, the sufferings of Mr. Garvie became so great they were obliged to leave him in the care of a friend, where death soon came to his release.

CHAPTER XI.

THE FAMILY OF AN OLD SETTLER TAKEN CAPTIVES.

Joseph R. Brown was one of the earliest adventurers in the then undefined limits of Minnesota. He has acted a conspicuous part in the various settlements, and, understanding the language perfectly, had often been an important agent in the adjustment of Sioux matters. His wife is a full-blood Sioux, whose mother still lives with her tribe. His present residence is a few miles below Yellow Medicine, and his family, at the time of the outbreak, numbered fourteen. Most of his children had been pupils of the writer when he resided in St. Paul, and therefore it was with no ordinary emotion that we received tidings of the massacre of the entire family. Mr. Brown himself, returning from the East, read the same in a St. Paul daily, while on board a steamer, and knew not to the contrary, till in the vicinity, he learned instead they were captives in savage hands.

On Monday, the 18th, Miss Ellen Brown went to see her grandmother at Yellow Medicine, and was by her informed and warned of the bloody intent. She returned home in alarm, but the family discredited it, to find it too sure on the following morning. It was earnest and hasty work then. Two teams were got ready, and they started for the Fort. Angus Brown,

Charles Blair, his brother-in-law, and hired man, remained to see the way things were going, and follow on horseback. They were joined by two men who had crossed the river and come upon them unawares. Apprehensive that the enemy might approach them in the same way, they turned the cattle loose and started on after the family. Blair rode ahead, and overtook them at Patterson's Rapids, where they were prisoners in the hands of about twenty Indians. This savage party averred they had as yet shed no blood, and did not wish to begin there, as all of these, except Mr. Blair, were allied to them by blood. They shook hands with him in a mock friendly manner, ordered him to dismount, appropriating his horse to their own use. The balance of the equestrian party, re-enforced by other refugees, were also taken prisoners, and from some strange freak the men allowed to go on with the rigid injunction "to speak to no one on the way"— the first instance where men in their power were left unharmed. which was owing to Sioux blood.

As the captive party proceed, half bewildered by the rapidly occurring events, and half doubting the reality of their experience, they are startled to its full consciousness by the sight of three dead mangled bodies. They, too, might be awaiting a like fate!

After various erratic movements on the part of their captors, they were taken to the top of Red Wood hill, and there compelled to listen to a discussion as to the disposition to be made of them. An old Indian woman, seeing their danger and desirous to save them, got off the

Browns, by secret manœuvre, to Little Crow's village, and into an upper room of the chief's house.

Here they remained, trembling with apprehension, till a late hour in the evening, when Little Crow himself came up, and kindly shook hands with all. Evidently, on his part, there was no hostile design. But he shook his head when Mrs. Brown spoke of ransom, and would not listen to it or encourage the hope.

He, however, assured them, they should all, except Blair, be safe from hostile hands, but refused to insinuate his destiny. He evidently wished his escape, and it was to facilitate this that he blew out the light before going down stairs. Little Crow went off into the village, and a young Indian soon came whom he had commissioned to aid Blair in escaping. Hasty preparations followed, which left him "shaven and shorn," as well as blackened and blanketed. Several times, suspicious ones tried to pull his blanket from his face, as he followed his guide through their village. When two rods beyond its limits, he was told to "go," and needed not a second bidding.

That night he went into a marsh, where, for half a day, he floundered in the mud, and then lay in the tall grass for four days, eating only two crackers, which the old squaw had given him when he left. Whenever he raised his head to reconnoitre, he held grass before his face — an Indian trick, but for which he would have been seen, for the woods around were filled with them. On the fifth day he crossed the river, keeping under cover of a log which he pushed before him, and at night reached the Fort in safety.

CHAPTER XII.

THE PANIC.

Despite the unbelief evinced in the "Introduction," the reader has seen it was not all a "scare," and a certain fertility of imagination enabled me to take a bird's eye view of the arena of three hundred miles, while the heart pulsates with fear for the safety of the enactors.

In every direction are seen men, women and children with streaming hair, *en dishabille*, or garments rent and torn, perhaps blood-stained, in wild confusion flying from the theatre of actual danger. Horsemen, frightened out of their wits, are flying through the country, giving the alarm, perhaps when there is no cause for it, and the people "flee for their lives," as if a dozen Indians were at their heels, and their tomahawks raised above their heads. Mothers go one way, children another, while perhaps the husband and father hides himself from sheer fright, or becomes powerless for action from the same cause. Some hide in the tall prairie grass; some seek the covert of the woods; some rush to the river and take to the nearest water craft they see, and others fly to the nearest village, to find it quite evacuated, and feel themselves comparatively safe in the deserted houses they enter.

One instance we know of, and were assured there were

not a few of the same order, where a mother, alone with four children, was preparing them for bed. A messenger called from without, that "the Indians would soon be upon them, and were murdering all in their way." The children were almost nude at the moment, the mother but little in advance of them and barefooted, threw one child over her shoulder, took her babe in her arms, bade the others, one on each side, to hold to her skirt, and thus, though raining hard, she ran eight miles, never laying down her burden or stopping for breath, while she saw an Indian on every stump, and a blanket in every bush; and this where there was not then an Indian within a hundred miles of them.

I hope my reader will not indulge a smile, audible or otherwise, at this panic scene, for "I myself" confess to a feeling akin to this, even though a citizen of St. Paul, a hundred miles or more away, though with no disposition to run. I wished to see it out, and then write it in a book for you to see what we suffered, my good friend. I had been over all this arena, and I knew the Indian from an acquaintance of fifteen years, and I knew no good of him. Now, the least street alarm would unseal the eye-lids and bring my nerve-quivering body to the window, for the Indians might even come here, and so cat-like were their movements, that the town might be half destroyed before an alarm was sounded! Many families actually went "below," while those from "above" were rushing here for safety.

Do you remember, reader, of the horrid "scare stories" of the nursery, about the Indians, and of the after lessons of our school books, and how the impression of terror mixed in the mind with the very name of Indian? You would have run then at the sight of a passive Indian, and these impressions were now having their fruition of fear. You, no doubt, would have done the same.

But it was not every where thus. Far up the valley, the alarm started, and like a wild tornado, it rushed on, till every house was filled in all the villages of this so lately quiet and beautiful valley; every strong building was barricaded, and hastily put in the best possible state for defense. Arms and ammunition of all kinds were concentrated with all speed, and brave hearts, men, yes MEN of will and purpose, resolved to do or die.

Still they come, those worn and weary refugees: One mother has dropped her darling infant by the wayside, and being hotly pursued, could not stop to recover it. A child has seen its parents, perhaps both, fall beneath a murderous bullet or tomahawk, and barely escape with life. Alas, "there is no more room in the inn;" in many hamlets, every house is an inn, and every woman a nurse, and, pitiable to relate, not a few are obliged to turn from what would gladly have been a friendly shelter to the covert of bushes, and the protection of Him who "carries the lambs in his bosom," and to the ministrations of those who

"Walk the earth unseen,
Both when we sleep and when we wake."

On the more remote boundaries, red lights darted athwart the sky in the night time, and dense pillars of smoke obscured the sun in the day—the light and smoke of burning houses and ripened grain-fields.

As if to add to one night of terrific horror, a storm of thunder and lightning, and wind and rain, fell on those shelterless ones, so lately in the homes of comfort. Vivid flashes made the darkness visible, felt almost, as in Egypt in the day of the plagues. It is no fiction, no fancy sketch, reader, nor was it a single instance, but innumerable, that when the heavens cleared, when the sun again rose on these roofless mothers, it rose, also, for the first time, on a new existence. A new life, a being of immortal destiny was folded in the arms and feebly clasped to the bosom of that mother. Yes, during surroundings like the above, many a child was born; many a sad-hearted mother prayed the angels would take it before it should know sorrow or be left to die from starvation and cruel want, or worse, to fall into the hands of the merciless savage.

Let the plate be adjusted so as to take in the scene entire; let the skillful artist daguerreotype the same in an actual life view,—would it all be told? Ah, no! none but the Divine Artist can daguerreotype the heart throbs, and mental and physical throes in these terrible days of panic and fright. Faithfully registered in heaven, it is kept for the wonder and admiration of the angels! Every pang is numbered, "every tear is bottled," for the future healing of those suffering hearts, on whom the calamity fell, not in righteous indignation and judgment, as on some.

True, much of the above described panic occurred where there was no immediate or present cause for it; yet it cannot be wondered at. Fresh excitement was constantly imparted by continual arrivals, as was new vigor to the flight by the fears which accumulated at every step. With all who participated in the panic, the cause to them was real. They suffered equally, in mind, with those who were flying from the actual murderous scenes, for such there were, as the reader has seen and shall presently see. They believed them to follow close in the wake of those who told the tale. In short, to be just upon them; hence, like the snowball gathering bulk and power as it rolls over the inclined plain, did this panic-ball roll on, depopulating the whole country in its course.

During that memorable Monday, Aug. 18th, the Indians ranged over Brown county, elated with the previous day's success, carrying death and carnage wherever they went. Those who here escaped their murderous hands, rushed to the charming little town of New Ulm, and, added to the population, made about 2,000 souls.

Gov. Ramsey, in his message to the Legislature, soon after convened, says, "Brown county, adjacent to the Sioux Reservation, has felt the worst effects of this calamity. It was peopled chiefly by Germans, and their neat cottages and fine farms gave evidence of the superior thrift and industry which distinguish this class of our foreign-born citizens. Driven from their homes, their property destroyed or plundered, robbed even of their household goods — many of them mourning wives, husbands, children and parents murdered — their beautiful and busy town of New Ulm, and their own homes a blackened heap of ruins:— these poor fugitives, many of whom cannot speak our language, are especially deserving our sympathies."

"In all probability, not less than 30,000 are involved, directly or indirectly, in the loss of life or loss of property, from pillage, destruction, or abandonment," and the details of each family or individual experience would make a volume of thrilling interest.

CHAPTER XIII.

ATTACK ON NEW ULM.

Fifteen miles below Ridgley, on the opposite side of the Minnesota river, at the mouth of the Cottonwood, was the neat little town of New Ulm, containing about 1,500 inhabitants. Nature had furnished an inviting site and been lavish with charms on the surroundings. Sad to say, a class of infidel Germans were first attracted by its beauty — were first to build here their homes. The original proprietors had stipulated that no church edifice should ever "disgrace its soil," under penalty of returning to the former owners. Thus, with no religious restraints, they became strong in wickedness, defiant of the restraints of the Gospel, and resolved that no minister should be allowed to live among them. One they drove from the place, and another was annoyed in every possible way. Even private Christians could not live in peace. They built a dancing hall, and the Sabbaths were spent in drinking and dancing. Wealth had rolled into their coffers, and they said, "our own hands have gotten it." As the crowning act of their ungodliness, some of the "baser sort" paraded the streets one bright Sabbath day, while Heaven was preparing the "vials of wrath" at Acton, bearing a mock figure, purporting to represent our blessed Savior, and labeled with vile and blasphemous mottoes; and the closing scene of the day was burning him in effigy.

Scarcely had the smoke of their unholy doings ceased to rise, as if calling for Heaven's vengeance, when, panic-struck, the enactors hide themselves as if from the wrath of the Almighty. The pleadings and threats of women to protect their homes were alike unavailing. New Ulm was doomed. The dance hall escaped the general conflagration, where "the wrath of man was made to praise Him," in being afterward used for worship by the troops stationed there. Yes, He who was here so lately derided and crucified afresh, was now worshipped and adored.

Recruiting for the volunteer service, some of its citizens found, on Monday afternoon, several dead bodies, horribly mutilated, a few miles back of town. Hastening home to give the alarm, this party was fired upon by Indians in ambush, some of their number and two horses killed. The panic, increased by the constant arrival of refugees, who had barely escaped the bullet, the knife or tomahawk, became terrible.

In expectation of an immediate attack, no man for the emergency was near. A few there were, brave, God-fearing men, who stood firm and unscared, ready to confront the danger, with a suitable leader.

Midway between St. Peter and Traverse, which are separated only by a school section, is the mansion of Judge Flandrau, forty miles from New Ulm. On Tuesday morning, while it was yet dark, the Judge was aroused by a violent rapping at his door. The startling news needed no repetition. Rapid movements ensued. Preliminaries were arranged for advanced action; the care of wife and child committed to an invalid relative from New York City, with peremptory orders to make the best time with a nag whose travelling qualities never won him a reputation for "fast," till past the line of danger. By noon of that day, his own house was closed, and he, with a company of one hundred and fifty men, true as steel, and of the best mettle, was ready to march to the "seat of war."

At four o'clock the same day, the dreaded assailants, three hundred strong, besieged the town. The entire population were huddled together, in houses, inside of two squares, and utterly powerless, from fright, when the first volley was fired. Fortunately, a party of eighteen men had preceded the main body from St. Peter, but vain were their efforts to rally the panic-stricken citizens. The Indians had first fired with long range guns, from the top of the table-land, and while they were advancing, this brave little body hastily organized and advanced to meet the skulking foe, who were now intrenched behind buildings, pouring their murderous volley into the town. The sure aim and true steel of these defenders of those who would not defend themselves, was made, in turn, to tell, and several red skins "bit the dust" in mortal agony. A man and woman, running through the street, to seek better security, were killed, and these were all who met death in this encounter. To increase the panic, and add to the horrors of the scene, several buildings were on fire, some of which were fired by the enemy, and others by friends, in order to get a better shot at the foe.

At six o'clock, Judge Flandrau arrived, to the great joy and relief of those who preceded him. His cavalry charged at once, drove them back, killing twelve or fifteen. The Indians, seeing they had encountered more than their match, gather up their dead, and retire from the field.

At the end of these two awful and ever memorable days, in which the soil of Minnesota drank the blood of more than one thousand of her citizens, by savage hands inflicted, eighty of these were in New Ulm and the immediate vicinity, the list made up by the remnants of slain families, who had sought refuge in other towns.

CHAPTER XIV.

ATTACK ON FORT RIDGLEY.

The thrilling events at Yellow Medicine, the weary prairie marches, neath a burning sun, the change of programme in rapidly varying events, did not abate the determined zeal of the young officer, on whom, now that Capt. Marsh had fallen, devolved the command involving the temporal salvation of the post, and the hundreds who had sought refuge there from the most wily of human foes. Nature's sweet restorer, rest, was forgotten — food was scarcely taken into the account of human needs, while the most active preparations to resist an attack went on. No little assistance was rendered by Mr. Wycoff, of the Indian department, having in charge their annuities on the way to the Agency, accompanied by J. C. Ramsey, A. J. VanVorhes and Maj. E. A. C. Hatch, since having been commissioned with the celebrated Hatch's battallion doing active and efficient service, for which it was originated.

So crowded was the garrison with refugees, that rigid discipline had to be kept over the citizens, as well as the soldiers, and the men were armed, or set to work on the defenses. Those were anxious working hours, greatly embarrassed by the presence of women and children. But the energy of their brave leader never failed him; everywhere present, he cheered the men in their work, infusing, throughout the ranks, his own indomitable spirit, while the Supreme Ruler held the savage hordes at bay, until they were comparatively prepared to receive them. No knowledge could be obtained from the outer world, and they knew not of the fearful work in progress at New Ulm, but were sure that this news-calm was no precursor of good tidings, and regarded the whole region as under savage blockade.

Foiled in their first attack on the doomed city, incensed by defeat, and thirsting for larger draughts of blood, these demon besiegers haste over the intervening space, designing a grand surprise, and capture of the fort. Very cautious and guarded was their approach, with flowers and grass fastened into their turbaned heads, that they might not be detected from the tall weeds and grass. But the watchful eye of sentinels discovered them on the west side of the fort, at noon, on Wednesday, Aug. 20th. At one o'clock, they had nearly surrounded them, and with horrid yells, poured a volley into the garrison. Several crawled even to the walls of a building, raised the windows, and fired several shots at Mrs. Jones, wife of the Ordnance officer, who was rescued from her fearful position by a squad from Co. C., one of whom, Mark Grere, lost his life, in the brave, soldierly act, for which the lives of three Indians at once paid the forfeit.

The excitement was intense. Men rally, in haste, to the conflict — women and children scream, in uncontrollable panic — the big guns fail to work, and investigation finds them stuffed with rags, the work of four half-breed soldiers, who had deserted, and gone over to the Indians, and were now encouraging them in their work of death. Had the courage of the assailants been equal to the opportunity, they might have rushed in, at this moment, and carried off, in triumph, the scalp of every person there.

But God overruled the savages' purpose, and the calm presence of mind which so characterized the commandant, through all this anxious siege, never, for a moment, forsook him; but, reckless of personal safety, even when bullet showers were thickest, he passed from post to post, cheering and encouraging his men, and had the satisfaction of seeing one savage fall by his own unerring aim. From the confusion came order, and the leader's spirit was soon diffused through the ranks, and every man stood firmly at his post. A six pound howitzer being ranged upon the foe, in the hands of Sergeant Jones, did deadly work. Some were seen to bound into the air, from its unwelcome effects, and all, for that time, were scattered like autumn leaves, in a strong wind. As darkness fell upon the brave but besieged company, the foe gathered in council so near, that the clamor of voices was heard, all that weary, working night. The day's battle had been sharp, determined and persistent on the part of the assailants; as sharp, more cool and decided, on the other. Two soldiers and two citizens killed, and one wounded, was the sum total of the day's casualties to the garrison.

The Fort buildings are mainly of wood, without walls or fortification, erected more for the purpose of government storage than military defense, hence in constant danger of being fired, as were also the citizens' buildings without. Several ignited arrows were shot into the roofs, but fortunately without effect. A timely rain, with thunder and fearful tempest, checked the night work, and gave the handful of weary men within the Fort, time to rally their failing strength and courage.

With no lightning speed had the news of the outbreak gone to the Executive department. The Eden Valley of the Minnesota had not yet seen its first decade since it passed from savage to civilized hands, from those who would now wrest it from its lawful and just purchasers, and telegraph posts had not had time to grow, even in this prolific soil. But messengers, disguised as Indians, had crept forth from those walls, and gone, with swiftest horse speed, demanding re-enforcements.

Impatient of delay, and distrusting their own powers of endurance, this struggling band continued daily, during the five days they were besieged, to send forth a "hurry up" for the relief desired.

Every hour was full of the most intense anxiety. If the battle ceased, it was only to be renewed with greater vigor.

Women huddled together, in almost breathless fear, children clung to their mothers in terror, and those too young to understand its nature, seemed conscious of impending danger. Sentinels stood on the "watch tower" with eyes keenly alert, and ever and anon a spyglass surveyed the direction whence re-enforcements were expected to come; officers and men stood at their posts all that weary night, not doubting but the attack would be renewed on Wednesday night. At daylight, on Thursday, 21st, the attack was renewed, but was less bold and spirited than on the previous day. The numbers seemed depleted, which was probably owing, in part, to losses of the previous battle, but more to scouting parties being out, plundering the country and extending the work of death. The Indians retired, after about four hours hard fighting, until six, when they again renewed their work of death, continuing it for an hour and a half, when, being warmly repulsed by our troops, again retired, leaving the little struggling, heroic band to another night of anxiety. Aside from an occasional alarm, nothing broke upon its quiet. It is surprising, how long and how much, in the face of danger, men can endure, without rest. O, how eagerly they waited re-enforcements, but still they came not.

On Friday morning, the Indians seemed resolved on one more desperate assault on the Fort, to retrieve the advantage lost by the three previous attacks. In anticipation of this, strong breastworks had been commenced, and though incomplete, afforded some protection.

At mid-day, the enemy were seen advancing, at a distance of two miles, in increased numbers, and all mounted. The ravine surrounding the Fort, gave them protection, till fully ready for action. For five hours, bullets flew like hail, and the guns were one continuous rattle; the battle was bitter and persistent. In one room, thirty-two balls were picked up, which had perforated the walls. One who was there, says, "All our previous engagements were as boys' play, in comparison with this. It was evidently expected to be the last, on the part of the enemy, for they confidently designed a charge and a capture. The first volley, discharged from the woods, the high reeds and out-buildings, was perfectly terrific. It seemed that all the incarnate fiends of hell were concentrated and let loose upon this little band, with all the fierceness of infuriated demons, crazed for blood and plunder. The fire was received with coolness, by our men, and returned in the same spirit. The officers and gunners were most exposed, yet only one man was killed, and but four wounded."

Too much praise cannot be awarded the officers and gunners; yea, every man in that seven days' sleepless watch and engagement, deserves a commission of high rank. Sergeant Jones, doing deadly execution with his big gun, really saved the post. At one time, a charging party was placed very near the fort, and the half-breeds within, distinctly understood and interpreted the order "to charge on and seize the cannon." But to thus charge with death, they had not the courage.

Early in the engagement, they had cut loose the mules and horses in the government stables, and attempted to fire some outside buildings.

The writer above alluded to, A. J. Van Vorhes, further says, under date of 25th, "After seeing themselves foiled in taking the post, their next game was to burn the barracks, in which are the government stores, the families seeking protection, &c. A number of fire arrows were found on the roofs, but, fortunately, they failed in their mission. Every preparation was made for a night attack, but the severe lesson of the afternoon, or a care for their plunder, prevented.

"About six o'clock, Saturday morning, this body of demons was seen approaching by the same route, but continuing along the ravines, and under cover of hills and woods, they passed by, most probably on their way to New Ulm, or vicinity, from which direction the fires of burning buildings were seen, all Saturday night.

"Since the battle of Friday, we have been undisturbed, but are in momentary expectation and preparation. The weather, perhaps, has had something to do with it, as we have had rain most of the day and night.

"Some three hundred women and children are here, for support and protection. This is a great embarrassment to the officers and soldiers. With them out of the way, a great point would be achieved. When the hospital becomes filled with them, as will be the case, unless removed soon, our position will be distressing indeed.

"What is the matter in St. Paul and Fort Snelling? Have re-enforcements been sent and cut off, or are we to be sacrificed to indifference and apathy? Let help be sent in such force that it cannot be impeded. With this point in the hands of the enemy, the Mississippi will share the universal desolation."

There was prompt response to the first note of alarm, and yet they knew it not. Every hour was an age to them. Lieut. Sheehan had written on the 21st: "We can hold out but a little longer, unless re-enforced. We are being attacked almost every hour. Our little band is being decimated. We had hoped to be re-enforced to-day, but as yet, hear of none coming."

Gov. Ramsey had hastened to Fort Snelling, where the new regiments were rendezvoused, and ordered four companies of the Sixth to march at once to the scene of disturbance, under Hon. Henry H. Sibley, whose long residence on the frontier, and thorough acquaintance with Dakota character, especially qualified him for the command to which he was designated. Seven other companies soon followed, under Col. Crooks, with orders to report to Col. Sibley.

We do not wonder that, in this severe siege, with no rest, day or night, save, as every other man, in turn, occasionally, in the lull of battle, slept on his arms a few moments at a time, the eye grew weary with watching, and the heart faint with waiting, and that, in this anxious solicitude, they should feel themselves neglected and uncared for. Hours were magnified into days, and days into weeks, to them, while relief troops were moving up the Minnesota valley.

'Twas a foot-sore march. The men, many of them just from the counting-room or law office, were not inured to hardness. Besides, there were unavoidable delays, over which, the Colonel commanding had no control. To meet the foe, unprepared, would be to rush to unbidden death, and the rifles were found to be useless, even in the hands of those most skillful in their use; therefore, they must camp at St. Peter, till the defect could be remedied, or others brought from St. Paul. Two mounted companies, under command of Col. McPhail, went forward and reached the Fort, August 28, after the walls of the wooden buildings were perforated "like the lid of a pepper-box," greatly to the relief of the worn-out men, and enabled the half starved refugees to go to a place of greater security. The night of the 30th was the first of rest, to the besieged party, for ten days. All now slept well, while the re-enforcements stood guard.

The Minnesota Third, a brave and gallant band as ever "sighted" rebels, was surrendered by their officer in command, to which they never assented, at Murfreesboro, Tenn., in July, 1862. They were at once paroled, the officers remaining prisoners of war. This well disciplined regiment was deemed a desirable force for frontier emergency; hence, a request from the Executive Department, to the War Department, responded to by prompt "orders" to report at Fort Snelling. On the day of their departure from the south, an "exchange" was effected with the rebel powers, and so they entered the home field, untrammeled by the shackles of parole.

To the Third was added the Seventh, which reported as before mentioned, so that Col. Sibley moved on to the fort, with a force of fifteen hundred men, where he arrived August 31st. But he found not an Indian to oppose him, though tokens of their doings everywhere met the eyes, and their dingy smoke wreaths had not yet ceased to rise from the ruins. Ghastly dead men lay here and there on the prairies, their bodies far advanced in decomposition, torn and fed on by hogs and prairie wolves, and tainting the air with their vapor. That night they were saluted by a few shots from the foe, with no serious effect.

We close this chapter with the record of Lieut Sheehan's promotion to a captaincy of the Company he so gallantly led, in the seven days of peril, — a merited honor, awarded by Governor Ramsey, 26th Sept.; and thereafter his military skill found wider scope on the tented fields of the South, in combat with a rebel foe. May his well-won laurels ever be green, and his name, indelible on the scroll of fame, never receive ambition's taint, but like the burnished gold, be reflecting more glory, when children's children shall recount, with pride, the valor and achievements of Thomas J. Sheehan.

T. J. Sheehan

Capt. T. J. SHEEHAN, 1st Minn. Vol.

CHAPTER XV.

SECOND AND FINAL ATTACK ON NEW ULM.

During those fearful and anxious days, while the engagement was going on at Fort Ridgley, this doomed village was unmolested. The time was well appreciated in intrenching their position, burying their dead, and in sending out scouting parties in various directions. One of these brought in thirteen persons who had secreted themselves in a slough to escape massacre.

The route of the Indians from the Fort was marked by the burning of buildings, the fires of which were seen at New Ulm, and intimated their approach to those preparing for their reception. When four miles in the distance, the foe were seen, and soon drove in the pickets, but all, save the still panic-struck inhabitants, rallied for defense. On they come, in all their fierce savage majesty. From twelve to five o'clock, the battle raged in the most approved style of savage warfare. With the rapidity of thought, they dodged from house to house, — fifteen of which, in less than half an hour, were in flames, — picking their man as they went. Their arms were the best, and their aim deadly.

The commander-in-chief, Judge Flandrau, was, during all these terrible hours, in a dense shower of leaden hail, cool, discreet and determined, constantly among "the boys," cheering them on, and these performed their part equally as well. More and more desperate the enemy become! Captain Dodd, well known in the State, makes an imprudent effort to drive them back by a mighty charge. Riding forward of the breastwork, shouting to his comrades, "come on," he becomes the target. His body is pierced by five balls, but heroically he keeps his saddle till he fell in the arms of his own people.

"At five o'clock was the turning point in the struggle. Now it seemed as if the Indians would capture the town. The remarkable gallantry of Judge Flandrau alone prevented this result, and a massacre, which for magnitude would have been without a parallel in the history of Indian warfare. He rallied his men, and, charging at their head, drove them out of the brush at the lower end of the town, the point whence they had inflicted the greatest injury upon the garrison.

"All night the burning of houses continued. Occasional guns were fired till ten, when they fell back, formed into three great parties, and had war dances, shouting and singing during the night."

During the fight, ten men were killed, and nearly fifty wounded. Theirs were carried from the battle-field, and the number not known — supposed to be not less than forty killed.

"As morning dawned, the enemy again came dashing over the prairie, 'spoiling for a fight,' and great indeed was their chagrin and surprise to find their breastwork but a few smouldering ashes. They gathered at the east end of the town, and seemed to be consulting what course to pursue. Finally, they collected a large drove of cattle, of which there were plenty all around them, and moving these as a breastwork, again advanced. But the cattle were not to be allied to such chaps, and soon commenced to make tracks for other parts, and the enemy, finding himself perfectly thwarted, skedaddled."

As these took up their line of march for parts unknown, they formed a train four miles long, of cattle, farm horses, and wagons, loaded with valuable booty, and several elegant "turn-outs." No wonder that, jubilant with success, they had made the night hideous with dance and song.

The next order in the programme of arrangements, was the evacuation of New Ulm. The entire region above, and on either hand, was desolated, depopulated, one-half of the town destroyed, and had it been safe to do so, there was no inducement for the people to remain.

Just one week had now passed since the first intimation of the rise of savage ire, and alas! what an incalculable amount of evil had been done. Where peace, plenty, and content reigned, there were heard now but the wails of anguished hearts, and seen but the desolation of hopes, the utter annihilation of earthly trust.

It was a mournful cortege which, on that Monday

morning, Aug. 25, took up its line of march for Mankato, twenty-five miles distant. Instead of ambulances for the eighty wounded persons, some of whom were little children, innocent of wrong, hacked and mangled in a most shocking and brutal manner, they were conveyed in hard running farm wagons, while scouting Indians watched from a distance, but happily leaving them undisturbed.

Such another company, perhaps, the world has never seen. Such a march, history never recorded. Here were mothers whose children, their shrieks still ringing in their ears, had been slaughtered before their eyes, — strong men "shorn of their strength," who in one day had passed from wealth to poverty, — homes in ashes, wife and children gone, some of whom wounded had crept away into sloughs or bushes to die, — wives bereft of husbands, children of parents, the heads of all bowed down in overwhelming grief and a sense of utter destitution. For their protection, the glittering bayonet gleamed, and yet a sense of the comparative security was no relief to the bitter anxiety of heart. In two instances, actual insanity occurred.

CHAPTER XVI.

BATTLE OF NEW ULM — OFFICIAL REPORT OF CAPTAIN FLANDRAU.

ST. PETER, August 27th, 1862.

HIS EXCELLENCY, GOVERNOR ALEX. RAMSEY:

SIR:—Events have transpired so rapidly, and my time has been so taken up since my last communication, that I cannot with certainty recall the condition of things existing at its date, but believe I wrote you almost immediately preceding the second attack upon New Ulm, which occurred on Saturday last.

During the morning we discovered a succession of fires on the Nicollet county side of the river, very near the bluffs, approaching us from the direction of Fort Ridgley. Our supposition was that the Fort had fallen, and the Indians were moving down upon the town, on that side of the river, to unite with another party on the side we were occupying.

As they increased in numbers very rapidly, I thought it best to send a detachment over to ascertain the design of the enemy, and if possible give him a check on that side of the river. Lieut. Huey, of Traverse des Sioux, volunteering to perform the service, I detailed seventy-five men with him, and they crossed at the ferry opposite the town, about nine o'clock, A. M. Very shortly after their departure, the Indians were discovered issuing from the woods above the town, in large numbers, and assembling upon the prairie.

I at once posted all my available force upon the open prairie, outside the town, about half a mile at some points, and at a greater distance towards the point at which I conceived the attack would be made, determining to give them battle in the open field, where I conceived would be our greatest advantage.

At nearly ten A. M. the body began to move towards us, first slowly, and then with considerable rapidity. The men were encouraged by their officers to stand firm and meet the attack, and all promised well. We had in all, about two hundred and fifty guns, while the Indians were variously estimated at from four to five hundred. I fixed the number at not over three hundred and fifty.

Their advance upon the sloping prairie, in the bright sunlight, was a very fine spectacle, and, to such inexperienced soldiers as we all were, intensely exciting. When within about one mile and a half of us, the mass began to expand like a fan, and increase in the velocity of its approach, and continued this movement until within about double rifle shot, when it had covered our entire front. Then the savages uttered a terrific yell, and came down upon us like the wind. I had stationed myself at a point in the rear, where communication could be had with me easily, and awaited the first discharge with great anxiety, as it seemed to me that to yield was certain destruction, as the enemy would rush into the town and drive all before them.

The yell unsettled the men a little, and just before the rifles began to crack, they fell back along the whole line, and committed the error of passing the outer houses without taking possession of them, a mistake which the Indians immediately took advantage of by themselves occupying them in squads of two, three, and up to ten. They poured into us a sharp and rapid fire, as we fell back, and opened from the houses in every direction. Several of us rode up to the hill, endeavoring to rally the men, and with good effect, as they gave three cheers and sallied out of various houses they had retreated to, and checked the advance effectually. The firing from both sides then became general, sharp and rapid, and it got to be a regular Indian skirmish, in which every man did his own work after his own fashion.

The Indians had spread out till they had got into our rear, and on all sides, having the very decided advantage of the houses on the bluffs which commanded the interior of the town, with the exception of the windmill which was occupied by about twenty of the Le Sueur Tigers, and held them at long range. The wind was from the lower part of the town, and this fact directed the larger part of the enemy to that point, where they promptly commenced firing the houses, and advancing behind the smoke. The conflagration became general in the lower part of the town on both sides of the street, and the bullets flew very thickly, both from the bluff and up the street. I thought it prudent to dismount and direct the defense on foot.

Just at this point, Capt. Dodd, of St. Peter, and some one else whose name I do not know, charged down the street, to ascertain (I have since learned,) whether some horsemen seen in the extreme lower town, were not our friends coming in, and were met about three blocks down with a heavy volley from behind a house, five bullets passing through Capt. Dodd, and several through his horse. They both turned, and the Captain got in sufficiently near to be received by his friends before he fell. He died about five hours after being hit. Too much cannot be said of his personal bravery, and general desire to perform his duty manfully.

Capt. Saunders, of the Le Sueur company, was shot through a part of his body shortly after, and retired, placing his rifle in effective hands, and encouraging the men. The fight was going on all around the town, during the whole forenoon and part of the afternoon, sometimes with slight advantage to us, and again to the Indians, but the difficulty that stared us in the face, was the gradual but certain approach, up the main street, behind the burning buildings, which promised our destruction. We frequently sallied out and took buildings in advance, but the risk of being picked off from the bluff, was unequal to the advantage gained, and the duty was performed with some reluctance by the men. In the lower part of the town I had some of the best men in the State, both as shots and for coolness and determination. It will be sufficient to name two as types of a class of the fighting men—Asa White and Newell Houghton, known to all old settlers. They did very effective service in checking the advance, both by their unerring rifles and the good examples their steadiness placed before the younger men.

We discovered a concentration of Indians on the side of the street towards the river, and at the rear of the buildings, and expected a rush upon the town from that position, the result of which I feared more than anything else, as the boys had proved unequal to it in the morning; and we were not disappointed, for in a few moments they came, on ponies and on foot, furiously, about sixty in number, charging round the point of a little grove of oaks. This was the critical point of the day, but four or five hours under fire had brought the boys up to the fighting temperature, and they stood firmly, and advanced with a cheer, routing the rascals like sheep. They received us with a very hot fire, killing Houghton, and an elderly gentleman, whose name I did not know. As they fled in a crowd at very short range, we gave them a volley that was very effectual, and settled the fortunes of the day in our favor, for they did not dare try it over. I think, after once repulsing them in a fair fight, we could have successfully resisted them, had they returned a second time, as the necessary confidence had been gained.

White men fight under great disadvantage the first time they engage Indians. There is something so fiendish in their yells, and terrifying in their appearance when in battle, that it takes a good deal of time to overcome the unpleasant sensation that it inspires. Then there is a snake-like stealth in all their movements that excites distrust and uncertainty, which unsteadies the nerves at first.

After this repulse, the battle raged until dark, without sufficient advantage on one side or the other to merit mention in detail, when the savages drew off, firing only an occasional shot from under close cover.

After dark, we decreased the extent of our lines of barricades, and I deemed it prudent to order all the buildings outside to be burned, in order to prevent their having come from behind which, to annoy us. We were compelled to consume about forty valuable buildings, but as it was a *military necessity*, the inhabitants did not demur, but themselves applied the torch cheerfully. In a short time we had a fair field before us, of open prairie, with the exception of a large square brick building, which we held, and had loopholed in all the stories on all sides, which commanded a long portion of our front towards the bluff. We also dug a system of rifle pits on that front, outside the barricades, about four rods apart, which completed our defenses.

That night we slept very little, every man being at the barricades all night, each third man being allowed to sleep at intervals.

In the morning, the attack was renewed, but not with much vigor, and subsided about noon.

During the day, a body of men appeared in the lower town, and turned out to be a detachment of one hundred and fifty volunteers from Nicollet and Sibley counties, under Capt. E. St. Julien Cox, which had been forwarded to our relief by Col. Sibley. They had about fifty Austrian rifles, and the rest were armed with shot guns and hunting rifles. Their appearance inspired us with gladness, as things were becoming doubtful.

I held a council of the officers, and we determined to attempt an evacuation of the town, carrying off all the inhabitants, women, children, sick and wounded, to the number of about two thousand. This movement was a very perilous one to undertake, with the force at our command, but the confined state of the town was rapidly producing disease among the women and children, who were huddled up in cellars and close rooms, like sheep in a cattle car, and we were fast becoming short of ammunition and provisions. I feared the result of another attack by a larger force, and all the people decided that they would abandon the town the first opportunity, as residence there was impossible under the circumstances.

At daylight next morning the barricades were broken, and the wagons taken out and put in motion. The scene was one of indescribable confusion and destruction. The poor people, naturally desirous of carrying off all they could, filled their wagons with boxes and baggage, to the exclusion (as we found before the train was complete,) of many of the women and wounded. I was, therefore, compelled to order all articles of a bulky nature to be tumbled out, and their places supplied by more valuable freight. It was hard, but necessary, and the inhabitants yielded with less reluctance than I had anticipated.

About nine o'clock A. M., we moved with one hundred and fifty-three wagon loads of women, children, sick and wounded, and a large company on foot. Lieutenant Cox took the general disposition of the escort, and the various commands were posted so as best to protect the whole in case of attack. It was a melancholy spectacle to see two thousand people, who a few days before had been prosperous and happy, reduced to utter beggary, starting upon a journey of thirty miles, through a hostile country, every inch of which we expected to be called upon to defend from an attack, the issue of which was life or horrid butchery. Beggary, starvation, and probable destruction were at one end of the road; a doubtful escape from the latter at the other. We took the latter alternative, and, under Providence, got through.

During the battle, we lost, as near as I can ascertain, about ten killed and fifty wounded. I can give you no accurate detail of either, as the casualties occurred among citizens, soldiers, and strangers. The physicians, of whom, fortunately, we had a good supply, may have kept some hospital lists, but I have been too much occupied to ascertain. I was satisfied to know the wounded were well cared for, without knowing who they were.

I was seconded, ably and bravely, by all the officers and most of the men of the companies, and many citizens from different parts of the State, and strangers who were present, so uniform was their good conduct, and valuable their services, that one could not be mentioned without naming all. There were several cases of abandonment immediately preceding the attack, which, if designed to evade the struggle, were disgraceful in the extreme, and unworthy of Americans. But as they may have arisen from other causes, I will not report the names of the parties.

Many narrow escapes occurred during the protracted fight. Several persons were shot through the hat. One young man received three bullets through the pantaloons in rapid succession, without being hurt in the least.

We did not burn the town on leaving, thinking possibly that the Indians might not return and destroy it, and not deeming it much of a defense for them, should they occupy it on our return.

It was my design that the country between New Ulm and Mankato, should be immediately reoccupied by our troops, and the ground temporarily lost by our withdrawal, regained at once by fresh troops, well equipped and capable of remaining on the field, and I looked for material of that sort for the business on my arrival; but not a soldier from the regular service, except Captain Dane, with one hundred horses, has yet reached that part of the country, which is at this moment utterly defenseless, except so far as he is capable of holding it. The citizen volunteers that went to the assistance of New Ulm, disbanded pretty generally on their return, being barefooted, overworked, and required at their homes.

I wish your Excellency would turn the tide of soldiers flowing into the valley, to the Blue Earth region, from which the whole southern portion of the State can be protected, and efficient co-operation afforded the column advancing upon the north side of the Minnesota.

Hoping my operations meet your approval, I am
Truly your obedient servant,
CHARLES E. FLANDRAU,
Commanding West of the Minnesota.

CHAPTER XVII.

THE MISSION PARTY.

Dr. Williamson, unwilling to believe there was any thing but a "scare," and yet fearing all things, sent away from Yellow Medicine, on Tuesday morning, the younger members of his family, while, with his wife and sister, he remained, to see whereunto the trouble would grow. For thirty years he had labored among this people — had a perfect knowledge of their language, and his soul was wholly engrossed for their good, both temporally and spiritually — in short, had been, as the others, a faithful, self-sacrificing missionary. This was the work to which he had devoted his life. His influence over them, was, under some circumstances, very great. Why should it not be now? He had seen individual dissatisfaction, but never a general uprising, and he was unwilling to interpret aright the demonstrations before him.

Mr. Riggs, under the guidance of a Christian Indian, had started, with his family, from Hazlewood, early on Tuesday morning, but was met by a hostile party, his team taken from him, and they escaped to a bushy island, in the river, where they were nearly devoured by mosquitoes. The first detachment of Dr. Williamson's household, hunted them out, and with them went on their way, numbering, in all, some forty persons, and not over six armed men in the company. Providentially, the terrible rain storm, which caused the battle at the fort to cease, until the "cords were lengthened, and the stakes strengthened," completely obliterated their tracks, so that they were not followed and murdered, by the war party which crossed their trail.

The Doctor remained until Wednesday, when, assured it was no longer safe to do so, they started, in an ox cart, guided by a Christian Indian, to overtake their family and other friends. Passing Beaver Creek Settlement, they found it entirely deserted. Inquiring of some Indians where the white people were, they replied:

"All gone to the fort, and you go, too, or you will be shot."

Nearly all there had been killed or made captive. In one instance, a war party started out of the Big Woods, with the design of crossing the trail of these parties, to kill or make them prisoners. "His-big-fire," a Christian Indian, known as Robert Hopkins, joined and kept with them until he had lured them from their purpose, and their intended victims had passed beyond the reach of their bullets, when he left the war path and returned to find the people of his choice — the Christian Missionaries.

On, the separate mission parties journeyed, scarcely knowing their whereabouts, or caring, so that they kept out of the way of the prowling savages, which, occasionally, were seen in the distance. It was woman's patience and faith which shone clearest, and buoyed up the sinking spirits of the men, during those desolate days and nights, suffering, as they were, for food, and often drenched to the skin with the cold, drizzling, and again the pelting rain. Even the children endured all this with a fortitude which shames complaining manhood.

At last, the two mission parties, having each been increased by wounded fugitives, to whom they had acted the "Good Samaritan," form a junction, and together make for the fort, where, unknown to them, the battle fury raged with the greatest violence. All were eager to enter its walls, thinking then all danger would be over. How every heart rejoiced at the prospect of being, once more, safe from fear, with abundance of food and rest!

Now they pass a sight which makes all hearts quail, and to thank God for their own deliverance, thus far. A mother and three children lay by the roadside, (the first time they had dared take to the road,) weltering in their own gore. And, near by, a sick woman had been burned, on the mattrass on which she lay, while her two sons were trying to escape with her. This filial love was rewarded by cruel death to each. Traces of massacre and butchery were more frequent, as they neared their destination, and their danger, where they had hoped security, was most augmented. The plains around were literally full of Indians, some of whom were seen at no great distance.

They now expected an attack, and drew up in battle line, with onward march, tightening their grasp upon their weapons, with firm resolve to die, rather than yield to the foe. They trusted in the living God, and He could and did deliver them.

Then they saw rockets ascend from the fort, and had no thought but that they were beacons, to guide them there, and not signals of distress, as they really were. There was then a lull in the battle storm, which was improved by Dr. Williamson and Mr. Hunter, who went forward, crawling on their hands and knees, and, as by miracle, avoiding the skulking Indians, and passing the blazing stables, enter the garrison, in safety. It was a wonderful exploit, which surprised all within the walls. But the long desired rest had not come yet.

The exhausted condition of the troops, and the crowded state of the barracks, made it inexpedient for more to enter, even could they escape the savage bullet or tomahawk. With sad disappointment, the tidings was received by the hastening party, and their hearts sunk within them. It was now quite dark, and the glare of burning buildings misled these scalp-seekers, and though passing but a few rods from them, their "eyes were blinded that they did not see them," and they hastened on, with rapid speed, still further away, in quest of their prey. With suspended breath, and fluttering hearts, they had heard them pass, and again, with as much speed and little noise as possible, push on their tired teams. From sounds they heard, death seemed lurking all around, but, trusting in God, they fainted not. In fording a stream, the exhausted teams gave out, and then they unhitched and let them graze, despite the danger. So tired and worn were all, that they sank down on the wet grass to rest, while one only, each in turn, rifle in hand, stood guard over their sleeping friends.

They knew these blood-hounds were upon their track, and that, just before daylight, was their time for attack, so, as this danger approached, they were again on the move. Four of their number now left, going in another direction. Scarcely were they out of sight, when their friends heard the firing of guns; afterwards the decayed bodies of these four men were found, where they fell, scarcely a mile from the main party. Thus had these again escaped death.

On Saturday morning, August 23d, after a vigorous siege of four days, the Indians, despairing of ultimate success, and ignorant of the decimated condition of the garrison, leaving a few men to prevent the arrival of re-enforcements, and starve the garrison out, they withdrew their main force, and moved for another attack on New Ulm. The Indians moved through the tall, dripping grass, in their approach to the doomed city; scarcely five miles away were passing the mission party, to whom their guns were visible, and by whom the rattle of the same was distinctly heard. They saw the burning buildings, as one after another lit the sky, with its glare, or sent up its lurid columns of smoke.

That night, another tragic scene was enacted, at Norwegian Grove, two miles from which they "encamped" in a deserted house. Weary and worn, they slept securely, while those who fled from it two hours before they entered, were already dead, though they then knew it not, nor of the bloody enactments, even then, at the "Grove." From this point, their dangers lessened, until all had been welcomed by friends, at various points, who had, during this memorable week, been mourning them as among the slain. They had "committed their ways unto the Lord," and he had, mysteriously, "directed their steps."

CHAPTER XVIII.

MASSACRE AT BIG STONE LAKE.

On the banks of Big Stone Lake, far away from white settlements, government agents had sent four men to cut hay, build a blacksmith shop and stables, preparatory to establishing an Agency there. They had, with them, John Julien, a lad of sixteen, for cook, whose parents lived near the lower Agency, and were among the first victims of the raid.

The first specified part of their work was done, and they were camped on the shores of the lake, cutting logs for the buildings. On the morning of the 21st of August, unaware of any danger, and sleeping in unconscious security, in their tent, they were suddenly aroused by a loud and repeated war whoop. They were scarcely on the feet before they were surrounded by fifty or sixty Indians, some on foot and some on horse.

Within ten paces of the tent, a volley was fired, killing one man, Henry Manderfield, instantly. Two others escaped, to be murdered by another party, when thirty miles away. Another, Anthony Manderfield, brother to the above, plunged into the ravine, on the brow of which their tent stood, was closely followed, and several ineffective shots fired upon him. Reaching the lake, he waded along the shore, for two miles, followed by three Indians, in a canoe. Seeing they gained upon him, yea, were about to lay violent hands upon him, by a dexterous manœuvre, he eluded their grasp, plunged into the bushes, where he remained concealed till the immediate danger was passed. He then pushed on, with bare and bleeding feet, in all haste, to the foot of the lake, and though, on one occasion, passing very near an Indian village, a rain, providentially, obliterated his footsteps, hence he was not followed.

At Lac-qui-parle, at the house of a half-breed, he saw Mrs. Huggins, whose husband had been murdered, and Miss Julia La Frambois, captives. He was kindly cared for, his bleeding feet bound up, and his stomach cravings satisfied. But they urged him away, with all possible speed, for they knew it was unsafe for him to remain. After four days of almost incessant travelling, with very little food, he arrived at Fort Ridgley, if not a better, a wiser man, for his experience at Big Stone Lake, and to avenge their treatment of him, and the death of his brother, by joining a cavalry company in defense of the frontier.

The boy, mentioned above, was taken prisoner, the details of which, we reserve for a separate chapter.

When the "Expedition" passed this point, in June after, George Spencer, and others, went over to see the ruins of his trading house. Here they found the skeletons of two human forms, one of whom, George recognized, by the shreds of clothing left, as the clerk in his own employ, when the outbreak commenced. The other, as in the employ of Louis Roberts, at another trading post, two miles away, who, in two days, lost

$80,000 by the Indian raid. Here they had lain, through autumn's rains and winter snows, till summer's heat had come, and were now, by friendly hands, buried, where, by savage hands, they fell. How many more such there be, their bones bleaching by sun and wind, yet remains to be seen.

CHAPTER XIX.

MURDER OF AMOS W. HUGGINS.

Some thirty years before this great Sioux tragedy was enacted, Revs. Riggs and Huggins, faithful and devout men of God, then in the vigor and prime of youthful manhood, and the heart's glow of richest earthly love, settled on the banks of Lac-qui-parle,* several hundred miles removed from civilized life. But they had girded them for the sacrifice, and the salvation of the red man, for whom Christ had died, as for themselves, was the impulse of their hearts. In due time, a son was given to Mr. Huggins, which the Indians learned to pet, caress and love.

Slowly their work went on, and after years of toil, these now toil-worn men and women were able to rejoice in some perceptible good to the people among whom they lived. Olive plants had increased around their tables, and though, to human view, their work seemed disheartening, yet could their hearts rejoice in His goodness, while they could still "thank God and take courage."

Amos W., the subject of this chapter, at the age of sixteen, was sent away, to finish the education commenced under the tutelage of his mother. Meantime, a change in the base of missionary operations took place, and this point was left for more urgent fields of

---
*The lake that speaks.

labor. Amos, having completed his education, returned to his father's house, bringing with him a fair young bride, to grace his frontier home. Government had designated him as its agent, teacher, and general superintendent of Indian affairs at Lac-qui-parle. On the very soil where his boyhood was spent, he dwelt, and among the very people of boyhood's memory. Thus, in quiet security, never dreaming of trouble, their isolation was not an unpleasant one. To these loving hearts, all the joys of earth centered at their own hearth-stone.

Employed as female teacher, Miss Julia La Frambois had long been a valued member of his household. Though a half-breed, she was a young lady of high cultivation, and spoke several languages fluently.

Two smiling cherubs blest their happy home, and a more bright and beautiful morning never dawned, than on the 19th day of August, 1862. It was Mrs. Huggins' twenty-fourth birthday, of which she says: "She little thought, when the morning dawned, so full of hope, and promised to be the happiest day of her life, it was to close, the saddest she had ever known."

Mr. Huggins had been in the field, superintending the work in which the Indians were engaged, and at four o'clock in the afternoon, returned home, bringing with him the oxen they had been using.

Previous to this, two Indians from Red Iron's village came to the house, seemed unusually talkative, asked many questions of Miss Julia, about the sewing machine she was using, but excited no suspicion. As soon as Mr. Huggins came up, they left the house, and the next moment the women heard the report of two guns. Julia rushed out, as the Indians rushed in, who, in a wild, excited manner, exclaimed to Mrs. H. :

"Go out, go out; you shall live — but go out — take nothing with you!"

In the strange bewilderment of the moment, she scarce understood their meaning, and from their manner, supposed that their enemies, the Chippewas, were upon them. Mechanically, she obeyed the imperative command, when she was aroused to terrible consciousness, by seeing Julia, kneeling by the lifeless form of her husband. "O, Josephine! Josephine!" was all she said; but it told the awful tale that *he was dead.* A ball had entered his back, passing through his body, killing him instantly. An ocean of grief swept over her soul, in that one awful and bitter moment. No time was given to adjust the lifeless form, but seeing they were really going to shoot her, unless she went away, she hastily threw over him a lounge cover, on which she was sewing, when she ran out; and with tearless eyes, but a bursting heart, left him there, without even a last kiss of those lips which would never again return this seal of affection. Julia had preceded her to Mr. De Cota's, a half-breed Chippewa trader, with a Sioux wife, who lived near, taking with her the darling little Letta.

When the heroic girl, with their host and hostess, returned to the tragic scene, (it was not deemed safe for the wife to go with them,) they found many excited savages gathered around, some ready almost to "gnash on him with their teeth," for the crime of being a white man; and others, among whom was the chief of the village, Wa-kan-ma-ni, or Walking Spirit, who denounced the deed, the latter saying, had he been there, he would have died before harm should have come to Mr. Huggins.

Before the sun went down, these friendly hands had buried him, without shroud or coffin, and with sad hearts, turned away, while the evil-designing Sioux pillaged the house, and divided among them, for their breakfast, the oxen, which he had driven from the field. With a brave heart, Julia had entered the house, even while full of pillagers and murderers, and secured some articles, which were afterwards of great value to them.

Among the relics of these spoils, were two pocket Bibles, one of which was the well thumbed companion of Mr. Huggins, the precepts of which he bound to his heart, as "the man of his counsel and rule of life." O, what a comfort was this, in the weary, anxious days of captivity which followed,— precious for the sake of him who had read and loved its teachings, as also the "hidden manna" of its leaves—the gracious promises which now fed her sore heart. Therefore, she trusted its teachings, and waited, while its Divine Author guarded her fatherless little ones, and kindly disposed the savages' hearts toward her.

CHAPTER XX.

CAUSE OF THE WAR — WHAT IS AN INDIAN?

We append the reply of one, to the above question, whose opinion is at least entitled to respect and consideration. His whole statement will be found of thrilling interest, and we cheerfully present to our readers the following statement of Mr. Spencer:

"Ever since the treaty, which was made in 1851, with the nation of Dakota or Sioux Indians, they have been finding fault, complaining that the government did not strictly comply with the stipulations of the treaty. While some of the causes of these complaints have been imaginary, there can be no doubt but that there have been good grounds for others. In regard to the management of affairs among the lower Sioux, where the recent outbreak originated, I cannot speak knowingly, as I have not resided among them since the treaty went into effect. But among the upper Sioux, the Sissitons in particular, with whom I have been engaged, in trade, for the past two years, there has been some cause for complaint, on their part.

"I have often heard Standing Buffalo, the Sissiton chief, complain about the whites not fulfilling their promises in regard to the location of mills, schools, mechanics, physicians, etc., among his tribe. It is true that the lower bands enjoyed all the advantages to be derived from these sources, but as they were located at a distance of nearly one hundred miles from the villages and fields of the Sissitons, they derived but little, if any, benefit from them. It is too often the case, that the parties who are employed by the government to hold councils, form treaties, etc., with Indian tribes, do not sufficiently understand the character of the parties with whom they are negotiating; and, consequently, although matters may go off smoothly enough at the time, difficulties are liable to arise in the future, the consequences of which may be disastrous.

"As there are other savage tribes, standing in the same relations to the government to-day, that the Sioux occupied, previous to the insurrection, it may be well enough to examine, minutely, one or two points connected with Indian affairs, which, if properly observed, may be the means of preventing a repetition of the cruel blow, by other tribes, which has been so fearfully inflicted by the Sioux. In the first place, let us examine the Indian himself. What is an Indian?

"Simple as this question may seem, yet it is one that, in my opinion, is not thoroughly understood by our officials, and others, who have Indian affairs in charge. In the great chain of nature, the Indian is a connecting link between the wild beast and the human species. In shape he is human, and has the gift of speech, and, to a limited extent, the use of language. In almost all his actions, he seems to be guided by instinct, rather than reason; to say that he possesses *no* intellect, might possibly be saying too much; but if he does, it seems to be so clouded and obscured, that it does not avail him much. Long association with the whites has developed, in some of them, the reasoning faculties, and shown them to be possessed of some little intelligence. So the same thing may be said of some animals, whose performances seem to be more the result of reason than instinct. The treachery of the Indian is proverbial. Unaccustomed to the comforts and luxuries of a home, there is, in his language, no word which answers to our word home. Accustomed, from infancy, to witness scenes of violence and bloodshed, and, as soon as he can speak, it is impressed upon his mind, that the greatest achievement he is capable of performing, is to dye his hands in the blood of his fellow-creatures, whereby he may become entitled to wear a scalp-feather. He soon learns to take delight in participating in the excitement of the chase, and in following the war path. His passions being subjected to no restraint whatever, his imagination is constantly taxed to invent some new mode of torture, to apply to the victim that may have been unfortunate enough to fall into his hands. The brutish propensities largely predominating, it requires but slight provocation to cause him to turn his murderous weapons against his fellow-beings. Poets may sing, and romancers may write, as much as they will, about the "noble savage," the "dignified and majestic bearing of nature's nobleman," the "generous traits of character" possessed by the "sons of the prairies," etc., but "distance lends enchantment to the view," and after having been, more or less, intimately associated with them, for the last ten years, I have been unable to perceive but a very few of those noble attributes which have been so plentifully ascribed to them. There are some individual exceptions, it is true. As you will find, among our own race, persons, who have been reared under the holy influences of Christianity, possessing the spirit of fiends, so you will find, occasionally, an Indian who is possessed of some feelings of humanity. Skilled to perfection in the peculiar craft pertaining to his calling, and his powers of endurance being almost incredible, when aroused, he becomes the most dangerous of foes.

"When difficulties and misunderstandings arise between civilized nations, they may be amicably adjusted by negotiation, or, that failing, a resort to warfare, conducted on scientific principles, but never losing sight of the great principles of humanity. But not so with a race of savages. Diplomacy is something unknown to them.

"When they feel that they have been wronged, they proceed (actuated solely by a desire for revenge) to wreak their vengeance upon defenceless, helpless women and children. Such being the state of things, how important it is that the government should see that the stipulation of the treaties now existing with those tribes who yet remain friendly, should be strictly and faithfully complied with. Since open hostilities have been commenced by one tribe, it will not require much to induce other tribes to follow their example.

"Another point, which is a very essential one, is the employment of competent interpreters — men who have a thorough knowledge of the two languages. It is my opinion, that more than one-half of the misunderstandings which have arisen between the Indians and the government, may be traced to the fact that the interpreter did not understand, himself, what had been said to him. As a general thing, half-breeds are employed to interpret.

"White men, who are capable of interpreting, cannot afford to accept the position of government interpreter, because the salary is so small that they can make more other ways. To explain what I mean, more fully, we will examine the languages. Ten thousand words will probably more than cover the number of words in the Sioux language, while our language is said to contain over forty thousand words. Now, the half-breed, of course, is raised among the Indians, and acquires his mother tongue perfectly. As he grows up, he becomes associated with the people of the frontier, and from them acquires his knowledge of English, which is not such English as is spoken among the elite. The person who has acquired his education, and has graduated from our high schools, speaks a different language, you might say, from the backwoodsman, who, probably, never saw the inside of a school-house.

"The excess of thirty thousand words in our language over that of the Indian, renders it very easy to say things which cannot be literally interpreted into the Indian tongue. In such cases, you can only convey the idea; that is, if the interpreter has intelligence enough to catch the idea himself. Now, our officials are generally intelligent and educated men. In councils with the Indians, they use the English language in its purity, to which the ear of the poor half-breed is entirely unaccustomed. He hears big sounding words; they are all Greek to him, and, under such circumstances, to convey the proper idea, is next to an impossibility. Under such circumstances, treaties are formed, and, when signed by all parties, the Indian is, half the time, as ignorant of the contents of the document, as a native of Africa. On the other hand, I have known instances where white men, who were wholly unfit for the office, have received and held the responsible position of interpreter for the government; men whose knowledge of the Indian tongue scarcely enabled them to carry on simple every day conversation. They were favorites of those in authority, and therefore received the appointment, the question of competency never being taken into consideration. Under such circumstances, it is the easiest thing in the world for serious misunderstandings to arise between the Indians and the government.

"Now, in regard to the Sioux, they knew that the Federal Government had been carrying on an expensive war for a long time; they believed that almost all our able-bodied men had gone South to take part in the war. The customary time arrived for the payment of their moneys and distribution of goods, and the Indians were assembled to receive them; but the money did not arrive.

"They were put off, with promises that, by such and such time, they should have their money, but were as often disappointed.

"Two months after the customary time for making payments had passed, when their agent volunteered to go into the service of his country, and taking almost every able-bodied man on the reservation with him, he left his post, to be gone, nobody knew how long. The Indians, finding that their agent had thus left them, without giving them any satisfactory explanations, were at once impressed with the idea that the Federal Government had ceased to exist, and that their money had been expended for the purpose of carrying on the war, and that they were left to take care of themselves, as best they could."

When they broke camp at Red Wood, and started for Yellow Medicine, Mr. Spencer says:

"A fine large flag, of the Hudson Bay Company, was flying out to the breeze, from one of the wagons in front, and a few American flags, which had been captured, were raised at different points of the procession.

"It did not occur to me, to inquire how they came by that emblem of British authority, but I supposed it to have been presented to some chief or soldier, many years ago, and it had been preserved until the present time. In the early part of the present century, British flags, medals, &c., were freely distributed among all the Indian tribes by the British traders.

* * * * * *

"Here much time was spent in counselling. Little Crow was very anxious to move up in a body, and place themselves under the protection of the English, at the Red River settlement, but a majority were against him. In the meantime, the attacks upon New Ulm and Fort Ridgley had been made, but their statements were so conflicting, and I was suffering from my wounds so much, that I took no pains to ascertain the particulars; one thing is certain, however, that they did not lose so many men as the whites have always supposed to have been killed.

"At New Ulm, the Sioux were assisted by some of the Winnebagoes, and the conduct of 'Little Priest,' in that engagement, was very highly spoken of by the Sioux.

"'Little Priest' is the head chief of the Winnebagoes, and lost two of his warriors in that attack. Messengers were sent from here to the Sissitons, Yanctons, Yanktonais, and to the governor of Selkirk Settlement, to inform them that they (the Mede-wa-kan-tons and Wa-hpe-kwtes) had declared war against the whites, and praying for their assistance. They considered it almost certain, that the western tribes would join them, and they confidently believed that the English would assist them. They say, that many years ago, the English gave them a small piece of artillery, and named it, 'Da-ko-ta-chis-tina,' or 'Little Sioux,' and promised them that, in case any difficulty should arise between the Americans and themselves, they could look to them (the English) for assistance. I could not hear, in any of my conversations with them, anything that caused me to suspect that secessionists had anything to do with it. If the tribes on the Missouri had been tampered with by secessionists, (which may have been the case,) this outbreak, I think, was no part of the programme.

"While encamped here, 'Standing Buffalo,' the head chief of the Sissitons, came down with about two hundred warriors, and, in a council with Little Crow, demanded the goods that had been taken from the Agency buildings at Yellow Medicine, as his property. This demand Little Crow refused to comply with, saying that as he had done all the fighting he was entitled to the plunder. Standing Buffalo then refused to take any part in the war, and threatened Little Crow or any of his people with death, if they came into his country for protection, in case they were defeated by the whites."

CHAPTER XXI.

LAKE SHETAK MASSACRE.

Lake Shetak, in Minnesota, ninety miles west of New Ulm, is the head-waters of the Des Moines river in Iowa. Attracted by its unsurpassed loveliness and fertility of soil, some six or eight American families, making a community of some fifty souls, united in a settlement on its banks. Industry was well rewarded, and comfort smiled a constant guest at their hearthstones. A weekly mail brought them tidings from the outward warring world, in the strifes of which they had no wish to mingle.

On the memorable twentieth of August, they went about their daily avocations as usual, till past mid-day, little dreaming of the terrible siege raging at Fort Ridgley, or the fate which awaited them ere the sun went down. So general was the onslaught from one extreme of the state to the other, it is hard to divest ourselves of the belief of preconcerted, pre-arranged action. Certain it is, that all acted under "orders" of the commanding general of evil; hence their death-dealing power.

Some two months before the outbreak, Mr. Phineas P. Hurd, formerly a resident of Steuben county, New York, but for three years a resident at Lake Shetak, with one man and a team, left home for Dakota Territory; since which time no tidings had come from him, and his wife was daily watching for his return; and his own heart too also bounded with joy at the anticipated welcome, as the distance hourly decreased between him and home.

The farm which smiled under the magic wand of cultivation, was left in charge of a Mr. Voigt, and the tidy, skillful housewife and dairy woman, was evinced by the cheerful aspect within doors, and the golden butter and rich cheese which sent their fragrance from the dairy room. Mrs. Hurd was an industrious woman and early riser; hence, before the sun was up or her children awake, she, with the hired man, was out milking the cows. On the bitterly eventful morning of August 20, 1862, while thus engaged, they are surprised at the appearance of some twenty Indian horsemen, and more at seeing her husband's horses among them. Suspicion was aroused and they hastened within, while the savages were dismounting, to be followed by the whole gang, who at once commenced an indiscriminate plunder. Beds were ripped open and the feathers sent kiting in the air; cheese, for which they have the greatest abhorrence of anything eatable, were pitched into the yard; trunks and drawers were rifled of their contents, and a ball was sent to the heart of Mr. Voigt, who fell dead with Mrs. Hurd's baby in his arms, as he was trying to hush its cries.

That was an awful hour; her home desolated, her husband, though her fears were not yet confirmed, a mangled carcass but a few leagues from the home to which he hastened, and now driven out with her undressed children, denied even a sun-bonnet or shawl, and life granted only on condition of giving no alarm, and starting across the prairie for the towns. Thus under an escort of seven Indians on horseback, with one child toddling by her side and another in her arms, she was hurried through an unfrequented trail for three miles, and then bidden to go alone, "to look not behind, nor tarry in all the plains," under penalty of sharing death with all the other settlers.

The August sun was shining with unusual brightness upon the suffering head of our heroine, and the thick matted grass was heavily beaded with dew, which also, soon set bleeding the bare tender feet of the pedestrians, and most piteously cried the little boy Willie, of only three years, to return home, and repeatedly asked where she was going. Alas, she could not tell him. Death by savage hands was behind her, and starvation with all its horrors before. The repeated firing of guns convinced her that her neighbors were suffering a like peril with herself.

It was some relief to her throbbing heart, when her little boy ceased to complain and manfully trudged along by her side, with apparent confidence in his mother's course, and the younger rested in blissful unconsciousness on her bosom.

Now burst upon the shelterless, weary wanderers, one of our wild western storms — that terrible storm of which mention is elsewhere made — which, sweeping over the prairies and bluffs, obliterated tracks, produced a lull in battle storms, and saved hundreds of hapless wanderers from savage hands and bloody death. So are often life's greatest discomforts, the soul's richest blessings. For three full hours the storm-king reigned supreme; the thunder and lightning were terrific, and the water fell in a blinding deluge, washing out the trail, and covering the lower portions of the prairie. But He who folds the lambs in his bosom, gave her strength to wander on, breakfastless and dinnerless though they were, to a slight, sandy elevation, where, supperless, she laid down her precious charge for the night, while bitterly her heart ached that she could not respond to her boy's pleadings for food; and there, her scant garments drenched to the skin, all that long dreary night, she leaned over her children, her own shivering body protecting them from the wind. Willie slept most of the night, but the baby worried almost constantly; happily its plaintive wail reached not the savages' ears, else a tomahawk would have sought its brain.

The second day was a duplicate of the first, till toward evening, when she had the additional trial of seeing her little boy become very sick, and his physical powers fast failing him; but the baby still slept and nursed, and so suffered less. At night she struck a road, and then understood her whereabouts. With all her foot-sore walking, she was but four miles from home, having doubtless wandered in a circle. Her heart sank within her and a sense of exhaustion before unknown came upon her. After two day's constant travel, her journey was just begun.

But, cheered by the fact that she was no longer lost upon the vast prairie, with woman's courage she pushed on in the road to New Ulm, till nature demanding rest, she halted for the second night. Willie's sickness increased, and he asked no more for food. In the morning he could no longer walk, but craved water from every spring or pool they passed.

To carry both her children was quite impossible for the exhausted mother, but her maternal love, of which we have no fuller or nobler exemplification, found practical development. Here let the reader pause and fix this woman and the circumstances surrounding her, in the mind's eye. Enter into her feelings if you can, after two days of fasting, watching and wandering, and tell me if history presents a more striking example of woman's heroism and endurance, as with the fire of determination in her eye, and firm purpose in her step, she conceals one child in the grass, and taking the other in her arms, passes over the first half mile, when she deposits this and returns for the other. Thus all that day she travels three times over the same path. We read of Spartan mothers and Cornelia's "jewels," but it is left for Minnesota mothers of 1862, to evince to the world the powers of human endurance in the strength of maternal love!

Take now another view. A distant cabin meets the eye, it revives her sinking heart and nerves her with the hope of rest and food, and on she presses, telling her boy of the relief so near. She enters, no sound breaks upon the awful silence, its inmates had either been murdered or had deserted it. She commences her search for food, but not an article could be found. In despair she sank down in unconscious exhaustion, to be aroused by the plaintive, pitiful cry of her boy, demanding the fulfillment of her promise for food, of which they had now been four days destitute. She now bethought of the garden, and thither she went, found some carrots and onions, of which she ate, but her sick child refused them. That night they slept in a cornfield, and she made her supper on raw corn, having no fire to roast it. The following morning, with as much joy as Hagar felt when she found the stream in the wilderness, and pressed therefrom the cup to the lips of her famishing boy, did Mrs. Hurd find the decaying remnant of a ham, not to exceed a pound. Of this she fed at intervals her starving boy, and had the blissful satisfaction of seeing him rapidly revive, and his vomiting cease. It was manna from heaven to her. She was here joined by some of her refugee neighbors, (of whom more anon,) and they continued together till they reached "Brown's," sixty miles from Shetak, where the inmates had been murdered. There they remained ten days, making themselves at home, while awaking to the terrible reality of their fate, realizing more keenly the bitterness of experience, and the dark uncertainty which awaited them.

CHAPTER XXII.

THE GENERAL ONSLAUGHT.

The note of alarm sounding from the door of Mrs. Hurd, soon extended through all the settlement, and was confirmed by the strange movements of the hostile foe.

The people at once aroused to their danger and collected in one house for defense; but finding they were insufficient in numbers and means to combat so formidable a foe, determined on flight. Women and children were hastily loaded into farm wagons, and the men on foot were as body guards for defenseless wives and children. Shaping their course towards New Ulm, the fate of which they had not heard, their anxious hearts beat with premature hopes of a safe asylum there. Alas, how little thought they, with all their fears, that separation and death was so soon to ensue, and that captives and fugitives, some of them were to pass through sufferings of which their own hearts had never conceived!

When but two miles on their journey, a fighting party of eight or ten Indians suddenly came upon them, ready for immediate action. Women and children hid in the high grass while the battle raged. Two of the men deserted at the onset. The others nobly stood their ground, till all the men were wounded, and Mr. Eastlick and eleven others killed.

The Indians, now regarding their work as complete, called to the women to surrender as prisoners of war, pledging life and protection if they did so; if not, threatening them with death as soon as their retreats could be hunted out. Their wounded husbands, hoping they might eventually be ransomed by Government, encouraged the surrender. Without a parting kiss, and scarcely a parting glance, they were driven away from husbands; and children in some instances, with scarcely an idea of what their fate was to be. Like a horrid nightmare dream seemed the experience of the day, — yea, of the last few hours.

The supposed dying husbands watched the receding forms of their families, till lost amid the foliage, and then nerving themselves to superhuman effort, assisted each other to their feet in trial to escape, — all save Mr. Ireland, who was left to die, and in his agony anxiously awaited the end.

When half a mile away, the captives were overtaken by Burton Eastlick, who for the love he bore his mother, had determined to follow, but she entreated him to return for the sake of his baby brother, only fifteen months old, which had been ruthlessly torn from her; with the injunction to save him, if possible, and carry *him in his arms as far as he could*, or till he reached some settlement. A sacred charge, and how regarded by this noble boy of twelve years we are yet to see.

No sooner had Burton received this charge, than with bursting heart, he obediently turned to retrace his steps, when the sharp crack of muskets made him look back in time to see his mother and three other women, together with several of the children, fall in death. Three bullet wounds in the head, back and knee of Mrs. Eastlick, had not produced the effect designed by the savages, and a young monster beat her on the head with the butt of his gun till she was quite insensible, and then with the spared captives, they hastened away.

When Mrs. Eastlick revived, darkness had settled upon the earth, like the pall upon her heart. Her last recollections were of her friend and neighbor, Mrs. Everett, lying near her quite dead, and her infant vainly endeavoring to draw sustenance from the source to which it had never before appealed in vain, and a little girl was crying over them in the bitterness of first heart grief. Now, these two children were dead, the Indians had returned and shot them.

To find her husband and see if he was really dead, Mrs. Eastlick crawled through the thick dew-matted grass to the battle ground. Cold and stiff she found him, and the little son of six years whom she left wounded in the feet, was with him—he too had ceased to suffer. Reader, picture to yourself that scene if you can! Silence sublime, reigning over all the broad expanse of earth and sky, and she alone with her dead, and there she must leave them. Again and again she kisses lips and forehead, and turns away in tearless agony, but firm, and resolved to find her wandering, living children.

Four miles from the main settlement of Lake Shetak, had resided the family of Mr. Myers. Early in the day he had become convinced that Indians, on hostile work intent, were prowling around. But there was no time or opportunity to confer with his neighbors, and so with a sick wife, on a bed in an ox wagon, with four little children, he started for some point of safety.

The wounded men, before mentioned, aided by an invisible power, had progressed about sixteen miles, and on the following day fell in with the Myers party. There was joy in that meeting, though their hearts were full of grief. The heavy, springless wagon in which they found a place, relieved, by change, their wounded limbs and broken bones; but slowly, very slowly, moved those plodding oxen along, and sadly their aching hearts kept time to the dull creaking of the lumbering wheels. Their undressed wounds were painful in the extreme, and why or how they lived through these weary days, is not in the scope of human mind to understand. Their only food was flour and water cakes, with no other ingredients, baked in the sun, they fearing to make a fire, lest the lurking Indians should be attracted by the smoke, and thus again put their lives in jeopardy.

They were unmolested by the way, but had several narrow escapes. On one occasion, they took shelter for the night in a deserted house, which had been sacked by the Indians. Scarcely ten rods distant was another house, where some Indians spent the night in feasting and plunder, but left, providentially, without making any discovery as to the occupancy of the other.

On approaching New Ulm, Mr. Myers left the team to go into town for assistance. When too near to remedy his error, for he was seen and pursued, he saw the Indians had already besieged it, the work of destruction was going on, and their horrid war whoop rung on the air. Happily he eluded pursuit, and though he could not return to his waiting, anxious family, he bent his steps for Mankato, twenty-five miles below, where he arrived in safety.

The wagon party, alarmed at his long absence, concluded some evil had befallen him, and sure he would not return, moved on, heading their oxen toward Mankato. Nervous, excited, anxious and alarmed at every sight or sound, worn out with suffering, hunger and waking, and constantly watching for Indian "signs," it was not strange they should mistake the encampment of U. S. troops for Sioux teepees. They left their wagon and hid in the swamp, but fortunately not till they had been seen by the soldiers, who suspecting the true cause of their movements, hunted them out and brought them into camp, where a safe escort into town was furnished them.

It was eight days since their wounds were received, to which neither lint nor bandage had been applied. But now, broken arms are set, putrid wounds dressed, and the poor sufferers made as comfortable as the circumstances would allow, in a town of only two thousand inhabitants, already crowded with refugees.

CHAPTER XXIII.

OUTBREAK AT THE NORTH.

Like a spark of fire in a magazine of powder, had been the war spark, ignited at Acton, and from the extreme north to the south-western boundary of Minnesota, the explosion was being felt. An electric chain, passing from village to village, through every savage heart, could scarcely have produced a more simultaneous uprising.

On the 24th of August, a party of Sioux crossed the the Red river of the north, at Breckinridge, where the entire "town" was comprised in a mammoth hotel—took possession of the horses, and slaughtered or drove off the cattle. Their next onslaught was on the "Breckinridge House," which was strongly barricaded by those who had resolved to defend it, or die in the attempt. Doors and windows were smashed in, and no living man was left to tell the tale. On the following day, a reconnoitering party drew up before the house, and scarcely had their eyes surveyed the destructive work, ere a large force of Indians sprang up, as from the earth. Their swift-footed horses, as well as their riders, saw the danger, and they reached the fort, in safety. A day or two after, another body of men went up to learn more of the true state of affairs. As they came near, a woman came forth from the saw mill, eliciting both their sympathy and protection. She wore but two garments, and these were stiff with the blood which, for twenty-four hours, had flowed from her wounded side, during which time she had not tasted food. Her home was at "Old Crossing," sixteen miles distant, where, with her son, she kept a "station," and with them lived little Jimmy Scott, her pet grandson, only five years old. The Indians attacked the house before breakfast. Young Scott was killed, and his mother severely wounded. She lay upon the floor, they supposing her dead, while they plundered the house. Then they came round her, kicking and punching her with sticks and guns, stripped off her dress, preparatory to mutilating her body, when the sound of approaching wheels drew their attention without, and they rushed for the prize of the farmer's loaded market wagon, she not daring to move a hand to staunch the blood of the wound, lest they should return, and note its change of position. But she opened her eyes, and saw little Jimmy, bewildered, and almost powerless from fright, and faintly whispered him to do the savages' bidding, — they *might* let him live.

The farmer had escaped to the woods, and greedy with venal desire, they did not pursue; but driving the wagon to the door, emptied the flour from the sacks, and drove off, taking little Jimmy, who, in obedience to his grandmother's injunctions, passively submitted to his fate. Not till the sound of the wheels had died on her ear, and no other sound broke upon the awful silence, did she again venture to open her eyes. Then she crawled to the door, where lay the ghastly form of her murdered son, her youngest born, and, faint from the bleeding wound, and without bonnet, shawl, or dress, she started. Fifty dollars in silver had been overlooked, when the Indians robbed the house, and this she hid in a haystack, with the provident hope of its doing good to some one. All that day, she walked and crawled, eating nothing but some savory herbs, that grew in her path. As twilight's mellowing influence fell over the earth, she crawled to the door, where she had hoped a friendly admittance. One glance, and she knew the fiends had been there; and though she did not know of the three dead bodies within, she turned to the saw mill, for shelter, and was found, as described. The ladies at Fort Abercrombie made her as comfortable as their own wardrobes would allow, and with kind surgical care, her wound was, in due time, healed. A party went down to "Old Crossing," to bury her son, and brought to her the money she had hidden. A few days after, others found the body exhumed, with a stake driven through it, into the earth.

The reconnoitering party entered the Breckinridge House, where they found the three dead bodies, with chains on their legs, by which they had been dragged from room to room, leaving a bloody trail, as the work of plunder progressed. They had now been several days dead, and were very offensive.

On further search, the stage of Burbank & Co.'s line was found in the river, the top cut off, the horses taken, and the driver killed. Articles of minor value were scattered around, and a distributing office had been improvised for the mail, letters and drafts were sent to the four winds of the prairie. Thus commenced the conflict, along the northern line of travel, and so few were the men and arms at Fort Abercrombie, that all who were there, and more, were needed for its protection.

Many of the people who were driven from their homes, could not get to the Fort, and so made their way to the nearest village. Thrilling tales are told of these life adventurers,—of their almost miraculous escapes, and providential guidance beyond the reach of savage hands. We remember of a man and his wife, with a little boy, of four years, whom they had brought forty miles, on their backs, coming into St. Cloud. Never had they a mouthful to eat, and never a loud word was spoken. Once or twice only, did the little hero whisper, "*I am hungry.*"

Another instance there was of a man shot at his own door. His wife drew him in, and bolted the door, when her husband continued to load the gun, which she fired, through the window, till the Indians, after several had fallen, withdrew, doubtless supposing a hidden force within. The husband, sure he must soon die, and feeling that every moment's delay but increased her peril, begged his wife to save herself by flight. Reluctantly she did his bidding, and after incredible hardships, by day and by night, she reached a friendly shelter. A few days later, some white men entered the dwelling, expecting to find only a putrid corpse. To their surprise, the man was still alive, though he had made repeated attempts to end his physical agony. In a short time, he was re-united with his wife, rejoicing in the failure of the dull butcher knife to perform his bidding.

CHAPTER XXIV.

SIEGE OF FORT ABERCROMBIE.

When the northern stampede began, Fort Abercrombie was garrisoned by only forty men, in command of Captain Vanderhock, with no protecting walls, or even embankments. The danger becoming known, messengers, with "life in their hands," were sent forth to warn the citizens, government and Red River trains, known to be on the route, which, it was rumored, the Indians had gone to intercept, and also to St. Paul, for military re-enforcements. The citizens at once banded with the troops for defense of the post, and soon completed a breastwork, from cord wood, covered with earth on the three most exposed sides.

The list of women and children soon swelled to sixty-two, who, being crowded into the soldier's quarters, the only bullet proof building, made a one room community of two hundred and fifty. Here commissary stores were brought, water was hauled, and whatever of comforts could be supplied for so large a family. Eyelids were held open in suspense, and the nerves of the women set quivering, at the least note of alarm. There was neither eating nor sleeping, only as each gnawed at hard tack, with which their pocket was supplied, when faintness from the cravings of hunger came over them, and slept on a blanket, which was rolled up for a seat, during the day. The men, in turn, kept guard without, while the women, even though all freedom from excitement was most desirable for some, energetically worked at cartridge making, or moulded bullets for hourly expected use.

The first show of Indians was on the 28th of August, when, in a daring, dashing manner, a large company of horsemen came in sight of the fort, and killed the herdsman, surrounded and drove off nearly three hundred head of cattle, and many of the horses and mules of the fort, which, in defiance of the guns, they entered the stables to obtain. A few, almost reckless men, went forth to dispute their right, and sheltered by the stacks of hay, actually drove them from the stables, and saved a few of the horses. The Indians fled to the woods, where Capt. V. thought imprudent to follow them, as the fort had poor enough protection at best. Take away the handful of men, and who would save it, if attacked from another side? The three successive days, the Indians bivouaced in sight of the Fort, their smoke revealing their whereabouts, while they barbacued and feasted.

At early dawn, on the morning of Sept. 1st, the actual siege of the fort commenced, and, for several hours, raged, with fearful power, against fearful odds. The loss on our side was comparatively small, only one killed and several wounded. Their casualties were unknown, as only two of their dead were left on the field; the prairie was strewn with cloths and paper, saturated with blood, which indicated more than it proved.

The brave little band at the fort was, by no means, idle. Every soldier and citizen worked with a will, in anticipation of a renewed attack, till, on the morning of the sixth — just as the sober gray was yielding to rosy tints — the pickets announced the enemy's approach. This band was variously estimated at from five hundred to one thousand strong, and spread themselves, the mounted ones ahead, in the form of a fan, till three sides of the fort were enclosed by them. As they wildly dashed on to the attack, their yells were most terrific, and their appearance hideous in the extreme. This was so unlike anything the men had ever heard or seen, that the first effect was not very cheering; but they rallied behind the breastwork, and though attacked at four points, fought with a coolness and heroism equal to anything we read of in history. Had they met this superior force of blood-hounds, with other than determined wills, all must have fallen into savage hands, and the buildings have been reduced to ashes. The fire from the howitzer scattered them like autumn leaves. One shell entered a log building, where many of the savages had taken refuge, doing deadly work. The blood on the floor revealed its effect. After three hours' hard fighting, the unequal conflict ceased, with a decided repulse to the assailants. Scarcely had their war whoops ceased to reverberate on the air, when a messenger, two weeks away, returned, with the cheering news of re-enforcements near. In forty-four hours, Mr. Hill had made the trip of two hundred and fifty miles, to St. Paul, and his demand for troops was promptly responded to; but these could not move with the celerity of fleet horses, nor could each man carry, in his haversack, sufficient food for his journey.

Though there were no more direct attacks, small scouting parties kept up a harassing fire from the opposite shore, where bushes and weeds concealed them. The dwellings, to which some of the families had returned, were being riddled with balls, and some persons had very narrow escapes. A friend of the writer was guest at the house of Mr. Stone, the sutler. After two weeks' fasting, the women went over, with the hope of being unmolested, while they should have a week's palatable rations prepared. They were seen, and a ball, sent to them, whizzed past their heads, and lodged in the casing of the door, as they were about to enter. Then, like "rain on the roof," they fell all around, while the inmates of the house lay upon the floor, almost breathless, with fear, till the bullet storm had subsided. Under circumstances like those named, personal ablution or tidy apparel, was not to be thought of, and for three weeks, the husband of the friend above alluded to, never removed his boots from his feet, only to shake out the fleas.

Under circumstances and with surroundings like those before described, the existence of three immortal beings was commenced. True, two of these had just opened their eyes, drew a few fleeting breaths, and then passed on to that eternal state, of which this life is but a shadow,—away from the cares and bloody strife which surrounded their advent into existence. In a soldier's bunk, partitioned from the main quarters by tent canvas, the chill wind whizzing between the logs, laid my friend, Mrs. L., pale, weak and senseless. Bravely had she endured the terrible siege, but the reaction came. The little one soon passed away. Her husband lay on a stretcher, in the same little place, for his wound was not healed. All are to leave — the band of women and children, whom a common misfortune had bound so closely, and almost made friends of uncongenial spirits. They drew around her bunk, for a last leave of one who had been a moving spirit in their midst — one whose manner ever endeared her to all hearts, high or low, rich or poor. She heeds it not. She realizes not that she is so soon to be left, with scarce a female friend, — and well may it be that she does not. Yet an All-wise Being had "ordained her unto life," even in such surroundings, and, in due time, the anxious hearts of friends, who could render no aid in this extreme need, but to wait and pray, was relieved by her presence among them, she quite satisfied with her eventful experience in frontier life.

Three weeks had they worked, watched, and waited, till, at last, when the suffering need is withdrawn, three hundred men are added to the number already there. These were decreased by death but eight, since the siege commenced, but several were helpless from wounds. Small parties were sent out daily, to reconnoitre, who, every little while, would discover an Indian, like a toad under a mushroom, his head popping from 'neath a bush, or from amid the weeds, tempting a shot, and these parties were, several times, surprised by superior numbers, when desperate fighting would follow; but the savages were always the vanquished party. Once, our men effected, by strategic movement, a backward retreat, and though leaving two dead on the ground, and others were wounded, they reached the goal in safety. One of this party actually died from fright, a few hours after his return. Another gave out, but with encouragement and aid, stood again upon his feet, just in time to send a ball to the heart of an Indian, who, at the moment, aimed at the heart of his comrade, though not in time to prevent a flesh wound in his leg.

The sad presentiment of the parents of a young man, in this rencontre, which was distinctly heard at the fort, proved literally correct. A few days after, a volunteer party went out to find and bury him and another, who was killed at the same time. The body of the last lay on his face, with his skull smashed in, and his brains scattered about, with eighteen bayonet thrusts in his back, and on one leg, a gash, nearly to the bone, from the hip to the calf of the leg.

The body of the other, Edgar Wright, had been ripped open to the throat, the heart and liver taken out, the lungs left on the chest, the head cut off, scalped, and stuck in the cavity of the abdomen, with the face toward the feet. The hands were cut off, and placed side by side, two feet from the body, but what was indicated by this arrangement of these organs, was not understood. In this case, as in those of a majority of the sufferers, the victim was void of offense toward their foe, and a young man of unblemished reputation, against whom they could have had no memory of wrongs to revenge. They knew him well, and had received frequent hospitality at his hand. This case is not an exception, for they have been most ingenious in devices of cruelty toward those who have most befriended them, and for whom they had professed most friendship.

We narrate these horrid facts, not because we love to dwell upon them — not because we are unmoved by the pen rehearsals, and the nerves can be quiet under it; but we give them, that the Indian sympathizers may see the diabolical natures of the foe our State has had to meet. We think it a mock philanthropy, which would screen these guilty, unprovoked wretches from merited justice.

CHAPTER XXV.

INDIANS AT SIOUX FALLS CITY.

Wherever the magic wand of civilization had passed, there went the human fiends, intent on bloody work. We have seen them in the interior; we have seen them at the extreme north; and now to the very southwestern corner of the State, and even a few miles beyond, in Dakota Territory, we see them as on other occasions, watching for a mark to shoot at. Sioux Falls City on the Big Sioux river, had just commenced an existence, and eight families were all its boast. Their nearest neighbors to the east were at Lake Shetak, sixty-five miles distant, and the nearest on the south at Yankton, about the same distance as the former.

Fortunately, on the 25th of August, a small military force under Lieut. Bacon, was stationed here, else doubtless there would have been a general massacre, and the world would have been ignorant of the transaction. Bright and joyous rose the sun on that sadly eventful day, and nought of earth or air evinced the dark pall to settle upon that little community, and rest with leaden weight on some.

Mr. Joseph B. Amidon, who had emigrated from St. Paul three years before, was, as also his wife, a former resident of Essex county, N. Y., and they were among the "first settlers" of this point. He resided on a "claim," one mile from the main settlement, and was with his son at work in the hay field, nearly a half mile from his dwelling. The supper prepared by the hand of his waiting, watching wife, remained untouched, for the husband and son came not from their toil. Anxiety filled her heart, strange suspicions un nerved her, though she knew not of the Sioux uprising. The clock struck ten, and unable longer to endure her suspense, she went to the soldiers' camp, her nearest neighbors. With soldierly promptness, they searched without avail the field where, during the day, they had seen the missing ones. Across the road was a cornfield, and thither now they repair, fearing they may have been decoyed there, and sure of 'foul play from savage source. Just as the morning dawned, the cold, stiffened bodies were found; a ball had pierced the father's heart, and earth had drank his blood. The soft plowed earth where they lay, showed very plainly Willie's severe struggles with death. Three balls had pierced his body, to the effects of which he yielded not easily or soon. They are taken to their now desolate home, where the wife alone awaits tidings from them. It is no marvel that she was well nigh paralyzed with the shock of sudden grief, and mechanically submitted to the bidding of others, as they prepared to bury her dead.

Scarcely was the dust to dust consigned, ere the Indians appeared, menacing for a fight, which was sternly met by the determined force. A sharp, brisk engagement ensued, in which seven Indians were made to "bite the dust," and which prevented the further execution of their base designs for that time.

In the rapid succession of events, came the news of the outbreak, and the Governor's order for the people to leave for some point of safety. Government conveyance and military protection would be furnished, but only one hour was allowed to prepare for departure. What an hour was that! How much must be crowded into it, and it is no wonder the brain should reel or the heart seem petrified with the sudden transition! But there was no alternative, savage eyes were even then watching their movements, awaiting the withdrawal of troops, for a general conflagration, which ensued a few hours later. This sad-hearted cortege, moving with the swiftness of ox and mule teams, are pilgrims and strangers in an unpopulated region, some of whom are obliged to make a circuit of a thousand miles, to reach a point two hundred and fifty miles distant. Such are the dangers of the way where moccasined feet stealthily tread.

CHAPTER XXVI.

THE HEROIC BOY.

We have seen Burton Eastlick following the captive party, and returning by the urgent desire of his mother. He had seen his mother shot, and supposed her dead. Beside his dying brother he watched till the angels bore his spirit above, placed the dear little form beside his idolized father, and with a bravery which would have honored men of mature years, affectionately took his baby charge, and commenced preparations to start, in obedience to his mother's dying wish. Mr. Ireland, who, it will be remembered, was *left to die*, remonstrated. "He could never carry out the design, and it was better that they die there together." But the boy was resolute and *firm.* "Nothing should deter him from the effort, — he would carry the baby as long as he could, — they *might* be saved." And so, folding his arms close about the child, he started. Mr. Ireland had given him some directions about his course, and other matters, which proved of use to the boy when alone upon his strange but holy pilgrimage.

The heroic spirit of the boy incited Mr. Ireland with new hope of life, and he said, "Why should I die here alone, when such a boy can do so much. I, too, will try and get away." And so he went, bleeding and suffering as he was, every rod gained increasing his desire to gain another. Ah, there is a Providence that watches our course and aids us in distress, and truly man is immortal till his work is done. We have, in more instances than are recorded in this work, been led more than ever before into a full, firm, unwavering belief in that Providential care and guidance which shapes our course in life so minutely as to number "the very hairs of our head."

An infidel world must admit the hand to be more than chance, which spared so many of this doomed settlement, protecting them in captivity, or succoring them by night and by day in efforts to reach the other settlements. Mr. Ireland's body had been the target for eight balls, three of which had passed through his lungs. His wife and two of his children were killed, and two daughters, Rosanna and Ellen, carried into captivity, and compelled to walk the entire distance to the Missouri river, being over seven hundred miles by the route they chose. This, and other incredible hardships which befell these girls, would seemingly have overpowered the physical energies, had not Divine aid been given them. He who said, "Call upon me in the day of trouble, and I will deliver thee," did not forget his promise, until they felt themselves safe with their rescuers, though strangers, such as their young hearts might well appreciate, and who in due time restored them to the arms of their father.

Can imagination paint the sufferings of Mr. Ireland during his weary wanderings of fourteen days, that followed his resolve for life? His wounds alone, with the kindest wifely care, and most careful nursing, should have allowed many anxious fears for the result. Weakened by the loss of blood, and the want of food, with naught but the bracing breeze, and the pure spring water, which none too frequently bubbled in his path, it is surely beyond the comprehension of mortal, how the frail fabric could continue to throb and beat with pain, while the fever's heat would nearly consume his vitals. How painful the progress, how bitter the thoughts of the future, for he knew not that one of his family lived, or *if* alive, but that a life fate worse than death was theirs, with faint hope of living to tell the tale of his horrid suffering, or much less to clasp to his heart the remnant of his once happy family.

Ninety miles, thick with dangers, lay before him, but our little hero, Burton, faltered not. True, his arms became *very* tired, but then he placed this precious burden on his back, and thus the first day he made sixteen miles, and thus he traveled on, making sixty miles in ten successive days. His food was raw corn and such as he could find in deserted houses. How carefully he munched the coarse, unpalatable fare, to relieve the baby cravings for its mother! How tenderly he folded him in his arms to shelter him from the chill night dews — how lovingly soothed his weary wail, lest the very breeze should announce their living to those from whom they fled — and how spasmodically hugged him to his heart, at the least real or imaginary note of alarm! Brave, darling boy! Did angels ever before witness a deed like thine! History's page furnishes nothing more noble, more deserving immortal fame! Thy name with the good and great shall live. We would fain impress on thy young brow the seal of admiring approval, and record with immortal pen the undying virtue of thy noble deed! God bless thee, noble boy!

The reader has seen the resolute mother, wounded, bruised and left for dead, crawling back to the battle field, finding her precious dead, and, with sublime purpose heroically turn from them for a lone, weary march over the now desolate prairies. She traveled by night and hid in the grass for several days, till almost exhausted from exertion and hunger. At the risk of being seen and murdered, she resolved on finding something to eat. So she crawled through the grass to a cornfield, but her stomach, so long empty, rejected the raw corn, and she became deathly sick and obliged to lie by for some time.

The friendly breeze cooled the festering, undressed wounds, which were occasionally bathed by a cool spring, and on she moved, an illustration of the powers of human endurance. At a deserted house she stopped over night, killed a chicken, and with her teeth, pulled the raw, bleeding meat from its breast. She continued very sick during the night, but the following morning, tearing the remainder of the chicken into strips to be dried in the sun as she went, she proceeds, and this, with three ears of raw corn, was all she eat during all those ten solitary days. Oh! the lonely night wanderings! — the anxious, listening days, when the very silence was painful — the terrible stomach cravings and the bitter heart throbbings for the loved and slain, as also for the living! But guided by an unseen hand, deliverance is sure to come. Joy, such as but the mother heart knows, was soon to commingle with her grief, such as for a time to make her almost forget its woes, and her weary, wounded body its pains.

From Sioux Falls City, in Dakota Territory, to New Ulm, August Garzene, a Frenchman, was employed in carrying the mail. Lake Shetak settlement lay on his route. All the little community were known to him. On his return route he meets Mrs. Eastlick, whom he at first scarcely recognizes, so jaded and changed is she. By dint of management, he gives her a seat in his single sulky, and at "Dutch Charley's", ere many hours, she folds to her heart her emaciated children, in whom the reader will recognize the *heroic boy* and his baby brother. We present the reader the sad, happy group, in their fugitive garments.

There, too, was Mr. Ireland, with eight balls in his body, whom the boy's courage had saved, together with Mrs. Hurd and her two children. These last had fallen in company several hours before and continued their less lonely course together. A glad meeting for hearts so mangled and torn! A few miles further they continue their pedestrian journey, where at "Brown's" they find more comfortable quarters, from whence Mr. Ireland is sent ahead to New Ulm for assistance.

MRS. EASTLICK AND HER CHILDREN.
(The Heroic Boy and his Baby Brother.)

Lieutenant Roberts, with twelve men and a team, was at once dispatched to their relief, and reached them about midnight. The following morning at daylight, with an escort of soldiers, they were on their way to join their neighbors at Mankato, who supposed them dead, when after fifteen days of intense suffering they enjoyed the luxury of food and rest, devoid of present fear.

Twelve bodies had fallen in death, at Lake Shetak, Aug. 20th, 1862. Twelve months and more, through winter's snows and summer's heat, the angels watched their unburied dust, while surviving friends plead for an escort of soldiers, to protect them, in the last sad burial rite. On the 28th Oct., 1863, they had the mournful satisfaction of consigning the beloved "dust to dust." Each body had retained its own living impress so distinctly, that there was no difficulty in marking the grave of each.

The beautiful farms there lie in waste, and the whole region is depopulated. Such is the work of savage hands, such the horrors of savage ire.

CHAPTER XXVII.

SIEGE OF HUTCHINSON.

The main body of troops, as we have seen, were marching up the Minnesota Valley, to the theatre, or centre of hostilities. Detachments or companies were stationed in the most exposed localities, some of whom had brisk skirmishes with the red foe, and others were left unmolested. Several companies of mounted citizens did efficient service, at various endangered points.

Captain Strout, with a company of fifty men, was stationed at Cedar City, whence all the people had fled. Here they were unexpectedly attacked by one hundred and fifty Indians. They fought like veteran heroes, until nearly overpowered by numbers, they retreated to Hutchinson, a town well fortified, eighty miles above the capital, and the first beyond the Big Woods.

From Cedar City, this savage band moved towards Forest City, making a determined assault, but successfully repulsed by the inhabitants, who had fortified the town, and made it quite a stronghold.

Thwarted in their last attempt, they advanced on Hutchinson, where Capt. Strout and his fifty men, to whom the citizens of town and vicinity joined themselves, valorously met the foe, and after more or less hard fighting, for two days, successfully repulsed them. Capt. Strout's dispatch, under date of Sept. 3d, says:

"I was attacked to-day by about one hundred and fifty Indians, about half of them mounted. They numbered full double my force, and fought us for two hours and a half. I threw my company into four sections, and in open order, pressed against them, as skirmishers, after which, as they so far outnumbered my force, I made a fierce march against their main body, which was still in front. Our loss, in the engagement, was three killed, and fifteen wounded. A number of the men were very much injured by exhaustion.

"I think I am safe in saying, that the Indians lost, in killed and wounded, two or three times our number.

"We lost most of our rations, utensils, tents, and some arms, from the excitement. Some horses ran away, others got mired, so that we lost nine, in all, from these causes.

"The Indians had excellent guns. They were bright, and carried better than our guns. They were dressed partly in citizen's dress, and many of them rode fine horses. Their ponies would lie down when they dismounted. Sometimes the Indians would rush up to within one hundred yards of my force."

Near the village of Hutchinson, lived a Mr. Adams, who, with his wife and child, were fleeing for their lives, to the protection of the town, when he, their natural protector, abandoned them to their fate. Finding themselves closely pursued, he threw the child, which he was carrying, and concealing himself in the grass, made his escape. She, possessed of a true mother's feelings, stopped to pick up her child, and was captured.

Her captor wished to take the child upon his horse, but she clung to it with an unyielding grasp. After repeated attempts to take it from her, the Indian became enraged, forced it from her grasp, and then shot it before the eyes of the agonized mother. These facts, I have from Mr. George Spencer, who had been a captive three weeks, when Mrs. Adams was brought into the Indian camp. During this time, he had heard no news from the whites, though many captives had been brought in. He says, "I told my friend (Chaska) that I should like to see the white woman who had just been brought in, when he immediately sent for her."

"I found her to be a very pretty and intelligent little woman, and from her learned the latest news in regard to the preparations which were being made by the whites to punish the Indians."

"In relating to me her history, when she spoke of the murder of her child, her first born and only child, she wept bitterly. Upon seeing which, the Indians inquired the cause. They then directed me to explain to her the reason why her child had been killed: that if she would have let the Indian take it, he would have brought it along safely." A poor apology for his barbarity, inhuman fiend, that he was.

CHAPTER XXVIII.

BATTLE OF BIRCH COOLIE.

The citizens of Minnesota had now begun to realize the horrors of a home war. Sorrow comes to their hearts, and sadness to their homes. Familiar faces, which went forth, but a few days agone, will be seen there no more!

The murdered dead remain unburied, and their nauseous effluvia taints the air, at Red Wood, and elsewhere. A detachment, composed of one company of cavalry, under Capt. Anderson, and another of infantry, under Capt. Grant, in command of Maj. J. R. Brown, were sent out, August 31st, by Col. Sibley, commissioned with the sad burial charge of these victims of savage brutality. At night, they encamped opposite the Lower Agency, and on the following morning, they find and bury about thirty bodies, in every conceivable state of mutilation, and mostly the heroes of Capt. Marsh's company. While this was being done, a detachment, having crossed the river to the Agency, were engaged in the same sad and unpleasant duty there. About eighty-five bodies in all, were buried by the two companies, that day.

Having re-united, they moved on, some three miles, to Birch Coolie, where they encamped for the night. There were no traces of Indians having been in the vicinity for many days, and a precaution against them was less in their thoughts, than personal comfort, when their camping ground was selected. Had they apprehended an attack, they would have sought the protection of the timber, not more than two hundred yards away, instead of the smooth prairie, the most unpropitious spot that could have been found for the ordeal which followed. Fortunately, the camp was made in the usual way, with the wagons packed around, and the teams fastened to them. The horses of the mounted men were fastened by strong picket ropes. A guard of thirty men and two non-commissioned officers, were detailed, and ten sentinels were on constant duty. Around the camp fire, the men talked over the horrid, sickening scenes of the day, till drowsiness settled upon their eyelids, when each, in their own respective tents, sunk into slumbers profound, unmindful of the sentinel's monotonous tread.

Sept. 2d was giving due notice of its dawning morn, in the sober gray which precedes its golden glimmerings of light, and an officer of the guard was completing his round with a new relief. The sentinel saw, by the waving furrows of the tall grass, that objects were moving stealthily along, in zigzag lines, not far away. Unwilling to give the alarm, without cause, he recalled the officer, and pointed them out to him. At this moment, came deafening war whoops from all sides, and the next, a raking cross fire poured in upon the unconscious sleepers. Most of the guard fell, some killed, and others wounded. The tents were riddled with bullets, and many in them were wounded, and others received their death shots, before aware of the presence of danger. Not sixty seconds of time was required for all this, and the utmost confusion prevailed, for a few minutes, and had the assailants charged into camp, a general slaughter would have followed. The panic and confusion of mind, which such hurried events create, gave place, in an almost incredibly short space of time, to calm, deliberate action. Every wounded man, whose hand could clutch a rifle, crawled from his tent, and with those uninjured, ranged himself at command, along the edges, behind the prostrate bodies of horses, wagons, or whatever else could answer for a temporary barricade. Thus on their faces, two and two, they worked. Some dug trenches with their bayonets, throwing up the earth with their tin cups, while others, loading as they lay, would rise on one knee, fire and fall, to repeat the process. Meanwhile, the hoarse braying of the animals, in their dying agonies, mingling with the groans of the wounded and dying men, is beyond the power of pen to depict. The first volley was the most deadly of any, for when the men were thoroughly roused, they deported themselves with the coolness and bravery of heroes and veterans, though they had been scarcely two weeks in the field. Every man was a host. It is but justice, to make some allusion to the honored dead, who fell here, in defence of our Minnesota homes.

Among the first to enlist in the renowned company of "Young Men's Guards," raised in St. Paul, for national service, was Benjamin S. Terry. When the burial party went forth from their encampment, at Fort Ridgley, Sergeant Terry volunteered to accompany them, though his company was not detailed. His object was to identify his bosom friend, George Spencer, by some specifications by which a stranger could not, as it would be far advanced in decomposition (for all supposed him dead.) This made known to Capt. Valentine, consent was given. No sooner was the alarm given, than, rifle in hand, he sprang from the tent, when a ball pierced his side and he fell, mortally wounded. Several times after his wound was dressed, he crawled from his tent, and took unerring aim at the head of a grass-hidden foe. He was perfectly aware of his situation, and before the sun went down, had fought his first and last battle with the Indians, and closed the more important life battle. He was a member, modest and unassuming, of the First Baptist Church, in St. Paul, and of three brothers, was the second who had fallen by savage hands; the first in 1852, while acting as their teacher and missionary, at the north. His body was afterward removed to St. Paul, and more than one eye was dimmed as they saw the friend for whom his own life had been given, with tearful heart and sad face, acting as first bearer at his second burial.

Corporal Wm. M. Cobb, of St. Paul, was a young man of many virtues, and the pride of his father's household. He received four bullets at one volley but still bravely fought on for an hour, when, exhausted from the loss of blood, he walked to the surgeon's tent, where his wounds were dressed. He lived until the next morning, but not to see the end of the fight. His dying injunction was *"not to give up the camp."*

Sergeant Wm. Irvine was among the bravest of the brave. For thirty hours he lay upon his face without food or drink, discharging his gun as often as he could "sight an Indian." He had just sent a message to Capt. Grant that he had killed three or four, when a a ball pierced his head, rendering him senseless. He died on his way to the fort, after relief had come to that worn out band.

These, with others, were afterward removed to St. Paul, and with suitable honors, buried in Oakland Cemetery. "So rest the brave."

All that day and all the night, that bullet shower raged. The little brave band was completely surrounded, and no possibility of sending for relief—unless heaven interpose, they must all die. Many a one lay soaking with his own blood, the soil of the trench he had dug with his bayonet and tin cup. On the morning of the 3d, the crack of the rifle is still heard, and its effect continues to tell upon our men. With savage yells and demoniac war-whoops the work goes on till nearly night.

In Capt. Grant's force were several half-breeds, who had fought valorously all the day and night. On Wednesday morning, the Sioux commander called out in his own language for these to leave the whites, come

H

over to their side, and they should have protection, assuring them that only the white blood was sought, and that they were going to charge at once and put every person to death. This was understood by all the half breeds, and by Maj. Brown, who translated it for Capt. Grant.

But Heaven interposed in the moment of greatest peril, and sent the boom of the approaching cannon, and at the same moment, an Indian horseman rode rapidly up to their commander, and was distinctly heard to say, that "two miles of white men" were coming to the relief of the besieged party, which was followed by the quick command to "cut them off — annihilate them!"

The pickets around Col. Sibley's camp at Fort Ridgley, fifteen miles distant, heard the firing early on Tuesday morning, and reported the same at headquarters, but the echoes from the woods and reverberations from the bluffs, prevented them from determining the exact point of compass from whence the sounds proceeded. Convinced that the burial detachment was in imminent peril, *somewhere*, two companies, with a few mounted men, with a six pound howitzer, under Col. McPhail, were ordered to their relief. As by intuition, their march was shaped in the right direction.

Bidding defiance to the men and terror inspiring gun, the savages hastened on to meet and annihilate them, leaving a few men around the camp, which they thought now almost defenseless. Little Crow had proclaimed to his people that Col. Sibley's army was composed of old men and little boys — hence but little to be dreaded in the conflict. But when they saw the formidable array, with all the modern paraphernalia of war, they deemed annihilation less sure, and concluded to defer it till the next day, while they demonstrated their prowess by firing from a distance, brandishing their hatchets, defiantly waving their blankets and sounding the horrid war whoop.

To the inexperienced eye of our men, the scattered horde of savages seemed greatly magnified in numbers, and they fancied themselves too weak to cut their way to the relief of the struggling, suffering band; therefore they bivouaced for the night, and returned a messenger for still greater re-enforcements. This messenger was the brave and intrepid Sheehan, of Yellow Medicine and Fort Ridgley renown. The Indians anticipating the design, tried to cut him off, chased him some seven miles, sending more than fifty bullets at him — but his work was not yet done. Col. Sibley, with his entire remaining force, took up the line of march the same evening, reaching the second detachment about midnight. At early dawn the column was in motion. As the sun rose, the sheen of bright muskets, in the hands of distant running Indians, was seen all around them, but quite out of range. They had delayed their attack for the stimulus of rest and food, but now, when they saw this column twice the length of the previous evening, they were powerless with wonder; unable to account for its sudden growth, and declared that "five miles of white men and a big gun were too much for them to fight."

A sufficient number of the enemy had remained at Birch Coolie to keep up a harassing fire. The main body of the Indians continued to brandish their burnished weapons, which flashed back the sun's rays, and louder and more defiant became the continuous war whoop.

Thus was each party deceived with the number and strength of the other. Our force continued to advance in battle line, their fire, however, having but little or no effect on the distant foe, unless it was to impart an impression of superiority in strength and discipline, and keep them in the distance, till they finally retired.

When first the group of conical tents appeared across the distant ravine, there were doubts whether they were friends or foes. To annihilate them if the latter, before they have time to remove, and to relieve them if the former, the march is quickened. Dead horses form the barricade, but not a sign of life appears. Had all been slaughtered and the relief come too late? Aye, *live men* were in the trenches and joyfully aware of the approach of friends, for they knew they could hold out but a few hours longer. The want of water alone would soon have made them powerless. Had the savage force remained undivided, they would doubtless even then all have been found slain. A strange, wild, but genuine joy reigned in camp. Some clapped their hands and laughed, others danced in delight — some gave praise to God, and others were mute with their real heart gratitude.

There was but little time for congratulation, for thirteen dead comrades lay unburied, and sixty more were suffering from wounds. "The hero of a thousand battles" no more deserves the laurel wreath of FAME than the heroes of Birch Coolie. For thirty-six hours, without food or rest, they had worked as none but heroes can, and had held their camp against three hundred savage foes.

Impromptu mattrasses of prairie grass, placed on the hard wagon bottom, served for ambulances, and at sundown they commenced their return march. At midnight, tired and worn out with fighting and marching, they entered camp at Fort Ridgley.

According to facts afterwards obtained from reliable sources, the Indian force at Birch Coolie was three hundred and nineteen men, who had come from their encampments at Yellow Medicine, with the design of separating in two columns and simultaneously attacking Mankato and St. Peter, in order to mete to them the fate of New Ulm, and had no idea of meeting any opposition by the way. The event proved that the detachment had been started from Fort Ridgley at the right time. Had these savages met with no check, they would have laid those flourishing towns in ashes, and many of the people would have shared the fate of those of New Ulm, and the adjacent country — and then it was their purpose to follow up this success (they never thought of repulse,) to St. Paul, attack it in the night time and reduce it to ashes, and more severely afflict the people than they had elsewhere. But God rules, and their designs were thwarted.

Those whose graves were made on the battle-ground were not the only victims of the Birch Coolie battle. One after another of the brave wounded swelled the list of dead, so that in ten days they numbered twenty-three. Of these, Robert Gibbons is worthy of special mention, being a humble Christian and prominent, devoted member of the Methodist Church in St. Paul. He had given two sons to the national army, and when a sudden home emergency arose, he joined a cavalry company to die the soldier's honored death, and when his remains were removed, to receive the soldier's honored burial, amid bleeding hearts and appreciating friends.

Mr. J. W. DeCamp had entered the ranks to fight in retaliation of the supposed death of his wife and three children. But he fell while fighting valorously, and though he reached the fort alive, he did not live to know but his worst fears were true.

Mrs. DeCamp was a companion in captivity with Mr. Spencer, and the utter neglect with which she was treated, was almost as unendurable as the surplus of of attention to others. She was claimed by no one in particular, and consequently, often went to bed hungry, she and her children, if indeed they were so fortunate as to find a blanket bed, on which to sleep. Our informant has himself besought the pity of the inhuman brutes and obtained something for her to eat.

One dark rainy night, according to a pre-arranged

plan, with no one to guard her, she found little difficulty in seeking the river, where a flotilla of canoes awaited herself and children, together with the family of her rescuer. For three days and nights they floated or paddled down stream in these open crafts, with the discomforts of a cold, drizzling rain, with insufficient clothing or food. But hope of a re-union with her husband, stimulated her desire for life.

On their way, they discovered a woman and five children lurking in the bushes, their clothes and flesh rent with the briers, and they were much emaciated from long fasting and anxious watching. This was Mrs. Robideaux, who was welcomed to their frail fleet, and made as comfortable as circumstances would admit. These were all brought safely into port by Lorenzo Laurence, a christian Indian, who jeopardized his life in this and other kindred acts, and with John Otherday, and others, is entitled to the gratitude and protection of white people for all time. These are evidences that the missionaries' labors have not been entirely in vain.

Simon, too, another christian Indian, and an old man, rescued Mrs. Newman and three children from the hands of their captors, and rested not till he had placed them in friendly hands at the Fort. But the bright hopes which poor Mrs. DeCamp entertained of meeting her husband went out when she reached her destination. Her brimming cup of sorrow overflowed at his grave, which had been made several days when she reached the Fort.

CHAPTER XXIX.

BATTLE OF BIRCH COOLIE — OFFICIAL REPORT OF MAJ. J. R. BROWN, COMMANDING DETACHMENT.

FORT RIDGLEY, Sept. 4, 1862.

Col. H. H. Sibley, Commanding Expedition in Sioux Country:

SIR:—In compliance with your order, I left the encampment at this post, on the morning of August 31st, 1862, to visit the different settlements between this post and Beaver River, to search for and bury all persons that could be found murdered, and at the same time, to examine the country about the Lower Sioux Agency and Little Crow's village, to mark all indications of the movement of the Indians, and the course taken by them in their retreat.

Capt. Grant's Company A, 6th Regiment; Capt. Anderson's Company of mounted men, several volunteers from the officers of the expedition, a fatigue party of twenty men, and seventeen teamsters, with their teams, formed the force of the detachment.

On the 31st of August, the detachment moved in a body and encamped on the Minnesota bottom, at the mouth of Birch Coolie and opposite the Lower Sioux Agency, having found and buried sixteen corpses during the day.

On the 1st of September, the detachment marched in a body to the river bank, when the mounted company, with one team and eight of the fatigue party, accompanied me across the river, under the protection of the infantry. After searching around the Agency, and becoming satisfied there were no Indians in the vicinity, Capt. Grant was directed to remain with his company, and twelve of the fatigue party, and sixteen teams, on the east side of the river, to bury what murdered persons could be found at the crossing and at the settlements, as far as Beaver river, and from the Beaver river to return to the upper timber on the Birch Coolie, and encamp.

I proceeded with that portion of the detachment that had crossed the river, to bury the dead about the Agency, and then proceeded to Little Crow's village, and from there I went alone to where the road leading to the Coteau de Prairie diverges from the Yellow Medicine road, to ascertain whether the Indians had gone to the Coteau, or continued up the Minnesota, towards the Yellow Medicine.

The road and the camps about Little Crow's village, indicated that the main body of the Indians had an immense baggage train, which had gone forward about six days previous, and a smaller baggage train coming from the lower part of the reservation, had gone forward two days subsequently, the entire force keeping the Yellow Medicine road.

In all our examinations, no signs could be found about the village, along the road, or at the river crossing, near the village, that any Indians had been in the vicinity for the four days previous. This was the united opinion of Maj. Galbraith, Messrs. Alex. Faribault, Geo. Faribault, and J. J. Frazier (who were among the volunteers,) and myself; and, as the Indians, when encamped near their villages, invariably visit them frequently, the general supposition was, that upon learning the approach of troops, the lower Indians had gone up to join the Yellow Medicine Indians, that they might subsequently act in concert in their defense against the troops, or in their movement west.

Having accomplished the object of my visit to Little Crow's village, I proceeded to the ford, near that village, and re-crossed the Minnesota river, and near sunset, reached the encampment selected by Capt. Grant, near the upper timber of the Birch Coolie, and about three miles from the Lower Agency.

The two divisions of the detachment buried, during this day, fifty-four murdered persons. Capt. Grant found a woman who was still alive, although she had been almost entirely without sustenance for fourteen days, and was severely wounded. She escaped from the massacre at Patterson's Rapids.

This camp was made in the usual way, on the smooth prairie, some two hundred yards from the timber of Birch Coolie, with the wagons packed around the camp, and the team horses fastened to the wagons. The horses belonging to the mounted men were fastened to a stout picket rope, between the tents and wagons, around the south half of the camp — Capt. Anderson's tents being behind his horses, and Capt. Grant's tents being inside the wagons, which formed the north half of the camp.

A guard of thirty men and two non-commissioned officers was detailed and organized — ten sentinels being stationed about thirty yards from the wagons, at intervals, around the camp, with instructions to keep a good lookout, and report any noise or other indications of the approach of Indians.

Nothing was reported from the guard, until half past four o'clock, on the morning of September 2d, when one of the guard called out, "Indians," and almost instantly afterward, a shower of balls fell upon the camp. The firing, for probably a minute, was entirely on the part of the Indians, during which time, many of our men were either killed or wounded; but the mortality among the men, at that time, was, by no means, as severe as might be supposed, owing to the protection afforded by the horses.

Capt. Anderson and his company promptly availed themselves of the protection afforded by the wagons near him, and opened fire upon the Indians.

Capt. Grant's company and the fatigue party promptly seized their arms, and commenced firing; but they, for some minutes, continued to expose themselves, imprudently, and, consequently, were very much cut to pieces. After the entire detachment became settled under the shelter of the wagons and dead horses, but few were killed or wounded, and the close firing on our side soon caused the Indians to withdraw to the shelter of the woods.

After the withdrawal of the Indians, the construction of rifle-pits was commenced in different parts of the camp, which, although the men worked with a will, progressed slowly, owing to the hardness of the soil, and the want of proper tools. Three spades, one pick, bayonets, tin pans, etc., constituted our means for excavation; and yet rifle-pits to the extent of about two hundred feet in length were completed. From the time the first rifle-pit was commenced, but one man was killed and two wounded, although the fire of the Indians was continued until the arrival of re-enforcements.

Although the Indians had great advantages over us in the early part of the engagement, I think that the mortality on our side, fearful as it was, did not exceed that of the Indians, judging by the numbers they carried across the prairie from the timber from which they fired. Our men were cool, and had orders to discharge their pieces only when a prospect of hitting a foe was presented.

About two o'clock, on the 2d of September, the report of a cannon, which we were confident was discharged by friends approaching to our relief, was hailed with joy, and as we were then in a condition to laugh at all the attacks of Indians upon our position, we felt confident that they would be cheated of a victory through starvation or thirst.

As the re-enforcements advanced, the Indians began to withdraw from us, and prepare for operations against the approaching force. We could see and hear the

Indians, and learned through them that the force was not large, and they hoped to cut it off. This gave us some uneasiness, because we feared the troops might attempt to cross the Birch Coolie about dark; but we soon learned they were halted, and that the Indians proposed to wait until morning to make an attack upon them. In the morning of Sept. 3d, we again observed the the manœuvers of the Indians, and could plainly hear their lamentations at the discovery that you with your entire force had reached Col. McPhail's camp during the night. From that time, the Indians had no hopes of either capturing us or defeating the re-enforcements. Still they kept up a fire on us until your van reached within two or three hundred yards of us.

The Indian force which attacked our camp, I estimate at from two hundred and fifty to three hundred, all well armed and many mounted on good horses.

Enclosed, you will find Capt. Anderson's report, detailing the force, operations, and casualties of his company. His officers and men (with the exceptions he indicates,) acted with the utmost coolness and courage. The captain, although twice severely wounded, continued in active command of his company until your re-enforcements reached our camp. To the prompt movements and energetic action of himself, and his officers and men, the early retreat of the Indians from the prairie, is in a great measure due.

Capt. Grant rendered important service in the construction of the main line of rifle-pits. Lieut.

Gillam, of Capt. Grant's company, with a small party, located themselves on the left of Capt. Anderson early in the fight, and did gallant service. Lieut. Baldwin, of the same company, also acted with cool courage in the different portions of the camp where his duties called him. Lieut. Swan, of the 3d infantry, (a volunteer,) was in charge of a party near and on the left of Lieut. Gillam, where he and his party did good service. Mr. Alex. Faribault, with his son, J. Frazier, and other volunteers, had position on the north portion of the camp, where good service was done during the continuance of the battle. Major Galbraith and Capt. Redfield, both volunteers, were wounded early in the morning. Maj. Galbraith received two wounds, but continued to assist in the construction of the rifle pits. Lieut. Patch, (volunteer) and Sergeant Pratt, of Capt. Grant's company, also rendered valuable service in the defense of the western rifle-pit.

There were wounded, of the volunteers, in addition to those mentioned above, Daniel Blair and Warren DeCamp, the latter very severely. Mr. J. C. Dickenson, of Henderson, and R. Henderson, of Beaver river, also volunteers, left the camp in company with four others at the first fire, and were probably killed. The body of Mr. Henderson was found a short distance from the camp.

Having received no report from Capt. Grant, I am unable to give the names of the killed and wounded of his company, and the fatigue party attached to it.

There were a few men who behaved badly, mostly,

I think, teamsters; but with these exceptions, the entire detachment acted with commendable coolness and courage. Probably the desire of Capt. Grant's company to charge upon the Indians, led to their exposure, and consequently so many deaths and wounds. After they took position behind the wagons, but few casualties occured.

It is a singular fact, that the woman found by Capt. Grant escaped unhurt, although she lay in a high wagon, exposed to the fire of the Indians, and which had several balls pass through it. The killed and wounded were reported to Van on the 3d instant, by Dr. Daniels, who accompanied the detachment. That report I believe to be correct.

Every horse belonging to the detachment was killed, excepting six, which were left at the camp, being wounded and unable to travel.

The tents belonging to the detachment were perfectly riddled, one having one hundred and forty ball holes through it. They are unfit for service.

   Very respectfully,
    Your obedient servant,
     JOSEPH R. BROWN,
Maj. Gen., 3d Division Minnesota Volunteer Mil.,
     Com. Detachment.

CHAPTER XXX.

WANDERING REFUGEES.

Alone, in the wild morass, through tangled bottom-land thickets, crawling in tall prairie grass, and subsisting on hazel-nuts for eight days, a mother wandered with her child. Her scant house covering nearly worn from her person, was poor protection from the chill night air, and the dew-beaded grass added to the discomfiture of her midnight ramblings. No Indian trail, even, marked the course for her feet to tread; but her upturned eye marked the course of the stars, and her uplifted heart sought guidance of Him who "stayeth the rough wind in the day of the east wind." The infant which nestled now quietly in her bosom, had ever been fretful, restless and loud crying. Often she detected the savage foe prowling upon her path. Then she would kneel and pray for deliverance, and that the pitying angels would keep quiet the babe, that its wail reveal not her lurking place — so would the danger pass.

Incredible as it may seem, this woman, Mrs. Almira Harrington of Leavenworth, Brown county, had a severe bullet wound in the back. The same ball had killed a man near her and severed a finger from the hand of her infant.

The first night of encampment by the sad New Ulm

cortege, on their mournful route to Mankato, was her rescue made. She was cautiously crawling through the grass towards the encampment, when discovered by a picket, who snapped two caps at her before he discovered she was a white woman, and but for their defect he would have shot her. This mistake occurred from her hailing him in the Sioux language — he very naturally mistaking her for one of the tribe. Her story is a very thrilling and affecting one, and given with no ordinary intelligence, as she is a woman above the ordinary grade of intellect. Her escape and rescue may be regarded almost a miracle.

The escape of Mrs. Caruthers, of Beaver Creek, from her captors, is hardly less remarkable than the former. Two Indians claimed her, both of whom determined to make her *his squaw*. The contest between them became fierce, each unwilling to yield his right. In the heat of the quarrel, one of their squaws, fearful of being supplanted in the affections of her lord, signified a readiness to aid her. She accordingly spirited Mrs. Caruthers and her two children off to a cornfield, from whence she made her escape, not waiting to know the result of the quarrel.

After being out two days and nights with little rest, she reached the Minnesota river, where she found a canoe and tried to paddle herself over. But "white squaw" having not yet learned "the light canoe to guide," found her frail craft playing funny antics, and resigning herself to its pranks, she laid down "the paddle," and floating on with the drift-wood five or six miles, was providentially thrown on shore near the Fort. She rapped for entrance, with one child in her arms and another on her back, and found a safe asylum there.

An amusing incident occurred with a young lady captive at the Lower Agency. The house of the Episcopal clergyman, Mr. Hinman, had been pillaged, and his clerical robes desecrated to savage use. With the red man, as with many white men, it is the dress that makes the man — hence their increased pomp and stately bearing when new blankets are distributed. No doubt he had looked in some time at the open door when the good man had been ministering at the altar, with an envious eye for his priestly robe. Now what could be more opportune? It was *his*, he had got it, and he would wear it — he would even honor his fair captive with the escort of his dignified self in pontifical robes. In self-admiration and self-congratulation he stalked around, vainly imagining himself the admired of fair eyes, when a witty thought struck him, and turning to Miss ——, he asked if she "belonged to his church?" The ludicrousness of the scene, despite the sadness, produced an *audible smile*, at which the poor fool was so elated, attributing it to his witticism alone, that he arose in ecstatic rapture, and for the moment forgot all but himself. The opportunity was seized for escape, and when the pompous wit came down to a level with the rest of mankind, "his bird had flown," and no magic could lure her from her safe hiding place.

A young man who escaped the murderous grasp, lay all that fearful Monday in his grassy concealment. He then moved on as best he could, till, finding himself nearly surrounded, he crept away in the grass, barely avoiding their savage clutches. Here he remained till a heavy rain came on, when, from a knowledge of their character, he felt he had little to fear. So he manœuvers till confident of eluding pursuit, and boldly pushes forth. From a high bluff he has surveyed the scene, and no signs of Indian for miles around. Down the hill he rushes with rapid strides, but at the base is brought to a dead halt. One hundred and fifty warriors at least are huddled together in the tall grass, not ten feet from him. The noise of the rain prevented the detection of his footsteps, and fortunately their backs were toward him, blankets drawn over their heads, and heads under their arms. Quick as if a thunderbolt had hit him, he drops to the ground and commences a worming ascent — hunger and weariness creeping upon him. Another day and night he rests, when again he resorts to the *creeping* process, and finally, succeeds in reaching a standing where erect locomotion is comparatively safe, to find not unfrequently in his path some freshly bleeding token of their inhuman deeds.

CHAPTER XXXI.

THE MANIAC.

When Captains Chittenden and Northrup, under Col. McPhail, passed up the Minnesota Valley, to raise the siege of Fort Ridgley, they were joined by Charles Nelson, a Swede, whose home at Norwegian Grove Settlement was burned the day previous by the Indians. He had seen the tomahawk cleave the head of his wife in her attempt to escape. His two little sons he last saw running for the corn, and the Indians in close pursuit. He, with bleeding feet, walked twenty-five miles to Henderson, where he met the troops, and supposing himself the only survivor of his family, joined them, thus to avenge their fall.

Passing the spot, so late his happy home, he seemed utterly stupefied with grief, and mechanically closing the gate of his garden, inquired, "When it would be safe to return." *His reason was gone!* This incident incited the following lines a few days after, while their writer, Captain Chittenden, was seated under the Falls of Minne-ha-ha, which our nation's poet has immortalized in his wondrous (?) song of Hiawatha:

> Minne-ha-ha, laughing water,
>   Cease thy laughing now for aye,
> Savage hands are red with slaughter
>   Of the innocent to-day.

DAKOTA WAR WHOOP.

Ill accords thy sportive humor
  With their last despairing wail;
While thou'rt dancing in the sunbeam,
  Mangled corpses strew the vale.

Change thy note, gay Minne-ha-ha;
  Let some sadder strain prevail—
Listen, while a maniac wanderer
  Sighs to thee his woful tale:

"Give me back my Lela's tresses,
  Let me kiss them once again!
She who blest me with caresses,
  Lies unburied on the plain!

"See yon smoke; there was my dwelling;
  That is all I have of home!
Hark! I hear their fiendish yelling,
  As I houseless, childless roam!

"Have they killed my Hans and Otto?
  Did they find them in the corn?
Go and tell that savage monster,
  Not to slay my youngest born.

"Yonder is my new-bought reaper,
  Standing 'mid the ripened grain,
E'en my cow asks why I leave her
  Wand'ring unmilked o'er the plain!

"Soldier, bury here my Lela;
  Place me also 'neath the sod;
Long we lived and wrought together—
  Let me die with her—O God!

"Faithful Fido, you they've left me;
  Can you tell me, Fido, why
God at once has thus bereft me?
  All I ask is here to die.

"O, my daughter Jenny, darling!
  Worse than death is Jenny's fate!"
*   *   *   *   *   *   *
Nelson, as our troops were leaving,
  Turned and shut his garden gate.

CHAPTER XXXII.
TALES OF SUFFERING.

Before the persistent and protracted engagement of Birch Coolie, Capt. Grant, on his route there, found a woman and four children in the swamp, who, for three weeks had subsisted on nuts and wild plums. They had seen no fire, found no covering but heaven's canopy, while rains had beat and fierce winds had blowed, and their now tattered garments were hardly sufficient for covering, and the chill autumn night air piercing to their very vitals. During this time she had given premature birth to an infant, which her own hands had buried. Exhaustion and constant fear made her a half wild woman, and she endeavored to elude her rescuers when first seen, by crawling deeper into the morass, and for some time she could not be made to understand that they were really her friends.

Her story is a heart-thrilling one. She had seen her husband and two children butchered, and her own back, incredible as it may seem, was the receptacle of seventeen buck-shot, which were not removed till after she was brought to St. Paul. Three of these were lodged in the bone, and none had entered the vitals, it having been a side shot. By superhuman effort and woman's dexterous skill, she and her two remaining children eluded her pursuers, and to her own were added two others, of a slain neighbor, which Providence threw in her way, and now, day and night, these four helpless little ones clung to her, begging for food and shivering with cold. She had not expected ever again to see a white person, believing herself the only one living in all that region, and had expected relief only in death.

During the memorable thirty-six hours while raged the bullet shower of Birch Coolie, this poor suffering woman, with the children, was lying quietly, as if fear and suffering had paralyzed the senses, in a wagon, protected only by a tent canvas. Several balls passed through the wagon box. Gradually she came to realize the change in her condition, and well did she appreciate the comparative comfort and kindness she received.

Soon after the terrible war whoop had rung through the State — before yet the people had regained mental equilibrium — the citizens of Saint Paul were startled by the bringing hither by their parents for medical treatment, two shockingly mutilated children, the first real exhibition we had here seen of savage barbarity. Four children were alone in the house, two of whom were killed outright, and the other two left, one of eleven years, with fourteen frightful tomahawk gashes about the breast, arms and head — the other, a mere baby, had three severe cuts on the head and face. No human skill could save them.

The mother with four other persons, was out of the house when the attack was made on it. Those with her were killed, and she barely escaped with life, and hid in the woods till nightfall. The husband and father, unprepared for the change in his home, after a day's absence, returns to find it desolate indeed — his mangled children lying upon the floor, and all in silence, save the groans of the two in whom life yet lingered. In that brief survey, how his agonized soul yearned for the presence of her who doubled his joys and divided his sorrows; nor was he long to endure the suspense. She had crawled from her concealment, when night shadows made it safe, to endure the anguished surprise with her other self. But there is no time for tears or even the burial of their dead,— they must fly with the mangled living.

A detachment of soldiers, sent up the Big Cottonwood for the purpose, found and buried nine bodies, all of which were terribly decomposed.

One man, evidently surprised at his meal, had fallen forward on the table.

A woman was lying across a wagon-rack, near which was the body of a man, doubtless her husband, with his head cut off and several bullet-holes in his body.

A child was found nailed through its hands and feet to a tree. Another literally skinned! O, the horrors of savage butchery! The world has no record of such inhuman acts.

The first process of torture is usually to strip them of clothes, and the varied and cruel modes would seem incredible, were they not authenticated beyond dispute; but we withhold the most saddening, soul-sickening pictures, for the pen revolts at their rehearsal; nay, there is no written language that would convey their full import. True it is, as often remarked during its progress, that the most horrid features of this Indian war will never be written.

A wife and several small children were, in one instance, butchered before the eyes of the husband and father, he being detained for the purpose of being made a witness. Prematurely hastening the advent of her infant, they threw it around her neck as she was bound to the tree, and turning to the husband said, "there, you go to St. Paul and tell them we are going to serve all the women there the same."

On the 27th of October, two months after comparative quiet had been restored to our borders, and troops, unmolested, were encamped at Yellow Medicine, the recent stronghold of the red man, and heaven's dews, heavy and chill, were nightly drenching the earth, two emaciated figures of the human form were brought into camp. They were Mrs. Boetler and her child, of three years old, who had wandered since the outbreak, not having seen a human being till picked up by the soldiers. There is no power in language to convey an idea of what she suffered, never seeing fire, and living mainly on raw potatoes, till, from extreme weakness, she could not speak above a whisper. She made her escape with three children, two of whom died from starvation. With her own hands she dug their graves in the sand and heaped them up with leaves. The little girl who lived was as weak and emaciated as herself, but with kind treatment, medical attention and good nursing, physical vigor returned, but a pall never to be removed, rests upon their hearts.

The foraging party which brought Mrs. Boetler into camp, buried forty-seven bodies, and left elsewhere, seventeen unburied. There is little doubt but hundreds have been left, unfound, till decomposition has taken place, and that the number of actual slain will swell to a larger list than we now have, while houseless, fireless wanderers roamed here and there till the last shred of clothing was gone, and cold weather upon them, they lay them down to die, having been the severest sufferers of the Indian raid.

CHAPTER XXXIII.

THE ATHENÆUM.

So vigorous were the measures, so determined the efforts of our troops, that ere one month had passed, the fast fevered pulse was quiet, fears were subdued, and midnight alarms ceased, save in night-mare dreams, resulting from the daily developments of blood and murder.

Minnesotians, with all their fertility of imagination, had never anticipated the sad fate which awaited her — that her fairest portions would be drenched with the blood of the owners, or that the most remote frontiersman needed any stronger protection than his own powerful arm and his own resolute *will.* The Indians, we all thought, would never dare molest a settler; not that they were too good to do it, but fear of the powers to whom they were amenable would prevent. But too late have they awakened to the need of strong frontier defenses — a cordon of military posts will be demanded, to protect from further incursions, extending from the Red river of the North to the Red river of the South.

The *direct* loss by savage hands was not much less than that occasioned by the panic and flight. Many of the dead found on our prairies were the victims of starvation, after having fled the actual danger.

Scarcely a town without the range of their savage

menace but gave shelter to the homeless; in many, citizens opened their own dwellings to give comfort and solace to the stricken ones. Societies were formed for their relief, food and clothing provided without stint, and for many weeks large donations from eastern cities, in money and goods, were daily received by the committees, and distributed to each "as they had need." The thanks of Minnesotians are due, and given in no stinted measure, for the prompt and ready co-operation in relief of these suffering thousands.

Take one example as a specimen of the congregating points. The vast German Athenæum of St. Paul, was given up to the reception of refugees. Benevolent hearts, beating in the breasts of noble men and women, were devoted to their needs. Through these and her own observation, the writer obtained an insight into the individual history of that one-roomed community, more than one half of whom were children. Arrivals and departures were of daily occurrence, and some days, five hundred persons were there to be fed, and many of them clothed, wholly, or in part, besides sleeping arrangements provided, and, as the weather was becoming colder, there was necessarily a large demand for bed coverings.

Many of these spoke only a foreign tongue, and a striking characteristic of all was the seeming extreme age — lines of grief and care. Nor is it strange. Most of these had been reduced from competence to penury. Garners were full, plenty smiled at their boards — the family circle was unbroken. One day, and O! how changed! Farms are dreary wastes, the stock driven off or roam, uncared for, over the prairies, houses and barns are pillaged, or a heap of smouldering ruins, and the family ranks invaded by grim and ghastly death. The panorama is a very sad one to gaze upon, and still sadder is the real life it represents. Dost wonder, reader, that premature age is engraven on the index of those sad, weary hearts? Alas! we only wonder that death has not set his signet there. Truly, woman was made to suffer and endure!

Here, at the Athenæum, is one family, whose beautiful country home, just without the village of New Ulm, was the admiration of all. Their carriage and elegant matched horses were conspicuous objects during the besieging of that town; for their buildings had all been burned, and their valuables seized upon. Their broad acres, teeming with golden plenty, were now one desolate waste, over which the cattle roamed, uncared for, and several thousands in money and promissory notes, were burned with the house. But all was naught, for the family circle was unbroken.

One little child, with violet eyes, of deep meaning, the only living member of its family, is being kindly nursed by a self-constituted foster-mother, who feels that Providence directed her to its rescue. This woman was fleeing from those whose war-whoop was ringing in her ears, when, stumbling over some object, concealed in the grass, she fell prostrate. Regaining her feet, she involuntarily cast her eyes backward for the cause of her downfall. The fall, rise, and seizure of the child was but the work of an instant, and with it in her arms, she soon eluded pursuit. Then, in her covert, she first looks upon the child. To her surprise, its mother, whom she knew to have been killed, was a neighbor and dear friend. The story being told, this darling baby-boy elicited no little interest from those who visited the building, and many of our best citizens desired to adopt him. But the foster-mother said "nay," its grand-parents were its rightful claimants, and her care would cease not till theirs commenced.

Another, with an eye of more than ordinary intelligence, dignity of mein and lady-like in deportment, had opened her house and larder to the heroic men who so nobly fought in defense of New Ulm, till the excitement of the terrible conflict obliged her to take her couch in real indisposition. Thus helpless she lay, while the bullets whizzed, and rattled upon the walls, and at last, necessity forced the alternative of firing the dwelling for better range of the foe. Hurried by her husband, she caught an ordinary dress, which was just thrown on (our lady readers will understand this), slipped her stockingless feet into slippers and made her egress at the front door as the savages made ingress at the rear. But her bright, intelligent boy of ten years, and her husband were saved, so she bore in silence the loss of all things else.

Here, too, is another; her husband died in her arms from a wound, a few hours after the battle. Her aged mother and herself each try in vain to hush the plaintive cry of the children in their arms, both mere infants, but recently, she says, "so rosy and fat," now so squalid and pale. Plenty smiled in her larder and cellar, and her wardrobe was rich and rare. The garments they wore away had become mere shreds, and their place is supplied by those of coarser texture than ever worn before. Her home and its contents are a heap of ashes, and with a bursting heart she sobs, "all would be nothing if he were only here." Though scarcely thirty, she looked like an aged grandmother of her own children, so terrible is such sudden grief to the heart.

As soon as possible, all who desired it, were furnished homes, either from private bounty or public resources, when a gradual improvement was apparent. The little squalid ones again smiled and crowed in healthful glee, and the burden of their mother's grief was lightened by the occupation of mind and the necessity for effort.

CHAPTER XXXIV.

THE CAPTIVE'S EXPERIENCE AS FURTHER RELATED BY HIMSELF.

"We remained at Little Crow's village five days, during which time all the Indians who had their villages below that place, moved up to our encampment, and in those five days the country for miles around was visited by the warriors, who dealt death and destruction to every person or thing within their reach. A great many female prisoners were brought in every day. I was the only white man ever taken and spared.

"There were three or four Canadians who had resided among the Indians a great many years, who had married Indian women and had children grown, who re-married with them; but they were not considered as prisoners, as they were allowed to retain their teams and other property. One of these men is said to have made his escape to the whites, but returned to his Indian family again after a few days.

"The attacks on New Ulm and Fort Ridgley were made while we were at this village, and after being convinced that they could not reduce the Fort, they made preparations for a move.

"In a short time the lodges were all struck, and their entire camp was in motion. A great many wagons were broken down on the journey in consequence of their being so heavily loaded. They supposed, of course, that a white man's wagon could carry all that could be piled on to it.

"As I was too badly hurt to walk, my friend got me a place to ride in a small one horse wagon, while he walked along by my side. The train of horses, wagons, etc., I should judge was about three miles long. After crossing the Red Wood river we had proceeded about three miles, when the body of a white man was pointed out to me, lying near the side of the road, upon his face. I got out to look at it, but it was so much swollen I could not have recognized it. But upon the shirt collar I read the name of 'Geo. H. Gleason.' He had then been dead about a week. Poor fellow, he had not a personal enemy among the whole tribe, but was universally beloved by all, both whites and Indians, but those savage fiends had sworn to spare none, not even women nor helpless children.

"About three o'clock of the second day's march we arrived at Yellow Medicine, where a large encampment in shape of a circle was formed, with the 'Ti-zo-ti,' or Soldier's lodge in the centre.

"I would here add that this Soldier's lodge, being composed of the bravest and wisest, governs the tribe. Their word is law, and from their decision there is no appeal. To it the chief must submit in silence.

"Here the Mission houses, the Agency buildings, and the house of Other Day were fired, also some other houses belonging to the farmer Indians.

"We remained here about two weeks, during which

time the battle with Capt. Strout's company was fought and the battle of Birch Coolie. Here, also, Gen. Sibley succeeded in opening correspondence with Little Crow. It was here, also, that Mrs. Adams was brought in a captive, some particulars of which will be found elsewhere."

From this point, two messengers were dispatched north, south, and west, as spoken of elsewhere, and from here he sent word to his friends that he was still alive, etc.

CHAPTER XXXV.

EFFORTS TO REGAIN THE PRISONERS.

Until after the battle of Birch Coolie, the Sioux had no doubt of final and complete success. The spirit of their leader had been infused into the mass, and for a time his scepter of influence was swayed in power. But a reaction comes. The whites have not all gone South, and those that remained had given occular demonstrations of their fighting qualities. Little Crow, the wily warrior Chief, feels his influence on the wane, and is often obliged to hide himself at night, to escape the fury of his dissatisfied soldiers, and then in the morning he convenes a council and all are ready to do his bidding, after he has feasted them to their full content.

Colonel Sibley had left a note attached to a stake on the Birch Coolie battle ground, as follows:

"If Little Crow has any proposition to make to me, let him send a half-breed to me, and he shall be protected in and out of my camp.
H. H. SIBLEY,
Col. Commanding Military Expedition.

The note was found and given to their male captive to be read to them. Little Crow desired him to pen the reply which he would dictate, but his arm, broken by the bullet, was not yet well, and he declined, but sent by the flag of truce which bore the reply, a message to his friends "that he was alive." The following is a verbatim copy of Little Crow's letter.

"Yellow Medicine, Sept. 7, 1862.

"Dear Sir:—For what reason we have commenced this war, I will tell you. It is on account of Major Galbraith, we made a treaty with the Government a beg for what little we do get and then can't get it till our children are dieing with hunger. It was with the traders that commence. Mr. A. J. Myrick told the Indians they would eat grass or their own dung, then Mr. Forbes told the lower Sioux that were not men then Robert he was making with his friends how to defraud us of our money, if the young braves have push the white man, I have done this myself; So I want you to let the Governor Ramsey know this. I have a great many prisoners women and children it aint all our fault the Winnebagoes was in the engagement, two of them was killed. I want you to give me answer by bearer all at present.

Yours truly,
his
LITTLE ⋈ CROW,
mark."

The following day the truce bearers returned with the following reply to the foregoing:

"Little Crow:—You have murdered many of our people without any sufficient cause. Return me the prisoners, under a flag of truce, and 1 will talk to you like a man.

H. H. SIBLEY,
Col. Commanding Military Expedition."

The above was not in accordance with the mighty warrior Chieftain's ideas, and the prisoners were still "held in durance vile."

The soldiers, the people and the press became impatient for the expedition to proceed. Col. Sibley was charged with remissness, negligence and a desire to favor the Indians. Still he kept his own counsels, unmoved by calumny and trusting his own superior judgment. He knew his men were undisciplined recruits, but never an army composed of better material. Halls of science, business houses and churches had contributed to swell the enrolled list. They must not be sacrificed, and to rush unprepared upon the enemy was madness. Besides, he knew the Indians well — habits, character and fighting proclivities — he knew, too, what would probably be the fate of the unhappy prisoners, should he be precipitate. The Indians held them for a specific end. Had the attack on them been made before they deserted their camp, it was their design to tomahawk every captive. This was not considered by his impatient slanderers, whose tongues were afterwards silenced, when they saw the wisdom of his plans and his courage in braving censure.

CHAPTER XXXVI.

CORRESPONDENCE BETWEEN COL. SIBLEY AND LITTLE CROW.

It was hoped that the checks which had been given the Sioux, with the practical knowledge gained of the fighting qualities of those with whom they contended, would cause the cessation of hostilities and the delivery of the captors. But always, in their mode of warfare, the danger is nigh when least expected. Fair, open field fight is avoided. Small guerrilla squads prowl through the country on fleet stolen horses, striking where they can wield the most successful blow, and before the alarm can be raised, are beyond the reach of punishment.

Coursing down the Minnesota valley, we find them in Blue Earth county on the 12th September, committing depredations and murders, where comparative security was being felt, and no supposition of an Indian within fifty miles. Four men, after taking their families to a place of safety, had returned to secure their crops, as many others had done, and were surprised and murdered, within one mile of a military company, stationed there for the protection of the neighborhood, This circumstance evinced the necessity of strong armed forces, where there was no apparent danger.

On the 12th of Sept., another flag of truce, with

another communication from Little Crow, was received at the "head-quarters." The bearer of the dispatch, had a secret for Col. Sibley's ear—*a dissatisfaction had arisen in camp*, confirmed by a private letter, secretly brought and delivered, and it was very evident that the war party among the Indians, had determined on a desperate stand against our forces. We give below a copy of Little Crow's second letter to Gen. Sibley:

"RED IRON VILLAGE, OR WAY-AU-AKAN.

"To HON. H. H. SIBLEY:

"we have in ma-wa-kan-ton band one hundred and fifty-five presoners—not included the Sisitons and warpeton presoners, then we are waiting for the Sisiton what we are going to do with the prisoners they are coming down—they are at Lake quiparle now, the words that I want to the governel il want to here from him also, and I want to know from you as a friend what way that il can make peace for my people—in regard to presoners they fair with our children or our self just as well as us.

"Your truly friend,
"LITTLE CROW."

We append the answer.

HEAD-QUARTERS MILITARY EXPEDITION,
Sept. 12, 1862.

To LITTLE CROW, SIOUX CHIEF:

I have received your letter to-day. You have not done as I wished in giving up the prisoners taken by your people. It would be better for you to do so. I told you I had sent your former letter to Gov. Ramsey, but I have not yet had time to receive a reply. You have allowed your young men to commit some murders since you wrote your first letter. This is not the way to make peace.

H. H. SIBLEY,
Col. Com. Mil. Expedition."

The following is the *private* letter named above, received at the same time as the other. The contrast of the two will readily evince the power of the christian over the savage Indian:

"WAY-AWA-KAN, Sept. 10, '62.

"COL. H. H. SIBLEY, Fort Ridgley:

"*Dear Sir:* — You know that Little Crow has been opposed to me in everything that our people have had to do with the whites. He has been opposed to everything in the form of civilization and christianity. I have always been in favor of, and of late years have done everything of the kind that has been offered to us by the Government and other good white people — he has now got himself into trouble that we know he can never get himself out of, and he is trying to involve those in the murder of the poor whites that have been settled in the border; but I have been kept back with threats that I should be killed if I did anything to help the whites. But if you will now appoint some place for me to meet you, myself and the few friends that I have will get all the prisoners that we can, and with our families go to whatever place you will appoint for us to meet.

"I would say further, that the mouth of the Red Wood, Candiohi on the north side of the Minnesota, or the head of the Cottonwood river — one of these three places, I think, would be a good place to meet.

"Return the messenger as quick as possible, we have not much time to spare.

"Your true friend,
"WABASHAW,
"TAOPEE."

Col. Sibley returned answer, as follows:

"HEAD-QUARTERS MIL. EXPEDITION,
Sept. 12, 1862.

"To WABASHAW AND TAOPEE:

"I have received your private message. I have come up here with a large force to punish the murderers of my people. It was not my purpose to injure any innocent person. If you and others who have not been concerned in the murders and expeditions, will gather yourselves, with all the prisoners, on the prairie in full sight of my troops, and when the white flag is displayed by you, a white flag will be hoisted in my camp, and then you can come forward and place yourselves under my protection. My troops will be all mounted in two days' time, and in three days from this day I expect to march. There must be no attempt to approach my column or my camp, except in open day, and with a flag of truce conspicuously displayed. I shall be glad to receive all true friends of the whites with as many prisoners as they can bring, and I am powerful enough to crush all who attempt to oppose my march, and to punish those who have washed their hands in innocent blood.

"I sign myself the friend of all who were friends of your great American Father.

"H. H. SIBLEY,
"Col. Com. Mil. Expedition."

As soon as the Expedition was provided with "bread and bullets for ten days in advance," the Col. issued his marching orders, and on the 18th of September crossed the Minnesota river, opposite the Fort, nearly two thousand strong, and in mud and rain, pushed on eager for the climax.

On their route the main body found and buried the body of Philander Prescott, an esteemed christian man, who for more than thirty years had been employed as interpreter, and had been one of the first victims of savage wrath. His history is peculiar and full of interest. When a young man he had found his way into the heart of the Sioux country, where, throwing off the restraints of civilized life, he adopted the habits, customs and costume of the tribe. He had married a squaw who bore him several children, who were growing up in all the ignorance which surrounded them. Thus he lived and thus he might have died, had not the Holy Spirit been commissioned with a message to his heart, reviving in even these dark surroundings the religious impressions of childhood. Deep and pungent conviction for sin was fastened "like a nail in a sure place," and he found peace at the feet of Jesus in the surety of pardon through his blood. Now arose the question of duty. The now christian man could not leave his wife and children in heathen darkness, and therefore resolved to give them, with their people, the benefit of his new life. So he came to the frontier and engaged as Interpreter, first at Fort Snelling and later at the new Agencies. His family had been educated in the walks of usefulness, and everywhere commanded respect. When the trouble commenced, his wife hid him in an oven, where he remained till the danger seemed comparatively over. Then he started for the Fort, a lone pedestrian, shuddering at the fresh tokens of savage wrath which often met his eye. But this was not long; the savage hounds were upon his track, and his aged body is left to decomposition without funeral rites, while his well-prepared soul basks in the light of eternal day.

CHAPTER XXXVII.

BATTLE OF WOOD LAKE.

Col. Sibley's force was camped on Wood Lake, three miles below the Yellow Medicine Agency. Thus far had they come unmolested by the skulking foe, but frequent proofs of their doings met the eye in the mangled and decaying bodies. Wherever their encampments had been, the ground was strewn with empty trunks, boxes, barrels, fruit and oyster cans, and various other indications of the quality and kind of spoils.

A scouting party, among whom was Other-Day, was sent forward on the 21st Sept., who having curiosity to gratify, hitched their horses for reconnoissance of the deserted Indian houses. A horse of their own party galloped up riderless, and Other-Day hastened out just in time to see an Indian riding off his own horse at full speed. His fire was without effect, but his flashing eye gave promise of success in a determination for revenge.

Where he was murdered, was found the body of George Gleason, whom it will be recollected was one of the victims of the first day's massacre. There was little else than a dried skeleton. His skull was broken in, and all his clothes gone, save his drawers and shirt. Some gold buttons with his initials, which the savages had overlooked, were the only means of identity. Around him were fragments of dispatches he was carrying to the Lower Agency, and other papers of both public and private interest. With sad hearts they heaped the earth over the remains of their once jovial, warm-hearted friend, and when all terror had fled that region, he was removed by Masonic friends to Shakopee, where, at last, the rites of a christian burial were given him.

A daring warrior of Little Crow came to the opposite shore the night previous to battle, counted the tents of Col. Sibley's camp, by which, seeing but forty-eight, he estimated a force of only three hundred men. *Their* number was seven hundred and eighty, and so they felt safe in risking a battle. The "braves," more honorable than their chief, overruled his intent of a night attack, reminding him of his boast that he could whip the white men, and now, say they, "let's show them by open day-light that we *can* do it." Crow's plan was to attack with a small force in front, sufficient to draw them from the ravine, and at a signal to be given, the ambushed Indians were to seize the baggage wagons and shoot the drivers. So confident was he of success, that their women were brought down to the opposite side of the river to carry off the spoils, while the men should do the butchering and *make a clean sweep* of the camp.

Early on the morning of the 23d, a foraging party was surprised, and conveyed the alarm to camp, while it was breakfasting. The Renville Rangers, under

Lieutenant Gorman, were sent at once to their support. In a few moments, the surrounding bluffs were covered with Indians, both on horse and foot, trying to circumvent the camp. The Third Regiment followed in support of the Rangers, who now pushed on a mile in advance, and were nearly surrounded, and barely effected a retreat. The artillery kept the opposite shore of the lake, clear. Two companies of the Sixth had a skirmish on the left, and the Seventh Regiment, under Lieut. Col. Marshall, made a gallant charge into a ravine on the right, and drove the enemy from shelter there. This charge is pronounced by all, as one of the most valiant and successful ever made. And when we reflect that it was by an undisciplined regiment, not two months from the quiet of home life, and most of them in their first fight, with those who had drank in the war-spirit with their earliest breath, we marvel that the brave Col. Marshall, with his young heroes, had not all been left in ghastly death, instead of driving the foe and leading his men out of that ravine, gloriously victorious.

Other-Day, too, proved himself on this occasion true as steel, and of great courage. He pushed forward of the lines, rushed in amongst the Indians, exposing himself to the fire of both sides, and several times being mistaken for an enemy, was fired at by our men. Finally, after he had shot three Indians, he was surrounded and led triumphantly into camp with two captured ponies, which more than squared up his account for the loss of his own horse.

During the fight, Little Crow was seen in the distance, riding a black horse, with a spy glass in his hand, which he used ever and anon, to see how the war was waging. It was a complete repulse to the Sioux, and from this time they were thoroughly convinced that the despised whites were more than a match for them.

Had the cavalry force been sufficient to follow up this repulse, the whole band might have been destroyed or made prisoners. But they being nearly naked, with no incumbrance but their guns and powder flasks, soon outdistanced the infantry and rendered further pursuit futile. But the back bone of the outbreak was broken—the power of Little Crow vanished as in air, and they sought their own safety by flight.

The aspect of affairs, as Col. Sibley moved up the Minnesota valley, was extremely threatening, and the difficulties under which he labored of no ordinary nature. Had he yielded to the almost unanimous desire of the people to advance, before being fully prepared, and his command been defeated or even temporarily repulsed, it is a fact which does not now admit of question, that there would have been a general uprising of all the savages on our border, embracing not only the entire Dakota bands, but the Chippewas and Winnebagoes also, which would have resulted in a repetition, upon a larger scale, of the murders and outrages committed by the lower bands of Dakotas. The imminent peril to the whole State of a premature movement, was constantly present to his mind, and con trolled every action throughout, notwithstanding the immense outward pressure brought to bear from every quarter. The obstinately contested but successful battle of Wood Lake, broke the power of the savage, completely demoralized the hostile bands, and relieved the entire frontier, teaching the savages a lesson they are not soon to forget.

CHAPTER XXXVIII.

COL. SIBLEY'S DISPATCH TO GOV. RAMSEY.

Wood Lake, near Yellow Medicine,
September 23, 1862.

To His Excellency, Gov. Ramsey:

Sir: I left the camp at Fort Ridgley on the 12th inst., with my command, and reached this point early in the afternoon of the 22d. There have been small parties of Indians each day in plain sight, evidently acting as scouts for the main body. This morning I had determined to cross the Yellow Medicine river, about three miles distant, and there await the arrival of Capt. Rogers' company, of the Seventh Regiment, which was ordered by me from New Ulm, to join me by a forced march, the presence of the company there being unnecessary by the arrival there of another company, a few days previous.

About seven o'clock this morning, the camp was attacked by about three hundred Indians, who suddenly made their appearance and dashed down toward us, whooping and yelling in their usual style, and firing with great rapidity.

The Renville Guards, under Lieutenant Gorman, were sent by me to check them, and Major Welch, of the Third Regiment, was instantly in line with his command, with his skirmishers in the advance, by whom the savages were gallantly met, and after a conflict of a serious nature, repulsed.

Meanwhile another portion of the Indian force passed down a ravine on the right, with a view to outflank the Third regiment, and I ordered Lieut. Colonel Marshall, with five companies of the Seventh Regiment and who was ably seconded by Major Bradley, to advance to its support, with one six-pounder under the command of Capt. Hendricks, and I also ordered two companies of the Sixth Regiment to re-enforce him.

Lieut. Col. Marshall advanced at a double-quick, amidst a shower of balls from the enemy, which fortunately, did little damage to his command; and after a few volleys, he led his men to a charge, and cleared the ravine of the savages.

Major McLaren, with Capt. Wilson's company, took position on the extreme left of the camp, where he kept at bay a party of the enemy who were endeavoring to gain the rear of the camp, and finally drove them back.

The battle raged for about two hours, the six-pounder and mountain-howitzer being used with great effect, when the Indians — repulsed at all points with great loss, — retired with great precipitation.

I regret to state that many casualties occurred on our side. The gallant Major Welch was badly wounded in the leg, and Capt. Wilson, of the Sixth Regiment, was severely bruised by a nearly spent ball in the shoulder. Four of our men were killed, and between thirty and forty wounded, most of them, I am rejoiced, to say, not severely.

The loss of the enemy, according to the statement of a half-breed, named Jos. Campbell, who visited the camp under a flag of truce, was thirty killed and a large number wounded. We found and buried fourteen of the bodies, and as the habit of the Indians is to carry off the bodies of their slain, it is not probable that the sum told by Campbell was exaggerated.

The severe chastisement inflicted upon them has so far subdued their ardor that they sent a flag of truce into the camp to express the sentiment of the Wahpetons, composing a part of the attacking force, and to state that they were not strong enough to fight us, and desired peace, with permission to take away their dead and wounded. I replied that when the prisoners were delivered up, it would be time enough to talk of peace, and that I would not grant them permission either to take their dead or wounded.

I am assured by Campbell that there is serious depression in the Indian camp — many having been opposed to the war, but driven into the field by the more violent. He further stated that eight hundred Indians were assembled at the Yellow Medicine, within two miles of the camp, but that the greater part took no part in the fight. The intention of Little Crow was to attack us last night, but he was overruled by others, who told him if he was a brave man, he ought to fight the white man by daylight. I am fully prepared against night attack, should it be attempted, although

I think the lesson received by them to-day, will make them very cautious for the future.

I have already adverted to the courage and skill of Lieut. Col. Marshall, and Majors Welch and Bradley, to which I beg leave to add those of the officers and men under their respective commands. Lieut. Col. Averill and Major McLaren were equally prompt in their movements in preparing the Sixth Regiment for action, and were both under fire for some time. Capts. Grant and Bromley shared the dangers of the field with Lieut. Col. Marshall's command, while Capt. Wilson, with his command, rendered efficient service. The other companies of the Sixth Regiment were not engaged, having been held in position to defend the rear of the camp, but it was difficult to restrain their ardor, so anxious were officers and men to share with their comrades the perils of the field. To Lieut. Col. Fowler, my A. A. A. G., I have been greatly indebted for aid in all my movements — his military knowledge and ability being invaluable to me, and his assistance in to-day's affair particularly so. To Major Forbes, Messrs. Patch, Greig, and McLeod, of my staff, who carried my orders, I must also acknowledge myself under obligations for their activity and zeal, while to Major Brown, also of my staff, though suffering from illness, it would be injustice not to state that he aided me materially by his exertions and advice. The medical staff of the several regiments were cool and expert in rendering their professional aid to the wounded. Assistant Surgeon Seigneuret, attached to my staff, is to be commended for his skill and diligence.

I am very much in want of bread rations, six-pounder ammunition, and shells for the howitzer, and unless soon supplied, I shall be compelled to fall back, which, under present circumstances, would be a calamity, as it would afford time for the escape of the Indians with their captives. I hope a large body of cavalry is, before this, on their way to join us. If I had been provided with five hundred of this description of force to-day, I venture the assertion that I could have killed the greater part of the Indians, and brought the campaign to a successful close.

Rev. Mr. Riggs, chaplain of the expedition, so well known for his knowledge of the character and language of the Indians, has been of great service to me since he joined my command.

I enclose the official report of Lieut. Col. Marshall. I omitted to mention Lieut. Gorman and his corps of Renville Rangers. They have been extremely useful to me by their courage and skill as skirmishers. Captain Hendricks and his artillerists won deserved praise to-day, and Capt. Sterrett, with his small but gallant corps of cavalry, twenty-seven in number, did good service also.

I send reports of the several Surgeons, embracing lists of the killed and wounded.

Very respectfully, your ob't serv't,
H. H. SIBLEY,
Col. Commanding.

CHAPTER XXXIX.

THE CHIPPEWAS.

While these barbarities were being enacted in the west and southwest, "tidings out of the north" troubled the political elements at the Capital. Indeed, all the surrounding counties are astir, for there are rumors of a Chippewa uprising. A dark, portentous storm seems about to increase the fury of the one already raging. Aye, rumor says, the Chippewas have joined hands with their hated enemies, the Sioux, and, henceforth, they will do battle together for the extermination of the whites, — that Agent Walker, they claim, has wronged them, and they will have redress. All this is not without foundation, and ere the excitement has reached its acme, Agent Walker shoots himself, some say, under the excitement of an insane mind, and more uncharitable ones say, from fear of his doings with them being fathomed.

At this juncture, Hole-in-the-day, the nation's head Chief, issued a proclamation, to the effect that he would not be responsible for the conduct of his people, after ten days, and desired all white settlers to leave the country, before the time specified. The Sioux raid had already depopulated many of the fairest portions of the upper country, and now, the few remaining and dwelling on the Chippewa reservation, fled to Fort Ripley or Abercrombie for protection, which were even then crowded with refugees, whom the Sioux had driven there.

A messenger came from Hole-in-the-day to Commissioner Dole, asking him to come with Judge Cooper, and make a treaty. These, with Senator Wilkinson and Paymaster Thompson, went at once on their mission of peace. It was said that Hole-in-the-day had assured his people that "we had all we could manage, with our brethren the South, and if they pleased to combine with the Sioux, their power would not be resisted. There surely was cause for alarm — alarm for the safety of the State, alarm for the fleeing inhabitant.

In due time, with a strong armed force, threatening in its aspect, the embassy seat themselves in council, when these are at once surrounded by a still stronger force of Chippewas, sending terror to the heart; and to their minds, bidding defiance to all treaty efforts. Two or three days were consumed in this way, each retaining their own military force on the ground, and refusing to be first to withdraw. There was no avenue of hope under such threatening skies, and a messenger was dispatched to Gov. Ramsey, to make all haste to be at the council. He lost no time, and with two or three others, was soon under way, and met Commissioner Dole, who considered himself fortunate in having escaped with his life, but deemed him hazardous in the extreme, in going, without a military escort. Therein was the trouble, but the Commissioner comprehended it not;

so giving all power into the hands of the far-seeing Governor, the two parted.

After an absence of three days from the Capital, the second corps of commissioners returned from a successful conference with the Chippewas. On the 15th Sept., all pending difficulties were declared settled, and they shook hands, in taking leave, more cordially than when they met, leaving them in a better state of mind than had existed for years. The public mind was relieved. This was the first rift in the savage war clouds. "Fair weather," saith the prophet, "cometh out of the north." This seemed a precursor of hope for the dying echoes of the war-whoop, on the other hand. Nearly every Chief of the nation was present, and appended their signature to a treaty of peace, involving perpetual friendship, made and signed at Crow Wing, Sept. 15, 1862, and in presence of the several bands over which each Chief bore rule. All hostile demonstrations now cease, and all return, in quiet, to their rude village homes.

Not months had passed since the painted savage, in our streets, or even any number of them, was no cause for alarm. Children followed them from street to street, and old men and maidens, last initiated into western life, were eager for an eligible position to witness the celebrated performance of the begging or scalp dance. To the ungratified eye, it was a coveted scene, and even those to whom it was no more a novelty, never lost the opportunity. But we have shown how vast a change a little time worketh. A red skin becomes a rare sight, and no more thought of, but in connection with rapine and murder. Women turn pale in affright, children scream in terror, and men involuntarily elevate the hand to the cranium, as if to hold fast their scalp, for a band of some forty Indians suddenly appear in front of the Capitol, on the morning of Sept. 22, demanding an interview with the Governor. The practiced eye could see they were not Sioux, whose bloody knives were still unsheathed; hence the alarm soon subsided, for policy forbade the violation of a peace treaty, not yet one month old.

This delegation represented twenty-one bands, each of which was accompanied by its Chief, tendering the service of the Chippewa nation to Gen. Pope, who was in command of the Department of the north-west, having its head quarters in St. Paul, to become our allies in fighting the Sioux. After trailing the "stars and stripes" through the streets, for an hour or two, while the people, in various humors, looked on its desecration, preliminaries for a formal reception and "talk," on the following morning, was being made.

The time designated being made known to them, they, prompt to the hour, were seated on the ground, their feet underneath them, in the usual manner, awaiting the *best bow* of the Governor, when he gave his "talk" in his usual felicitous humor. He welcomed them to the city, forgave past indiscretions of some of their young men, in taking property of the whites, which he was sure they all now regretted, and was happy that the Chippewas had never shed the blood of the white man, as their bad brothers, the Sioux, had done. He said that Gen. Pope, the great war chief, who had lately come to fight these bad Indians, was not ready for them now, but would send them word when he wanted them to go upon their war-path. He regretted that they were not here an hour earlier, as they then could have witnessed the deliberations of the great council of the State.* He wished them a happy journey home, promised them a good supper that night, and a ride on the fire wagon† to St. Anthony.

The above brief speech was responded to with the usual grunts and "ho, hos," and being concluded, the Chief, Berry Hunter, assured the Governor that the words he spoke "went right into his ears, and they were good, and though he was an old man, he had not lost his reason. That they had come down to show their white brothers they felt very friendly, and never desired to have any other feeling toward them."

Big Dog, another Chief, desiring to display his oratorical powers, as also his warrior prowess, came forward and said "his hands were very red — he had painted them on purpose, so that when he came to imbrue them in the blood of the Sioux, they would show no stain."

After some more like unimportant speeches, of which these are samples, the council broke up in seeming satisfaction, but, doubtless, as much from the promised feast, as any other cause, to which, at the appointed hour, they did ample justice. And the following

---

* An extra session of the Legislature had just adjourned.
† Cars.

morning opened their eyes in wondering pleasure, as they swiftly rode over the prairie, but dodging, in alarm, at the shrill notes of the engine whistle.

CHAPTER XL.

THE CAPTIVE'S PERIL.

Perhaps it was the *power* of the whites, and the fear of merited punishment, or the influence of Chaska, whom his white friend had impressed with the evil of their doings, which made dissatisfaction apparent in the Indian camp, and incited the resolve for a separation. "The leaven" was surely "hid in the meal," and was working with its own hidden effect for the formation of a friendly camp. Believing this to be the case, Little Crow and his adherents, daily threatened the life of the captive, Spencer. Chaska was the "head soldier" of his chief when the work began, who had relied on him to carry out his monster plans of ruin and death, but against the whites he would not "move so much as one of his fingers." Threats were made, hard quarrels resulted from his pacific course, and the disposition to be made of the "white man." Armed and mounted men almost daily rode to the door of the lodge demanding "the white man to be brought out." And this, when he was too weak to stand alone, supported by the strong arm of his red friend, with the hostile guns aimed at his heart. Then Chaska, brave and fearless, would aim his double-shooter, with *"Shoot if you like; kill him if you will; but two of you will come out of your saddles if you do."* They knew his spirit, and did not care to risk a *test* of his steel on their own person; so for that time the danger would pass, to be repeated in a few hours. Their tent had a large hole dug in the center, where he was concealed when danger was known to be near.

"For the most part of the time," (we quote his own language,) "for ten days previous to the arrival of our forces, I was kept concealed, in consequence of numerous threats made, and an order issued by Little Crow that Ta-o-pi, my friend, and myself, should be put to death.

"The friendly Indians, however, guarded me faithfully, notwithstanding I was considered by many as the cause of placing their lives in danger. The night before the battle of Wood Lake, I was disguised and sent to a lodge in a different part of the camp, in consequence of two or three armed Indians who had been discovered lurking round the lodge in which I usually staid, evidently with the intention of trying to get a shot at me.

"Another time a squaw came in and whispered something to my friend, who instantly seized his gun, and bade me put on my blanket and follow him. As I followed, he hurriedly told me that Little Crow and two others were prowling around, and intended to fire into the lodge where I was. I was taken to a neighboring lodge and placed in the hole already dug, and carefully concealed, where I passed a long and sleepless night, with a guard of ten or twelve Indians around on the outside. These and similar occurrences happened so frequently, that I at length became indifferent, and did not care how soon death might come.

"My bodily sufferings were very great, but nothing when compared with my mental anxiety. Being threatened with death so often, sometimes I almost prayed that some of their attempts to kill me might prove successful. I thought that death would be a relief to me.

"Being constantly with my friend, I received the best of treatment from him and his wife. But the female captives were, with very few exceptions, subjected to the most horrible treatment. In some cases, a woman would be taken out into the woods, and her person violated by six, seven, and as many as ten or twelve of these fiends at one time. There was, I believe, but one captive killed; that was a boy, who had in some way offended his captor, who deliberately shot him dead.

"With the exception of being almost devoured by fleas and other vermin, which always infest the Indian lodge, my situation was as comfortable as it could be under the circumstances. Before leaving the Indian camp, my friend restored to me my ring, pin, watch, money, clothes, and, in fact, every thing I had about my person when I was taken.

"I oftentimes contemplated making my escape, or at least attempting it; but my wounds were not sufficiently healed to allow me to undertake it. I am satisfied that, had I been perfectly well, I could very easily have stolen a pony and gun, and knowing the country well, I should not have had much difficulty in escaping.

"The battle of Wood Lake was fought, and the Indians were thoroughly convinced that the whites were more than they could successfully contend against, and sought safety in flight.

CHAPTER XLI.

THE FRIENDLY CAMP.

The day of redemption was drawing nigh; hearts were to be relieved of the bitter anxiety, and the sufferings of the captives in the Indian lodges, to end. Of the formation of the friendly camp, Mr. Spencer gives the following particulars:

"While yet at Red Iron's village, Ta-o-pi, Ma-za-ku-ta, Wa-kin-yan-wash-te, my friend, in accordance with the instructions received secretly from Gen. Sibley, attempted to form the friendly camp, or in other words, to form a separate encampment from the main camp, and to get as many of the captives as they possibly could into their possession, and remain firm, and when the whites came up, to deliver themselves and the captives up to Col. Sibley.

"Several attempts were made to establish this camp, but no sooner would the lodges be set up, than hundreds of armed Indians from Little Crow's camp would come over and push down the lodges and force them back into the main encampment. Some few friendly Indians made their escape, taking captives with them, and succeeded in getting into Fort Ridgley.

"White Lodge left us at this place with his entire band, taking away with him about fifteen captives. They went over toward the Missouri river. One day, when most of the warriors were absent, a party of about twenty-five lodges made another attempt to camp by themselves. They were this time successful. They pitched their lodges in a small hollow, and determined to intrench themselves and fight rather than to again be forced back with Little Crow's party. They accordingly dug large square holes in the centre of the lodges, in which to place the women and children in case of an attack; so that the little camp was in quite a defensible condition. After it was thus fortified, several other Indians who had not the courage to join in at first, came in, and in a few days our camp numbered about one hundred and twenty-five lodges, and fighting men enough to hold it against all the warriors that the opposite party could bring against it.

"Standing Buffalo, the Sissiton Chief, and Wa-a-na-tan, the chief of the Cut Heads, came down while we were at this place and held council with Little Crow, and determined not to take any part in the war against the whites.

"A great deal of credit has been given to Wa-ba-shaw, a well known chief, for assisting in the formation of the friendly camp. But I can see no just cause why he should have the credit of doing an action which justly belongs to others. After the battle of Wood Lake had been fought, and upon the return of the Indians; hastily holding a council, Crow and his followers determined to flee to the plains. Wa-ba-shaw started off with them, and returned and joined the friendly camp only the day before our forces came in sight. His conduct was most cowardly all through the whole trouble.

"Our camp remained firm, and two days after we had the most welcome news that the 'Long Trader' (the name by which Gen. Sibley is known among the Indians,) with his troops, was in sight.

"It was to me a glorious sight. I had been in captivity forty days, and during most of that time my life had been in imminent danger almost every hour. When I rolled myself in my blanket to take a little rest, I knew not whether I should awake in this world or the next. I was now about to be released, and take my friends by the hand. Could it be a reality, or was it only a pleasant dream, such as I had often had, to be again dispelled by sounds of the well known war-whoop, which would warn me to betake myself to my place of concealment? The gleaming of the bright bayonets in the sun, the sound of the ear-piercing fife, and the rattling drums, were sufficient to convince me that it was not a dream, but that I was saved.

"Too much praise cannot be awarded to Colonel Sibley, whose thorough knowledge of Indian character has so successfully enabled him to accomplish the objects of the expedition.

"The rescue of his unfortunate countrymen, who were held as captives, by a savage foe, was ever uppermost in his thoughts, and though others may censure him for not coming up to their expectations, we, who have been rescued, will ever hold the name of Henry H. Sibley dear in our hearts."

CHAPTER XLII.

CAMP RELEASE.

Two hundred and twenty captives had been aided into the friendly camp, and now hearts beat with exultant hope of no distant release. To what brutal indignities had they been obliged to submit! How the heart revolted at the loathsome retrospect!—wives, mothers, young ladies, and young girls, almost children, had met the same fate.

The fairest, most cultivated, and most attractive of the youthful women, was Miss Mattie Williams, of Painesville, Ohio, who, at the time of the outbreak, was residing with an uncle, seven miles up the Yellow Medicine river. Each sought their own safety, in whatever direction circumstances seemed best to indicate, neither person or company waiting to see the course of the other. Mr. and Mrs. Reynolds, the uncle and aunt of Miss Mattie, were nearing a place of safety, when a party of armed Indians were seen making toward them. What was to be done? The reeking, jaded horse, just ready to fall, could not be urged out of a walk, and the first thought was to abandon the buggy and trust their own locomotion for safety. But he being a large man, was dissuaded by his wife, who suggested the strategy of playing Indian. By the time they had their blankets adjusted in the most approved

Indian style, the savages were sufficiently near to suppose them of their own people, and so made off in another direction, leaving them to a safe terminus of their route. Miss Williams, with a German servant girl, was in an open buggy, with a Mr. Patwell, and they had begun to feel safe from pursuit, when set on by a gang of these worse than blood hounds; the man was killed, the German girl was wounded, so that from the wound and other brutal treatment, she died in four days. Miss W. was hit by a spent ball in the shoulder, but its pain was forgotten, in the terrible anguish that followed, in the experience of forty days' captivity. Occasionally, she would find the fragment of a book, or some coarse needle work, with which to kill time, else it was all given to bitter reflections on the sad reality of her lot. O! how my heart yearned toward her, as she modestly alluded to the indignities, the cruel, brutal treatment which may not be penned, and I felt, and I still feel, that the man or woman who would stoop to calumniate the fair fame, for such a cause, of one who has thus suffered, deserves to be *branded a coward and a brute.*

Forty nervous, anxious days, forty restless, sleepless nights, suffering from cold and leaking tents, though never from hunger, forty days clad in Indian costume, suffering in every way that savage passion could devise! A soft, dewy mistiness creeps from the heart to the eyes as we contemplate the horrors of that life, which time and again she prayed might end. But the hour of release drew near. A giant mind with strong will, had every energy of soul bent to this one object, and its accomplishment was sure. With nervous joy she wrapped her blanket around her on the night of the 25th September, for the last time in that Indian camp, and laid her down, not to pleasant dreams, but to blissful waking visions of release.

How her heart fluttered and beat in turn, lest the hope should be thwarted! Nor was she alone in her night vigils. In every tent in that encampment "eyes were holden" from sleep. Only the infants slept unconsciously, as if fear, care or pain had never visited the earth. Were those weary days, those anxious restless nights indeed to end? was the one absorbing thought, — and memorable for this will be that last night in Indian camp. At the first dawnings of day on the morning of the 26th, the camp was astir, and preparations went forward for the reception of their distinguished guests. Personal decoration was the absorbing theme of the "Master of Ceremonies." Paint of every hue was in active demand, together with eagle's feathers, beads, and wampum, and white flags were displayed all through their village.

At noon, a flag of truce, consisting of a stolen bed sheet, tied to the end of a pole, went forth to meet the approaching "Expedition." Great indeed was the captive's joy on the sound of the martial music, and at the sight of the bright gleaming bayonets in friendly hands! The Indians, squaws and pappooses, were arranged in a circling wall around the camp for the reception of their guests, or in awe at the strange and imposing display. Col. Sibley marched his column partly around their encampment and went into camp near the river. Some of the men whose families were held captives were allowed to go at once to them, and O! the joy of such meetings! Who shall paint the scene? In due time, Col. Sibley and staff went over to take formal possession of the camp. Around him crowded those from whom the blood-stains were scarcely washed, with every protestation of friendship and the constant declaration of "me good Ingian."

Col. Sibley, from his great magnanimous heart assured them, that the really innocent had nothing to fear, while the guilty ones would meet the punishment their deeds merited. He now demanded the unconditional and unreserved surrender of all the prisoners. The preliminaries being concluded, the waiting, trembling captives were brought forth and delivered up to him who had spent anxious days and sleepless nights devising for the accomplishment of this object. He says of it: "I conducted the poor captives to my camp, where I had prepared tents for their accommodation. There were some instances of stolidity among them, but for the most part, the poor creatures, relieved of the horrible suspense in which they had been kept, and some of the young women freed from the loathsome attentions to which they have been subjected by their brutal captors, were fairly overwhelmed with joy." This camp very properly took the name of "Camp Release."

Another, in speaking of the circumstances, and the profound joy which made them speechless, says:

"We brought them into camp and did all we could to make them comfortable, for every heart was moved at the recital of what they had suffered."

Many of these were so overwhelmed with gratitude they could have fallen to the ground, doing reverence to their rescuer. One of his officers said to him— "Col. Sibley, *I would sooner have the glory of your achievement to-day, than the proudest victory ever won in battle.*" There was no audible reply, but his manhood was stirred within him, and his soul-full eye was far more emphatic than words could have been. He had accomplished the sublime purpose of his heart, this great good to more than two hundred helpless beings. What mattered to him the vile reproach of envy, or the clamorous tongue bidding him rush on to mad extermination, which would have brought inevitable death to every captive. He had the proud triumph resulting from a fearless discharge of duty, and to his own quarters he took the only adult male captive, caring for him as a "father careth for a son whom he loveth."

CHAPTER XLIII.

INDIAN PRISONERS.

After proper attention to the rescued, the next "order" in the military programme was the erection of a jail in the centre of Camp Release. Some were detailed to cut the logs, others to haul them in, and others to throw them up and firmly bolt their corners; and before nightfall, the huge pen was completed, ready for occupants. These were brought in by Col. Crooks. with an adequate armed force. Those absolutely free from suspicion were unmolested. The prisoners were put in chains, and a strong guard set around the jail. A military commission, composed of Col. Crooks, Lieut. Col. Marshall, and Capts. Grant, Bailey, and Lieut. Olin, to which two or three others were afterwards added, was convened for the trial of the guilty.

No more formidable Calendar was ever brought before human tribunal. Four hundred and twenty-five men arraigned for criminal trial! Every precaution was taken that no injustice should be shown, and all testimony was required to be written down, that it might be easily recurred to, in case of any after questioning of their innocence. Those who plead "guilty" to charges, had their cases soon disposed of. The equivocation of the guilty parties, who were allowed to testify in their own case, was often, to say the least, very amusing, and their statements devoid of all reason and good sense. Many would admit they fired in battle, but generally insisted it was at random, and nobody was hurt! A plea supposed to be valid by the one who rendered it, was that the horse he stole was a very *little* one, and, of course, his crime not very great, and that the oxen he took were for the gratification of his wife.

A man in the vigor and prime of life declared that his gray hairs should attest *his* innocence, and some young men, that their hearts were too weak to face fire. A strange admission for an Indian. Another batch would insist that when the battle raged, they were lying flat on their faces, writhing in physical tortures, such as in babyhood would have been relieved by a dose of catnip tea.

A small army of culprits vowed they had crept under a wonderfully capacious stone (which nobody ever saw there,) during the battle at Fort Ridgley, and did not emerge therefrom till all was quiet. A still larger number averred that an unsocial spirit kept them from fighting, and then again that they were in the rear of the several battles feasting on roast beef and green corn, and for the truth of the last assertion they called on the Great Spirit, Heaven and Earth to witness. One had his tender sympathies so wrought upon to see his kin killing the whites, that he lay down to sleep and did not wake till the battle was over.

Cut-Nose, whose bloody deeds are before recorded, was condemned for the same, and a companion in crime

CUT NOSE.
(The Wholesale Butcherer.)

for having butchered nineteen persons, both made most solemn protestations of "me good Indian," with strongest avowals of friendship for their accusers, proving, very conclusively, that many, in the friendly camp, were as black in crime, as any who went at large, unwhipt of justice.

All ages, from boys of fifteen to infirm old men, were represented by these criminals. One said, he "was fifty a great many years ago, when he quit counting." The characters were as diverse, if the physiognomy was a criterion, as the persons represented by them.

The party engaged in the captivity of Mattie Williams and the murder of Mr. Patwell, were doomed to the punishment their deeds merited. A very old man was identified by two boys, one of more than usual intelligence. Their families had escaped from the vicinity of Beaver Creek, and arrived almost within hailing distance of the fort, when met by the Indians, who told them, if they would return to their homes, and give them their teams, they should not be injured. They accepted the alternative, but when nearly home, the Indians suddenly fired into the party, killing several, and then took the uninjured women and children prisoners. The stolid old wretch was made to confront the witnesses, who identified him as having taken unerring aim at more than one of the party. It was a thrilling scene, the boy hearts swelling with emotions unutterable. "I saw that man shoot my mother," burst forth from one of the boys; and "I saw him," said the other, "shoot a man who had kneeled down to pray." Another was recognized by Mrs. Hunter, as having shot her husband, and taken her into captivity.

Several of the Renville Rangers, who, it will be remembered, had deserted, were brought before this tribunal. They had been in all the battles, and fought with a determined daring, equal to the fiercest of the full bloods. Of these, particular attention was drawn to a young Hercules, about eighteen, bright, intelligent; and competent for a vast amount of evil. He declared he was outside the fort, when the Indians surrounded it, and was thus unintentionally thrown into their ranks, and that his hands were as free from blood as his heart from guile. The evidence, however, proved him to have taken the first scalp at Wood Lake, from an old grey-headed man and former comrade, and received therefor one of the two belts of wampum, which had been promised by Little Crow, as a reward for killing the first white man. One greatly amused the Court by asserting that he was the sole cause of the war. He was an old sore-eyed man, of lymphatic temperament, and had been living, he said, near New Ulm. The benevolent whites had supported him, and their lavished kindness incited the jealousy of the other Indians, — hence the war.

Thus might we multiply instances of strange fabrications and flimsy subterfuge of falsehoods, which, in detail, would crowd a larger volume than this. But enough has been given to show their duplicity and their guilt. Three weeks of patient, unremitting labor, was given to this business, ere Camp Release was broken up, and still it remained unfinished. The troops were ordered "below," and the Court adjourned to the Lower Agency, where the work of death had first commenced. Surely, no more appropriate place could have been found.

While at Camp Release, Col. Sibley was very justly promoted to "BRIGADIER GENERAL OF VOLUNTEERS," and the same was confirmed by the U. S. Senate, one year after.

CHAPTER XLIV.

CAPTIVITY OF MRS. SOPHIA JOSEPHINE HUGGINS.

Driven away from her husband, as the reader has seen in a former chapter, it was very natural that Mrs. Huggins should look to the one for protection who had evinced a kindly spirit toward her, and believing they would be more safe with the Chief than elsewhere, she, with Julia and her children, went to his house the same evening.

As they passed through the village, many squaws came out, with a show of grief, in the usual way of laying the hand over the mouth, groaning, &c. The men loafed at their tent doors, smoked their pipes and said nothing, pretending not to see them. They were kindly received by the Chief's wife and other members of the lodge, her mother, and their son, Na-ho-ton-mana, a lad of fifteen years. A buffalo robe was spread for them at the further end of the lodge, and this "seat of honor" was always reserved for her, so long as she remained a member of the family. On one of her own pillows, at night she rested her throbbing head, and many other articles from her own house were around her, reminders of the day's experience.

That was a dreadful night. Men went and came to consult their Chief, and loud talking was heard all over the village. Only the children slept sweetly and soundly, as if in their own little crib at home, with a loving father near. So hurried and stunning had been the events of the previous evening, that all seemed more the result of some mental hallucination than actual reality.

The choicest cut from her husband's oxen was set before them for breakfast, but when she thought that he slept his last sleep, she wept but could not eat. The pent up waters of the heart had happily found vent. Thank God for tears! without them, grief's consuming fires would soon destroy the powers for intelligent action.

News of their captivity having reached the ears of Mr. John Lagree, on the opposite side of the river, some distance away, he came with kindly proffers of a home to these women, promising, as he thought, greater security. Walking Spirit left them to their own choice. Their route lay through Lame Bear's village, where they saw many reminders of the past — Indian children dressed in their own children's clothes — her husband's writing desk and their own chairs, besides evidences that they were not the only sufferers. This was on Wednesday, the 20th August, the day of first attack on Fort Ridgley, about eighty miles away.

The hearts of these women were sad and lonely in the extreme, and their anxiety none the less from an ignorance of the extent of the trouble, and the fact that Lagree and a Frenchman who staid with him, were in turn watching without, or sleeping with a loaded gun at their side. On Thursday, dreadful tidings came from the seat of Indian war. All the Missionaries and Government officials, it was said, were killed, and so for more than one long anxious week had *everybody* believed. How precious the promises of holy writ, when grief was so poignant and anxiety so distressing. And now, Mrs. Huggins must be robbed of her only earthly comforter and counsellor. Julia's brother, hearing of her fate, had come disguised as an Indian, to take her to his home at Yellow Medicine. It would not be safe for the mother and children to go with them, and therefore she must abide her time of release, and suffer all her FATHER's will. That night Mr. Manderfield, who had escaped from Big Stone Lake, came in. The women bound up his bleeding feet, and for the time forgot their own sorrows in efforts to relieve his sufferings and preparing him with comforts for the remainder of his way. He bore the first tidings of their fate and whereabouts to white friends below, who from that time were busy with thoughts and devising plans for her release. On Friday morning, Julia bade her companion in captivity adieu, and in Indian costume went forth by the side of her brave brother, on their tedious and perilous journey.

An invitation at this juncture was received from De Cota, to return and make her permanent abode with him at Walking Spirit's village. So after the sad leave-taking of Julia, attended by Lagree, she and her children set out on horseback. As they trotted on through the woods, she imagined every tree hid a lurking foe, ready to spring out and shoot them, for she had now become very nervous from continued excitement and suspense. At Lame Bear's village, Lagree, who was a Chippewa half-breed, seeing many Sioux about, feared to go further, so getting an Indian woman to "pack" Letta, she took little Charlie in her own arms, sick and weak though she was from having eaten nothing that day. Presently an old squaw came running after her, signifying a desire to relieve her of the physical burden. So she put him on her back, pappoose fashion, with which the little fellow seemed quite content.

Her fears were destined to no abatement, for but a little out of the village four hideously painted warriors were lounging by the roadside; but she hid herself behind the women as best she could, and passed unmolested, probably they not detecting her nationality. Again, in passing through a piece of woods, she was desired to go ahead, but trembling with fear, while the women manifested even greater alarm, the cause of which she could not understand.

Now came another sore trial for this "bruised reed." Faint, sick, tired and hungry, she came to the door where she expected a friendly welcome, and in response to their invitation she had made this weary day's journey. Mr. De Cota, her recent neighbor, silently smoked his pipe without the door of his lodge, deigning her never a look, while his squaw wife, coldly, though not unkindly, motioned her on to the chief's house. Her sensitive, sore heart well nigh sank within her. What would be her next step, if thus coldly received at Walking Spirit's? The old chief was away, but his wife, anticipating the wants of the exhausted woman, brought her water and food, and arranged for her to rest, almost tenderly looking after her comfort.

We are glad that we have comparatively small record to make of women being the aiders and abettors of the transactions which brought such dismay to our frontier. As a general thing, they have "fed the hungry and clothed the naked" when in their power to do so. True, they have been subject to their liege lords, and obliged to do their bidding; but whenever left to themselves, we are convinced that the fundamental elements of *true womanhood* live in the hearts which beat beneath their dirty short gowns and rusty old blankets. Remove the shackles which the men inflict upon them, and they would soon arrive to the dignity of white women.

It is but justice to De Cota to say that he was loyal to the whites, and would have received Mrs. Huggins according to his invitation, had his courage been adequate to the occasion. But he knew his own scalp was in danger, and the least provocation would jeopardize his life yet more. Things around him looked stormy enough, and his Sioux wife could not save his scalp to the rightful owner, should any act of his excite their displeasure. Not long after he took his wife and went to his own people, and for several months thereafter was in government employ, carrying the mail through the trackless region from Pembina to Fort Randall.

CHAPTER XLV.

MRS. HUGGINS IN CARE OF WALKING SPIRIT.

The old chief was from home, trying to quell the war-spirit of the young braves, and did not return till Mrs. Huggins had been several days domiciled in his lodge. The usual gutteral salute — "ho-ho-ho-," sounded very cheerily and pleasant, as he extended his hard brawney hand, by which she understood she was very welcome. This increased her confidence, which he seeing, made still greater efforts that she should not feel it misplaced. The language of his actions she knew was very kind, though she understood little of his spoken vernacular. In this assurance, she says her "poor, weary, anxious heart felt comforted. This old man was my friend and protector, I could here find something like rest, quiet and security."

For the six successive weeks she remained a member of the chief's family, regarded more as a distinguished guest than a powerless captive. We rejoice that there are some alleviating features in the wretched Dakota character — something to evince them not hopelessly "the children of· wrath." We believe them, bad as they are, the creatures of God, objects of his care and government, but O how fallen, how totally depraved. Under like influence, with the same Heaven-born privileges as the white race through generations past, the results would be equal. Even worse savages than the North American Indians — those whose richest feasts were upon the putrid bodies of their slain enemies, have been brought under the teachings of the holy influences of christianity. "Christ has been formed" in their hearts the hope of glory, and "the wrath of man has been made to praise him." So it may be, so it will be with these. All nations "shall call Him blessed," for the mouth of the Lord hath spoken it, and we are no ways sure but the Lord will overrule this initiatory step for their elevation to the great platform of religious, christian nations.

For ages, the Indian has known naught but his present life, and from infancy, has been taught that his highest achievement was to take the scalp of an enemy. Hence their glory in the number of scalp-feathers they are entitled to wear.

Not from Walking Spirit and his family alone, was this lone captive the recipient of favors. All the women of the village seemed desirous to outvie each other in this regard, and invariably addressed her in the language of kindness and respect. They would often say, "white woman feel sad; I want to shake hands with her." But their style of living soon began to tell seriously on little Charlie's health, then the women sent milk for him, and would come and take him out for the air. For days they lived only on potatoes and corn, and then occasionally beef or dog meat, and once in a while they had coffee and sugar. Those who were well provided with food for the day, often sent for her "to come and eat" with them. She had learned to make a virtue of necessity, and the practical illustration of the adage, "when in Rome do as Romans do," and a cheerful, pleasant conformity to the society in which she lived, conciliated her into favor. Once she was sent for at bed time, to "come and eat." Though not hungry, she went, as it was not policy to refuse. A piece of nice carpet was spread for her to sit on, and a white towel for her plate, which was one of her own, and one of her own dishes to drink from; the bill of fare, consisting of potatoes, rice, dried apples and cold water. She says of the culinary department, sometimes, when she thought of the dirty dishes her food was on, the dirty kettles it was cooked in, and the dirty hands which prepared it, her stomach rebelled. But she tried to keep away such troublesome thoughts, and make the best of what she had. She well appreciated the kindness which sent one of the women to Yellow Medicine to bring up flour and other articles for her use, and one cold frosty morning, another came cautiously behind her and threw a warm shawl over her shoulders; though part of the stolen booty, we credit the kindly spirit which evoked the act.

One of her great perplexities was the means of ablution, which Mrs. Walking Spirit remedied by obtaining from a neighbor a half powder keg. She had no other convenience for washing clothes than an old iron heater, which had been used for a dog dish. This she cleaned, and made subserve her purpose.

Once or twice she was privileged with a tub and washboard, which had been her own property. She was thankful to get clean clothes, though they went unironed.

All this time, not one of the young men of the village was allowed to speak to her, and there was a commendable pride, as they expressed it, "in keeping her very carfully." No work was ever demanded, or even expected of her; yet occupation lightened the burden of grief, and so she would assist her hostess in sewing, cooking, and even at times brought water from the brook. Many of her own articles of dress were returned to her, and she was permitted to wear her own costume; but it was hard to see her children's clothes, of which they were in real need, worn by Indian children, and very painful to see the clothes of her murdered husband on the persons of those, if not his actual murderers, who had "consented unto his death."

The children became great favorites, were petted and caressed, and afraid of no one, and this partiality came near causing her the severest heart-pang she had known. The chief's wife had a brother who lived far to the north, and had no children, and whom she had induced to think could get Mrs. Huggins to give to him her little girl. The proposition was made through a French interpreter, but her decided "no" gave no little offense, especially to the old woman, the man's mother. He was very angry, but the presence of the chief awed him, for he would not suffer the child to be taken without her consent; but the offense was never forgiven, nor could she feel the same measure of confidence in the offended party as before. The former fondness of the old woman for the children was changed to indifference or hate, and she was ever afterward very cross to them. This, however, Mrs. H. allowed to pass unnoticed, and thereby prevented any serious quarrels; yet she lived in constant fear of their being taken by stealth, and would never again trust them alone in her care. She now watched them closely when they were packed around the village by the squaws, who had before done it, eliciting no special anxiety from the mother, and at night folded them in her arms, while she dreamed of a horrid waking to find them gone.

With nothing to distinguish one day from another, Mrs. H. soon lost the days of the week, and afterward learned that several Mondays had been kept by her as the holy Sabbath day. O, how the Christian woman longed for the privileges of the sanctuary, or even the quiet of home retirement, where she could worship God, with "none to molest or make afraid." But the time for her removal from the red-heated furnace had not yet come, but the "form of the FOURTH" was with her. The refining, purifying process was not yet complete, and she girded her soul with patience to endure all her Father's will.

CHAPTER XLVI.

THE ALARMS.

There was a mighty host of "Northerners" coming directly through the village. They had many carts, and some of the warriors were on foot and some on horse. The village was in great alarm.

Mrs. Huggins was hurried out to look at them, in the distance, and then to a tent, with orders to suffer no noise from the children, until these were entirely passed. The caravan halted just past her tent, and their tumult so excited the children, that they cried to go out, and it was some time before they were frightened into silence. There were, at least, six men to a woman, in the crowd. The excitement was intense. Men, women and children were running about, as if frightened out of their wits, all of which the hidden woman could see through a hole in the tent. But formidable and unwelcome as were these visitors, they must be fed. This was the only hope of a pacific turn in affairs, had they come for evil. The young warriors, eager for display, galloped around, firing off guns, and making other demonstrations of their prowess. Then rang forth on the serene air, the stentorian voice of a would-be mighty chief. With a high head, proud look and stately tread, he stalked back and forth, as he delivered himself of the eloquent speech which was burning in his soul, threatening to consume him. For several hours, our heroine lay in her concealment, when all was again quiet.

Now came a time when the village was deserted, and Mrs. Huggins was alone, with the nameless old woman, for many days. From night till morning, and from morning till night, she trembled with fear, and closely hugged her children to her heart, lest, in an unexpected moment, they should be torn from her, but, guarded by the divine hand, she was safe.

A week or two after the advent of the "Northerners," a detachment of the band returned. Walking Spirit invited them to his lodge for a feast, more to concilitate peace than from any real friendship. He guaranteed protection to his captive, and directed her to sit behind him at the door, doubtless for quick egress, in case of trouble, while his guests would fill the lodge. With two loaded guns beside him, they sat down to the feast, no other woman being allowed inside, only to bring the food, which was fried bread and coffee, to the door. Several of the guests were attentive to the children, feeding and allowing them to drink from their own cups. After considerable speechifying and meaningless parade, the crowd dispersed, much to her relief.

One day, the chief handed her a nice looking letter, written in Dakota language. She was unable to read it for him, but waited, with anxious forebodings, the imparting of its contents, and yet with faint hopes of some feeble glimmer of light for herself and children. But instead, the contents were such as to make the friendly chief declare himself "very angry," so angry that he threw the letter into the fire, in retaliation of the base insult. Good Day, its author, had proposed to buy the captive for a wife, and hence her protector's rage.

On another day, she was told to stay very closely in doors, that a "bad man was in the village, and would kill her." She was alone with the children, and wholly engrossed with her sewing, when, of a sudden, the blanket door was thrown up, and a fierce looking, hideously painted young man, with an elevated drawn sword, stood before her. A child from a neighboring lodge, followed him in, eyeing first one and then the other, with a look of terror. With great self-command, after the first moment of surprise was over, she bent her face to her sewing, yet trembling so violently, she could scarcely hold her needle. But his scrutinizing gaze over, he went away, without speaking. Then she drew a long breath, and thanked God, that she and her children were alive. A moment after his leave-taking, the chief, panting and blowing, sprang through the opening. Her's was no feigned joy at seeing him, as she smilingly said, "You frighten me, coming in such haste."

"You frighten *me*," he replied, as he sat down to rest. "I was afraid you would be killed before I got here."

Some women then came in, and told her about the angry man. His wife, for whom he was in search, had run away from him, and therefore had he come to the chief's house. Thus was she in constant alarm — her nervous system agitated with the most harrowing fear, and was often hid, by her protector, from threatening dangers.

News from below became more and more exciting, and, finally, the battle of Wood Lake determined the terror-stricken Indians on flight. "To go or not to go," was left optional with the captive. She could not go alone to her friends below, nor could Walking Spirit now go with her, as he had hoped to do, as all the region was filled with the hostile, fleeing foe. So she committed herself to the guidance of Providence, knowing thereby she should not be led wrong.

All was now the bustle of preparation. Corn and potatoes were to be gathered and prepared for the journey, or buried. One, acquainted with their life habits, and unacquainted with present incentives, would have thought them suddenly metamorphosed into a provident, working people. Some pounded corn from the cob, others parched it or bagged it up for the journey, and others were packing the household goods. Our heroine was no idler, and, therefore, made herself as useful as she could. She assisted to put up five sacks of corn and potatoes, for family provisions by the way.

All being in readiness to depart, the story was circulated, that all the white prisoners were killed, and that retributive justice would soon fall upon the Indians. Walking Spirit would have remained, had he dared, but discrimination between the friendly and unfriendly Indians, he thought, would not be made in the swift winged justice upon their track. The innocent was liable to suffer with the guilty.

Hosts of Sioux were daily arriving from below, with whom many of the villagers "fell in," swelling each arrival to quite a caravan.

CHAPTER XLVII.

LEAVING FOR THE PLAINS.

The chief's family, still reluctant, were the last to go. Mrs. Huggins had not yet made her decision known. She was perplexed, if not in despair, but she still trusted Him who said, "call upon me in the day of trouble and I will deliver thee." When all was ready, the question to *go* or *stay* was again submitted, and her answer "I will go," pleased her protector, and prompted a renewal of "faithful care." To her and her children was accorded the privilege of riding on the rear top of the load, while Mrs. Walking Spirit, on foot, led the old horse which dragged the load on poles — her mother carried a large pack, and his son led the colt, while he himself drove the oxen. The cow, by especial request of her hostess, was led by Mrs. Huggins.

Methinks I see them now filing across prairies; through dark ravines; up beetling bluffs and in the forest shade; while, with mighty force of will, her severe heart-struggles are forbidden vent. To lighten the load, in the ascent of hills and through mud-holes, our heroine, often, with a child on her hip, and fast hold of the rope which was attached to the cow's horns, performed the unromantic trip of wading ankle deep in mud, and then sat down in the grateful shade of some ancient tree, panting for breath.

The first day of the journey, these were exclusives,

though in sight of the main caravan. At night their tent was pitched in a beautiful valley, and when the horses were "staked" and all other matters properly attended to, as in well regulated families, they drew around a sumptuous board "groaning" with skunk meat and potatoes.

The calm quiet, the sublime silence of the night was a real luxury to the ardent soul of Mrs. Huggins. It was sweet to reflect on the constant care of Him whose presence fills the universe. Nature had spread around, her sweetest charms, in which a heart like hers might revel both day and night. Early next morning, before the family had breakfasted, an excited horseman rode up with tidings which brought all who understood it to their feet, followed by hasty arrangements to go. Falling in with another company, the greatest haste continued till the middle of the afternoon, they, meanwhile, eating nothing, and with only a little parched corn for the children, who became tired, sick and fretful. For four successive days they continued the same haste, the little boy daily growing weaker and weaker, and it was so hard to see him droop thus, with no means to relieve him, and to feel that very soon this precious comfort might be taken from her. Then there was the fear of starvation haunting her, or that Walking Spirit might be overpowered by Little Crow or some of the Northerners, and she be taken away from him. While her only employment was *to think*, it is not strange, that, with all her firm and steadfast faith, she was thus in soul perplexed. Then again, buoyant hope would cheer her heart, for she knew that friends were earnestly praying for her safety and release, and she believed that when the divine end was accomplished, the severe discipline would cease. In the presence of danger she ever relied on the judgment of others, to "lie down and cover up," without inquiring as to the why or wherefore — trusting the promise "He shall cover thee with his feathers, and under his wing shalt thou trust," and so was she "not afraid of the terror by night nor the arrow that flieth by noon-day."

CHAPTER XLVIII.

RELEASE AND RETURN.

The reader has seen the main body of troops at Camp Release, from whence, on the day following their arrival, General Sibley dispatched four of the most trustworthy half-breeds and Indians, with instructions to follow up the fleeing Indians, and bring back Mrs. Huggins and children, with as much expedition as possible.

The fourth and last outward bound night, Mrs. Huggins was made to understand that many bad Indians were in the very large encampment. They had many cattle, horses and wagons, and she counted eighty yoke of oxen, and knew that all were the trophies of their raid upon the whites. Hope now well nigh died from her heart, for in the midst of the great darkness, how could she think of deliverance as near? So in the physical as moral world, often when least expected, the greatest blessings come. The following morning, a message was brought to the chief, which produced a counter movement on the part of his family. The white lady was not made to understand the reason; perhaps they designed a joyful surprise, but she dare not hope it augured any good to her, and the suspense threw her into a feverish anxiety, from which she did not recover till it was practically demonstrated. When at noon they camped, the family bustled about in preparation for visitors, — thus much she knew.

While wondering and waiting for the strange arrival, her heart gave a sudden bound of joy, for the familiar faces of her rescuers were before her. Intuitively she understood their mission. Two letters from General Sibley to Walking Spirit and herself were read, and he declared at once his intention of strengthening the escort by returning with her to Camp Release. Such was the joy of her heart that sleep came not that night to her eyes. The mind was active in the past, present and future.

While Mrs. Walking Spirit got the breakfast, Mrs. Huggins repaired the wardrobe of her husband, that he might appear as respectable as possible in the presence of superiors. When she finished, she returned the thread and scissors to his wife, who pressed her to retain the latter, as a parting gift and a memento of her love.

We will note at this point the release of two little German girls and a half-breed boy, who were in the main encampment. This, to their honor be it said, was more than the duty assigned their rescuers. One of the girls was very beautiful, whose mother was at Camp Release when she arrived there, and after clasping her to her heart in wild joy, she looked to Mr. Riggs, and emphatically asked, "Where is the other?" He *could not tell her*.

The first night they camped at Big Stone Lake. Lame Bear and some of his people were there, who extended to them the hospitalities of their camp. The excitement of joy and its reaction, after all she had passed through, had nearly prostrated Mrs. Huggins' nervous energies, and with a thankful heart she that night sank upon the comfortable bed which was made for her, and awoke refreshed, ready to go on her way rejoicing.

Passing over the same ground she had in going out, with no incidents worthy of note but a satisfaction of daily drawing nearer home, we find them, in less time than when outward bound, approaching Camp Release. When but a few miles out, they passed twelve warriors, savagely painted, smoking on the grass. Murder flashed from their eyes, and there was evident cause for alarm, though some of the men halted to shake hands and smoke with them. But as they drove rapidly away, a close watch was kept over the shoulder, till fairly away from any danger of their following. That night the camp was in sight of Lac-qui-parle. They resorted to Sioux stratagem as a precaution against enemies, by leaving their wagons and camping some distance from the road. There was little sleep; every ear was alert for sounds of a wily foe, and they suffered much from cold, as autumn frosts had come, and the night winds were very chill.

With kind consideration, they halted on the following morning for Mrs. Huggins to visit the grave of her husband, around which they drove stakes by her request, to protect it from careless intruders. They allowed her time to linger over every familiar spot associated so closely with him who slept near. How desolate all appeared,—and with heart even more des olate than all, she turned away, and for her children's sake, nerving her soul with energy to battle a little longer with life.

Eight miles further, and they entered Camp Release, which is to be memorable for all time in the history of Minnesota. The reaction, of a system wrought up so long to the highest tension, had come; but with the kind care and sympathy there bestowed, she and pining little Charlie rallied wonderfully during the two weeks in which the trials of guilty Indians still progressed, before being sent down to the anxious hearts awaiting her. To one who has thus suffered, — to one who has thus been released, nought but gratitude the most profound could ever arise toward her temporal deliverer, and to Him who disposes the hearts of men to do His will, and brings out all things according to His own hidden plans.

CHAPTER XLIX.

REMOVAL TO CAMP SIBLEY.

On the 23d of October, the condemned and uncondemned prisoners, chained two and two, were loaded into wagons, twelve or fifteen in each, and under a military escort started for Camp Sibley. Here the trial was resumed in a log house, formerly owned and occupied by a half-breed named LaBatte, "for unromantic kitchen purposes, but from hence to pass into history and be immortalized." The main building separate from this, had been deeply stained with the blood of the owner, whose native affinity did not save him from the murderous scalping knife. From the ashes of his dwelling in which he was burned, after having been shot, the soldiers drew forth his charred remains. But a few steps away was the store of Nathan Myrick, where Lynde, the first victim, DeVill and Andrew Myrick were killed. With such reminders of their guilt before them, how could they hope for pardon? We wonder that fair and impartial trials were given — we wonder at the staying hand which prevented their execution *en masse* — and we wonder at the patience of the commission in the long, tedious trial!

But this heavy criminal calendar was at last cleared, and of the men arraigned for trial, three hundred and three were sentenced to be hung, and twenty to imprisonment. They were removed to Mankato, where an immense jail had been prepared, there to await the execution of their sentence.

As the train of guarded prisoners neared New Ulm, the citizens who had returned to their homes came out pell mell — the women leading the van, assailing them with axes, stones and clubs, in retaliation for murdered husbands and children. Even at the point of the bayonet the infuriated mass rushed into the midst of the soldiers, determined to return an equivalent for the past. In several instances the guns were turned aside, or the axe warded off as the fatal blow was about to descend. One woman actually cleft the jaw of an Indian with a hatchet, and another fractured a skull, so that the victim died in a few days. Some eight or ten were badly wounded before the assailants could be driven off. We regret to have this retaliatory act to record, but we aim to give a true and impartial history of the main events. Still we will not too harshly condemn. They had suffered much, and were still smarting under the terrible blow, and a half frenzy seized them when they saw the authors of their misery. Doubtless, more serious would have been the results, had they foreseen that in fixing the day for their execution, the Chief Executive would have been moved with pity for the guilty wretches, and ordered the punishment of all but thirty-nine suspended.

This fact becoming known, some two hundred men, whom suffering and bereavement by savage hands had made desperate, armed with hatchets, knives, and other death-dealing implements, on the 8th of December, forced their way through the guard at Camp Lincoln, near Mankato, with the avowed intention of dealing to the murderers the merit of their crimes. Col. Miller, prompt and resolute in the discharge of duty, had them surrounded and prisoners, before they could effect anything, but released them on a pledge to abstain from further attempt at violence. Gov. Ramsey issued a proclamation, urging upon the citizens not to throw away the good name Minnesota had hitherto sustained, by any rash acts of lawlessness which were not necessary to the ends of justice, of personal security, or even private vengeance. "Our people," he says, "have had just cause to complain of the tardiness of executive action in the premises, but they ought to find some reason for forbearance in the absorbing cares which weigh upon the President. If he should decline to punish them, the case will then come clearly within the jurisdiction of the civil authorities."

CHAPTER L.

REMOVAL OF THE GOOD INDIANS TO FORT SNELLING.

The army of "good Indians," men, women, children and half-breeds numbered some eighteen hundred. On the 7th of November these took up their line of march for Fort Snelling, under escort of Lieut. Col. Marshall's command, all of which made a train of four miles in length.

The "winter quarters," previously prepared, was an immense pen in which their teepees were set according to latest approved city surveys — with streets, alleys and public square. Around and without, armed soldiers paraded day and night for six successive months, and the Government outlay for their support was little less than $2,000 per month; while the hundreds of worthy women and children whom their own tribe had made widows and orphans, were mainly dependent on their own exertions, or the benevolence of a sympathizing public. Visitors daily thronged the enclosure with "passes" from the post commander, and when admitted, a disgustingly filthy sight met the eye. The streets were the receptacles of all the offal of the lodges, where barefooted women and children splashed around in the filthy snow slush, as much at home as my reader on a velvet carpet with neatly slippered feet.

Here we saw old Betsey, whom we knew before the State was a State, or the Territory had a name, and without whom its history would be incomplete, so identified is she with frontier life and pioneer experience. Her ugly old phiz is seen in every Photograph gallery in the land, and readily recognized by every street urchin. Everywhere she has warm personal friends, and it is her proud boast that none of her family have taken part in the raid against the whites. Even she, old as she is, was pattering around barefooted, as lithe as a girl of sixteen. Then we bade her good-bye, supposing it the last time, and she actually kissed our hand at parting. But when the encampment was broken up to go to the new "hunting grounds," by the earnest desire of her farmer son, Ta-o-pee, old Betsey was permitted to remain with him, so we may have a chance for another parting kiss.

It will be recollected that Ta-o-pee was very active in the formation of the friendly camp, and for the release of the prisoners, and made the first move in that direction. Wabashaw, too, was there. These had kept aloof from crime, using every means to subdue the rage of their red brothers. When an answer came from their letter to Col. Sibley, the utmost caution was requisite to conceal the fact from others. Great excitement that night prevailed, in their camp, on account of the letter Little Crow had received, the contents of which, when interpreted by Spencer, was proclaimed by Little Crow, in thunder tones, to the clamorous throng, which crowded around his tent. Ta-o-pee had a secret for the white man's ear, which he managed to communicate. There was an assenting nod to the request that he be in readiness to read the letter, the first favorable moment. Excitement run high, and the tent was full, till far into the small hours of morning — Ta-o-pee, with nervous anxiety, hidden beneath a calm exterior, frequently coming in and going out again. At three o'clock, all was quiet; now was the time; the moment was an important one. They knew that evil, designing ones were prowling around, suspicious of everything; so, throwing a blanket over their heads, that the light might not be seen from without, they, underneath it, struck a match, lighted a candle, and in a soft whisper, read the important missive, which the reader has before read, and which was the first hope-inspiring note of a temporal salvation.

Chaska, too, with whom the reader is so well acquainted, came also with the train. While, in various ways, making himself useful to our people, he was charged, by envious ones, as having taken life before he rescued his friend, for which charge, he was a long time under guard, awaiting trial. He was honorably acquitted, and engaged as scout to the expedition, the following spring. Having renounced his tribal birthright, he was, to all intents and purposes, a *white man*, faithfully doing his duty, whatever and wherever it might be.

CHAPTER LI.

PROTEST OF SENATOR WILKINSON AND OTHERS.

With the groans of the wounded still deadening our ears, and while the echoed shrieks of the already dead, still reverberate from bluff to bluff, and while he still lies in wait for our heart's blood, sympathy for the "poor, wronged red man," is being roused, in some parts of our nation. We love the EAST — the soil which our infant feet trod — we love its people and its lofty principles of right, but we ignore their argument of the Indians' wrongs. *Our nation's pampered proteges instead.*

In discussing the removal of the *"good Indians,"* we confess to a desire to see them turned loose on Boston common, as Congress was memorialized to do by several thousand citizens of Minnesota. Had the tragic scenes, of which we have given but a faint outline, been concentrated for one stereoscopic view, in any Eastern city, had their streets been drenched with blood, as were our prairies, had fire and ravishment come to *their* homes, as to ours, we think we know the New England heart well enough to say, that quite as little leniency would have been desired for the perpetrators, as by us.

We think the protest against Presidential clemency, from Senator Wilkinson and Representatives Aldrich and Windham, worthy of immortal record, and here re-produce it for the benefit of our readers, yet to be.

"*To the President of the United States:*

"SIR: — We have learned, indirectly, that you intend to pardon or reprieve a large majority of the Indians in Minnesota, who have been formally condemned for their participation in the brutal massacre of our people, in the months of August and September last. If this be your purpose, as representatives from that State, we beg leave, most respectfully, to protest against it, and we do so, for the following reasons:

"These Indians were condemned, most of them, upon the testimony of women, whom they had carried into captivity, after having murdered their fathers, husbands and brothers, and who were treated, by these Indians, with a brutality never known before, in this country, nor equaled in the practice of the most barbarous nations. There were nearly ninety captives, who were wives and daughters of our neighbors and friends. [This does not include the children.] They were intelligent and virtuous women — some of them were wives and mothers — others were young and interesting girls.

"These savages, to whom you propose to extend your Executive clemency, when the whole country was quiet, and the farmers were busily engaged in gathering their crops, arose with fearful violence, and travelling from one farm to another, indiscriminately murdered all the men, boys and little children they came to, and although they sometimes spared the lives of the mothers and daughters, they did so only to take them into captivity, which was infinitely worse than death.

"Mr. President, let us relate to you some facts with which we fear you have not heretofore been made acquainted.

"These Indians, whom (as we understand,) you propose to pardon and set free, have murdered, in cold blood, nearly or quite one thousand of our people, ravaged our frontier for more than one hundred and fifty miles north and south, burned the houses of the settlers, and driven from their homes more than ten thousand of our people. They seized and carried into captivity more than one hundred women and girls, and in nearly every instance treated them with the most fiendish brutality.

"To show you, sir, the enormity of these outrages, we beg leave to state a few facts, which are well known to our people, but delicacy forbids that we should mention the names of the parties to whom we refer.

"In one instance, some ten or twelve of these Indians visited the house of a worthy farmer, who at the time was engaged with his sons stacking wheat. They stealthily approached the place where the honest farmer was at work, and seizing the opportunity, shot the father and two sons at the stack. They then went to the house, killed two little children in the presence of their mother, who was quite ill of consumption, and then took the sick mother and a beautiful little daughter, thirteen years of age, into captivity. But this is not all, nor is it the most appalling feature of this awful tragedy. Its horror is yet to be revealed. After removing these unhappy prisoners to a lodge some two miles away, these fiends incarnate, after placing a guard over the weary and exhausted mother, took her little one outside the lodge, removed all her clothes, and fastened her back on the ground. Then they commenced their work of brutality on this young girl. One by one they violated her person, unmoved by her cries, and unchecked by the evident signs of approaching dissolution. This work was continued until the Heavenly Father relieved her from suffering. They left her dead upon the ground. This outrage was committed within a few feet of the sick and dying mother.

"There is another instance of a girl eighteen years of age. We knew her well before and at the time of her capture. She was as refined and beautiful a girl as we had in the State. None had more or better friends; no one was more worthy of them than she. She was taken captive by these Indians, her arms were tied behind her and she was tied fast to the ground and ravished by some eight or ten of these convicts before the cords were unloosed from her limbs. The girl, fortunately, lived to testify against the wretches who had thus violated her. Without being more specific, we will state that nearly all the women who were captured were violated in this way.

"Again there was a little boy brought to St. Paul (whose father and mother had been murdered,) whose life was spared as a witness of the horrid nature of this massacre. His right eye was cut completely out, it had fallen from its socket and perished on his cheek. His two little sisters, aged respectively six and four years, were also saved, but in an awfully mutilated condition. Their tender arms had been mangled with the savages' knives, and otherwise fearfully wounded and left on the ground for dead.

"Mr. President, there was no justification or pretext even for these brutalities. We state what we know, when we say that the Sioux Agent, Mr. Galbraith, has labored faithfully and efficiently for the welfare of these Indians. The Government, as you know, has built a house and opened a farm for every one of these Indians who would reside upon and cultivate it. Missionaries have labored zealously among them for their spiritual welfare. There has been paid to them yearly the interest upon $2,000,000. Farming implements have been purchased, and farmers have been employed by the Government to improve and cultivate their lands.

"These Indians have been called by some, prisoners of war. There was no war about it. It was a wholesale *robbery, rape and murder*. These Indians were not at war with their murdered victims.

"The people of Minnesota, Mr. President, have stood firm by you and your administration. They have given both it and you their cordial support. They have not violated *law*. They have borne these sufferings with a patience such as but few people ever exhibited under such extreme trial. These Indians are now at their mercy; but our people have not risen up to slaughter them, because they believed that their President would deal with them justly.

"We are told, Mr. President, that a committee from Pennsylvania, whose families are living happily in their pleasant homes in that State, have called upon you and petitioned you to pardon the Indians. We have a high respect for the religious sentiment of your petitioners; but we submit that is a bad taste, indeed, that it is entirely unbecoming them to interfere in matters with which they are so little acquainted, and which relate entirely to the security of our own people.

"We *protest against the pardon* of these Indians, because, if it is done, the Indians will become more insolent and cruel than they ever were before, believing, as they certainly will believe, that their great father at Washington either justifies their acts or is afraid to punish them for their crimes.

"*We protest against it*, because if the President does not permit these executions to take place under the forms of law, the outraged people of Minnesota will dispose of these wretches without law. These two people cannot live together.

"We do not wish to see mob law inaugurated in Minnesota, as it certainly will be, if you force the people to it. We tremble at the approach of such a condition of things in our STATE.

"You can give us peace, or you can give us lawless violence. We pray you, sir, in view of all that we have suffered, and of the danger that still awaits us, *let the law be excuted — let justice be done our people.*"

CHAPTER LII.

CAUSE OF THE DAKOTA UPRISING.

Hitherto we have scarcely hinted at the *cause* of the strange and sudden uprising of this powerful tribe; but such effects have had their birth in design. Mr. Spencer said to the writer, that had he been less a sufferer while a wounded captive in their hands, had not his life been daily threatened so that he had little hope of living to transmit the truth to the world; in short, had he foreseen what he now sees, he might have probed the whole matter, and the moving impulse would have been made known to him. He heard nothing from them to confirm the view we here present, or by which he would feel justified in declaring it to be an offshoot of the rebellion. This is, however, a synopsis from reliable sources, to which he had no access at the time, and we shall leave the reader to deduce his own conclusions.

However deep and long they slumber beneath the rubbish of sloth or fear, the fires of discontent, of envy and hate, are ever burning in the savage heart. Sooner or later they will burst forth in wild volcanic throes, when peace treaties are forgotten, the buried tomahawk exhumed, and woe to the defenseless victim over whose head the scalping-knife is flourished. In every normal savage heart exists a principle of reckless hate towards the whites, which, stimulated by real or imaginary wrongs, needs no avalanche of argument to start the missiles of death. Like a spark of fire in a magazine of powder, the ignition is as sudden, the results as terrible. That the great Sioux raid of '62 was somewhere premeditated, plans intelligently matured and admirably arranged for secrecy, is beyond a doubt. Strategy is the art of savage warfare, secrecy the guaranty of success.

We have seen squads of daring, determined warriors, all over the counties of the north, west, and south-west, striking a simultaneous blow on the settlements, desolating an area of four hundred miles in extremes, filling the woods and marshes with starved, panic-stricken women and children, bestrewing the fair prairies with corpses of men, and desolating the fields of ripened plenty. No magic pen could portray, no master pencil paint the horrid, sublimely tragical events of the horror-stricken plains. The reaper lying dead in his swath, with his sickle in his hand; cattle roaming at large, and bellowing in inquiry of the midnight that has suddenly fallen upon their noon; while the huge, swollen bodies of others, were mingling their nauseous affluvia with the headless bodies of men; hogs were rooting in the long ringlets, or feeding on the fair cheek of beauty, and dogs going mad from the same, — in short the tide of desolation was sweeping over all.

Some hidden leaven has been at work — from fur-clad Pembina to blood-dyed Secessia had the lump been leavened, till it became a *risen* mass of duplicate rebellion. Investigation shows conclusively that Secessia had sent her emissaries not only to the Dakotas, but all other tribes of the north-west—fostering a spirit of unrest, magnifying mole-hill grievances into mountain realities,—inciting the barbarous war-spirit dormant in their hearts, and infusing a death-dealing fury wherever the war-king should stride. The hope of a savage menace to the frontier, involved the one that the north-western troops, everywhere noted for their valor, would be retained and recalled from the national field to subdue a savage foe. Hence they prated of wrongs, and encouraged a hope of a re-possession of garden Minnesota, glittering in wealth and happy in the quiet of well-earned homes. That the task was no difficult one, the double subtlety of rebellion taught, for it assured them that all the fighting powers were engaged with a southern foe. Thus the whole gear was in complete running order, before the war horse was bid to move.

It has been conclusively proven, that runners, ever after the great rebellion began, were going back and forth among the various tribes, and particularly to effect their object with the Minominees, who utterly refused complicity. God was on the throne of heaven, and thwarted much of the base design.

In one of their grand councils, convened in Wisconsin, for the purpose of discussing the war theme, it was emphatically stated, on the authority of a head chief, that all the western tribes were going to join the South, and that there would be a general uprising among the Indians, in the summer, 1862.

There is no doubt but the Chippewas did seriously contemplate an alliance with the Sioux, at one time, but being discountenanced, by the prudent foresight of some of their own number, it was timely nipped in the bud, by the wise policy of Gov. Ramsey.

A Lieut. Colonel, in Ashby's rebel cavalry, wrote from Virginia, under date of Aug. 20, 1862, to his brother-in-law, of Columbus, Wisconsin, advising him, and defining ways and means for so doing, to haste to the Confederate lines for safety. But if he failed in this, to seek an asylum in Illinois, giving, as a reason for the warning, "a general uprising of all the Indian tribes in the north-west, about the first of September." Even then it had commenced, but the Divine hand had held in check all but the wrathful Sioux, and Little Crow had dared to attempt what some of the nations of Europe dare not risk.

What fearful guilt rests upon the murder plotters — the proxy desolaters of the fair land and domestic peace, for that secession is the root and base of the wide-spread ruin, we think the evidence admits scarce a doubt, but so secretly, so adroitly manœuvered, that scarcely can the horns of the beast be seen, pushing this way and that, like the one of which the prophet speaks, and like it, destined to a final overthrow. The enormity and magnitude of the desolation, can be somewhat comprehended, by the figures on which we rely for data.

It will be recollected that 30,000 persons were actual sufferers, in flight, loss of property, and loss of life.

Two thousand, nine hundred and forty persons claimed redress from Government, for the loss of their earthly all. The total amount of claims for losses sustained by the above, is $2,600,000. For the disbursement of these claims, the annuities, which are forever forfeited, are appropriated, an arrangement, than which none could be more just or equitable.

May God yet make the wrath of these Sioux to praise him, and so overrule all these trying events, as to result in both individual and national good, temporally, spiritually and eternally.

CHAPTER LIII.

PREPARATIONS FOR THE EXECUTION OF THE CONDEMNED INDIANS.

As soon as the President's order, postponing the day of execution, from the 19th to the 26th Dec., was received, the military authorities at Mankato commenced preparations for the execution. The gallows, twenty-four feet square, so arranged as to afford room for the hanging of ten, on each side, was erected on the levee, opposite the "winter quarters" of the condemned. The people felt that justice was being defrauded of its dues, and that the gallows might have been of more extended capacity, had the President been less squeamish.

On Monday, the 22d of December, the condemned prisoners were separated from the "suspended" ones, and removed to a strong stone building, where every precaution was taken to secure their safe keeping from the hands of violence, which was feared from excited, misguided, but injured men.

On the afternoon of the same day, Col. Miller, the officer in command, through his interpreter, Rev. Mr. Riggs, announced to the prisoners, the decision of their "Great Father" at Washington, in these words:

"Tell these thirty-nine* condemned men, that the

---

*The death sentence of one of this number was afterward suspended.

Stephen Miller
GOVERNOR OF MINNESOTA

commanding officer of this place has called to speak to them upon a very serious subject, this afternoon.

"Their Great Father at Washington, after carefully reading what the witnesses testified in their several trials, has come to the conclusion, that they have each been guilty of wantonly and wickedly murdering his white children. And for this reason, he has directed that each be hanged by the neck until they are dead, on next Friday. That order will be carried into effect on that day, at ten o'clock in the forenoon.

"That good ministers are here, both Catholic and Protestant, from amongst whom each one can select a spiritual adviser, who will be permitted to commune with them constantly, during the four days that they are to live.

"That I will now cause to be read the letter from their Great Father at Washington, first in English, and then in their own language." (The President's order was now read.)

"Say to them now, that they have so sinned against their fellow men, that there is no hope for clemency, except in the mercy of God, through the merits of the blessed Redeemer; and that I earnestly exhort them to apply to that as their only remaining source of comfort and consolation."

The prisoners received their sentence very coolly, some smoking their pipes, composedly, during the address; and one, apparently more hardened than his fellows, when the time for execution was designated, quietly knocked the ashes from his pipe, and re-filled it while another slowly rubbed a handful of kinnekinnick, preparatory to a good smoke.

The preference of clergymen being signified, the Colonel and spectators withdrew, leaving them in consultation with those selected.

During the four days which intervened, before the sentence was to be executed, nearly all had made confession of their guilt, to their spiritual advisers, but felt it "a shame" for them to suffer the penalty of their crimes, while others, equally as guilty, went unhung. Their confessions, made to and written out by Rev. Mr. Riggs, were generally done in a cool, truthful manner, though with some exceptions, and these were checked by the others, and told that they were all dead men, and that there was no reason why they should depart from the truth. They dictated letters to their families or friends, expressing the hope that they would join them in the world of the Good Spirit.

On Tuesday evening, they extemporized a dance, with a wild Indian song. It was feared this was a prelude to something else which they might attempt, so their chains were thereafter fastened to the floor. Mr. Riggs says it was probably their death song which they sang. Those who had friends in the main prison were allowed to receive a visit from them, and then they parted, to meet no more till in the spirit world. These partings, with the messages conveyed to absent wives and children, were sad and affecting, and many tears were shed. Good counsel was invariably sent to their children, and in many cases they were exhorted to a life of Christianity, and good feeling toward the whites.

Several of the prisoners were completely overcome during this leave-taking, so that they were obliged to suspend conversation. Others laughed and joked, unmoved and unconcerned as if they had been sitting around a camp fire smoking their pipes. One said he was old, and even though uncondemned, he could not have hoped to live long, and that he was dying innocent of white man's blood, and he hoped thereby his chances would be better to be saved — that he had every hope of going "direct to the abode of the Great Spirit, where he would be always happy."

As the last remark reached the ears of another, who was also speaking with his friends, he said, "Yes, tell our friends that we are being removed from this world over the same path they must shortly travel. We go first, but many of our friends will follow us in a very short time. I expect to go direct to the abode of the Great Spirit, and to be happy when I get there; but we are told that the road is long and the distance great, therefore, as I am slow in all my movements, it will probably take me a long time to reach the end of my journey, and I should not be surprised if some of the young active men we will leave behind us, will pass me on the road before I reach my destination."

In shaking hands with Red Iron and another Indian, this same man said, "Friends, last summer you were opposed to us. You were living in continual apprehension of an attack from those who were determined to exterminate the whites. You and your families were subject to many insults, taunts and threats. Still you stood firm in your friendship for the whites, and continually counselled the Indians to abandon their raid against them. Your course was condemned at the time, but now we see your wisdom. You were right when you said the whites could not be exterminated, and the attempt indicated folly. You and your families were prisoners, and the lives of all in danger. To-day you are at liberty, assisting in feeding and guarding us, and we shall die in two days because we did not follow your advice."

The night before the execution, Col. Miller received an order from the President, postponing the execution of Ta-ti-mi-ma, the Sioux name for David Faribault, a half-breed, and a former pupil of the writer. He was convicted for murder, and the capture of women and children; but there were strong doubts among those best acquainted with the subject, of his guilt of murder, and this belief was daily strengthened by new evidence. Hence the respite.*

The last night allotted them on earth, they smoked and chatted, or slept as unconcerned as usual, and seemed scarcely to reflect on the certain doom awaiting them. "As we gazed on them," says one who visited the prison at a late hour that night, "the recollections of how short a time since they had been engaged in the diabolical work of murdering indiscriminately both old and young, sparing neither sex nor condition, sent

---

*He has since been unconditionally pardoned.

a thrill of horror through our veins. Now they are perfectly harmless and look as innocent as children. They smile at your entrance and hold out their hands to be shaken, which appear to be yet gory with the blood of babes. Oh! treachery, thy name is Dakota!" The Catholic priest spent the entire night with them, endeavoring to impress upon them a serious view of their condition, and before morning dawned, his efforts were rewarded by the privilege of baptising several, who also partook of the communion of that church, before leaving the world. They wished their friends to know how cheerfully and happily they met their fate, devoid of all fear or dread.

CHAPTER LIV.

THE EXECUTION.

The spiritual advisers of the condemned Indians were all with them, early on the morning of the 26th December, and were now listened to with marked attention. They had gaily painted their faces, as if for grand display in the begging dance, and, frequently, their small pocket mirror was brought before the face, to see if they still retained the proper modicum of paint. They shook hands with the officers, bidding each a cheerful good bye, as if going on an ordinary journey. Then they chanted their monotonous, but very exciting death song.

The irons being knocked off, one by one, their arms were pinioned with small cords, and the wrists fastened in front, leaving the hands free. Songs and conversation gave a cheerful appearance to the scene, while they moved around, shaking hands with each other, the soldiers and reporters bidding the frequent "good bye." This over, they arranged themselves in a row, and again sang the death song, after which they sat down for a last general smoke.

Father Ravoux, the Catholic priest, now addressed them, and then knelt in prayer, some of them responding, while they were even affected to tears. The long white caps, made from cloth, which had formed part of the spoils taken from murdered traders, were placed upon their heads, leaving their painted faces still visible. Their repugnance to this was very evident. Shame covered their faces, and they were humiliated by it, as chains and cords could not do. The singing ceased, and there was little smoking or talking now. The three half-breeds seemed most affected, and their sad countenances were pitiable to behold.

Crouched on the floor, they all awaited their doom, till precisely ten o'clock, when they were marched in procession, through a file of soldiers to the scaffold, crowding and jostling each other to get ahead, as a lot of hungry boarders rush to the dinner table in a hotel. At the scaffold they were delivered to the officer of the day, Capt. Burt.

As they commenced their ascent to the gallows, the air was made hideous by the repetition of their death song. It was a moment of most intense suspense — every breath in that immense throng seemed suspended, when one of the baser sort improvised an exhibition of his contempt of death, and the lookers on, in the most vile and indecent manner, accompanied by foul impromptu song, insulting to the spectators, and such only as the vilest could conceive or execute — a mockery to the triumph of that justice whose sword was suspended by a hair over his guilty head. One young fellow smoked a cigar after the cap was drawn over his face, he managing to keep his mouth uncovered. Another smoked a pipe till the noose was adjusted over his neck.

The general aspect of the scene was intensely solemn, though there were many little incidents which, under other circumstances, would have been ludicrous in the extreme. Thirty-eight men awaiting the moment when one blow would launch them into eternity! Did civilized world ever look upon the like before? All who looked, approved the sentence, and would, had it been ten times as large.

The silence was awfully intense — then came three, slow, measured and distinct beats on the drum, by the signal officer, Major J. R. Brown, when each of the condemned clasped hands with his next neighbor, which remained in firm grasp till taken down, and then the rope was cut by Mr. Dooley, who, with his family, were among the Lake Shetak sufferers.

One loud and prolonged cheer went up as the platform fell, and then all relapsed into silent gaze at the thirty-seven bodies which hung dangling in the air. One rope had broken, and the body it held was upon the ground. This incident created a nervous horror in the vast assemblage and complete satisfaction to the morbid curiosity which led them to be eye witnesses to such a spectacle. Though there was no sign of life remaining, the body was again suspended. There seemed to be but little suffering — the necks of nearly all were dislocated by the fall, and in just twenty minutes, life was declared extinct.

The bodies were placed in four army wagons, and with Company K, under Lieutenant Colonel Marshall, of the Seventh, for a burial party, were deposited in the one grave, prepared for them, on the sand bar, nearly in front of the town.

The other condemned Indians were chained in their quarters, that they might not witness the execution, and when the death song of their associates in crime fell upon their ears, they crouched themselves down, with their blankets over their heads, and kept perfect silence, seeming to feel all the horrors of their situation, and that a like retribution to them was not long to be delayed. All day they were much dejected.

The disposition of the military force, amounting to 1,419 men, as also the entire arrangements for the execution, were most perfect and complete. Great credit is due Col. Miller for devising and carrying out so successfully his well directed plans, and for preserving the quiet, order and discipline which distinguished the day.

CHAPTER LV.

THE CONDEMNED.

During the winter, those whose death sentence had been postponed, continued to receive spiritual advice, as before the execution.

Those who, from daily intercourse with them, were best prepared to judge, felt that the Spirit of God came into that jail of guilty ones, for whom Christ died, with mighty and convincing power, — that darkened understandings were opened to receive the truth, and hearts, all stained and blackened by crime, were regenerated by His blood. Others hardened themselves against the truth, and would none of "the reproofs of the Spirit."

As a fruit of the change, one hundred and fifty became earnest scholars, and soon learned to read the Bible and Hymn Book, in which they took great delight, and often held religious service among themselves. Whether, indeed, these were true converts to the christian faith, we leave it for a religious world to judge, and the day of final account to decide. But this we do know, that they were never in so favorable circumstances for *thought* and for the mind to receive lasting impressions. Their roving, unsettled life has been the greatest drawback with which the Missionary has to contend. They would not stop to *think*. Now they had no other employ, and the time for instructing them was well improved by those who had long sought their souls' good. If "Christ died for the chief of sinners" surely he died for them, and great sinners, with enlightened consciences, have been pardoned.

During the winter, several deaths occurred in the jail, so that when those whose sentence was suspended, were removed to Davenport, Iowa, they numbered but two hundred and sixty-three men, with whom went sixteen women for cooks and laundresses. The quarters there provided for them was an immense prison pen of boards, inclosing four large shanties clustered in the center.

A decided improvement is noticed by those who visited them there, and before they left the State. Instead of dozing and idling away their time, as was their wont, they were often seen reading, writing or solving the first lessons on the slate. Habits of industry, too, were formed; it may be because compelled to do so, but cheerfully they set about cleaning camp, digging wells, or whatever work assigned them. Thus are we led to conclude that a transforming power has been at work, and though those who, when they visited them, and looked, for the first time, upon an Indian, went away disgusted, it argued not that a decided change for the better had not taken place.

CHAPTER LVI.

THE WINNEBAGOES DECLARE WAR WITH THE SIOUX.

An Indian, a savage, untamed, unchristianized Indian, be he Sioux, Chippewa or Winnebago, *is an Indian*, wherever you find him. They delight in cruel deeds, and are ready to join any tribe with whom they are at peace, in war against a weaker party.

At the commencement of the outbreak, the Winnebagoes, not as a tribe or band, but many individuals distinguished themselves with their allies for bravery and daring, entering as vigorously into the battles as the aggressors themselves. But the tables are turned. The Sioux are driven away, and now war is declared upon them by the Winnebagoes, and more to curry favor with the victorious whites, than for any other cause, probably hoping the removal of their families deferred, while the men take the "war-path" against their enemies. Certain it is, that some other motive than pretense of friendship for the whites, has instigated so small a tribe as the Winnebagoes to take up arms against so powerful a nation as their Sioux neighbors, with whom they have heretofore been on friendly terms.

The scouting Sioux, left behind, are hunted out, and no opportunity for a good shot is allowed to pass unimproved. Instances occurred, where as brutal, barbarous treatment was given the Sioux, by these enemies, as they were ever guilty of towards the whites. The bodies of their victims would be mutilated, hearts would be torn out, large knives run through their centre, and then hung upon poles.

A scalp dance was even improvised in the streets of Mankato, in which all the warriors, squaws and children, joined. One young Winnebago brave paraded the main street, with the tongue of a Sioux warrior, recently murdered, apparently torn from his mouth, and swollen very thick, stopping, as occasion occurred, to gratify the morbid curiosity of passers-by.

The Indian, whose tongue had given such mortal offense, had a wife of their own tribe, with whom he had lived, during the winter, among her own people. Hearing of the murder of two of his own people, by them, his Sioux blood was aroused, and he declared his intention of imparting the information to the tribe; only his wife knew of his design, when he left, but he was overtaken and murdered before he left the reservation, hence the exhibition we have seen.

But not serious or of long continuance were the frontier troubles with these two tribes. One fled beyond the reach of harm for the winter, and it was only with skulking parties that they could deal, while they remained. The return of spring brought a change. The Winnebagoes no longer held their Reservation in the very Eden of the Minnesota Valley. Far up the Missouri river, their home is now where they could "worry and devour each other," with less molestation than before, was it not for the vigilant care of the Agents and the watchful eye of Government.

CHAPTER LVII.

AN ALARM.

During the winter of 1862–3, comparative quiet was upon the borders and throughout the State. Military forces were stationed all along the frontier, to protect the most exposed portions, and prevent further incursions. Marauding parties of savages lurked in the Big Woods, and, as often as opportunity offered, murdered those in the most depopulated districts, stole the horses, and committed various depredations, in the more distant settlements.

As winter advanced into spring, they became still more daring, and horse thieving more general. Little Crow had sent thieving parties all over the State, and things again assumed an alarming aspect, though by no means so formidable as before.

Col. Miller, still at Mankato, was early awakened, one morning, to read and act upon the following alarming dispatch:

MEDALIA, April 17, 1863.

COL. STEPHEN MILLER:

DEAR SIR:—This morning, at two o'clock, two men from a detached post, on the south bend of the Watonwan, reported here, with the information that the settlement was attacked yesterday morning, by a large party of Indians, estimated by the Lieutenant in command, at not less than fifty. We have but one man killed and three wounded, and one boy, ten years of age, was killed. The Indians have taken all the horses they could get hold of—one belonging to Government. Lieutenant Hardy writes, that he thinks the Indians will renew the attack this morning. I shall start re-enforcements at four o'clock, and send for the wounded. We will need a surgeon to attend to the wounded, also a force of cavalry, with which to pursue the Indians. Your ob't servant,

T. G. HALL,
Capt Co. E, 7th Reg't Volunteers.

The settlement attacked, after this long quiet, was distant, to the south-west of Medalia, about twenty miles, and from Mankato forty-eight miles. A detachment of twenty-one men, from Company E, of the Seventh Regiment, under Lieut. Hardy, was engaged in building a stockade, which was unfinished when the attack was made. This was at dawn, on the morn of the 16th of April.

As soon as the alarm was given, messengers were sent to collect the settlers in the stockade, and the force was deployed so as to cover their flight as well as possible. One woman, Mrs. Targerson, was wounded in the thigh, before she left her house, where one man was killed, and another severely wounded with arrows. The wounded man grappled with the foremost Indian, broke two arrows, grasped his gun, and fired at them, when they fled. Mrs. T.'s wounds retarded her running, so that the Indians soon overtook her, when they beat her over the head, in a most cruel manner, with the butts of their guns. This act was seen by some soldiers, who started for her relief, when the Indians fled, and she reached the stockade, without further molestation.

The Indians appeared to be well armed, but had no horses, except what they stole in that neighborhood. They also drove off cattle belonging to the settlement.

As soon as orders could be given, one company of cavalry and two of infantry, under command of Lieut. Col. Marshall, were on the way to the theatre of danger, and reached Medalia, the same night, from whence, the following morning, they proceeded, meeting the wounded party, in charge of Lieut. Hardy, for whom he was seeking a place of more safety and comfort.

Upon the receipt of the same intelligence at Fort Ridgley, Lieut. Col. Pfender, commanding there, started a cavalry company, of fifty well armed men, to unite with Col. Marshall's command. This swelled the cavalry to one hundred, which, with several teams, with forage and ammunition, started, on Sunday morning, the 19th of April, in pursuit of the Indians. The infantry companies were left at Medalia and the stockade, deeming a strong force essential to guard against another attack.

The companies in charge of Col. Marshall, scoured the country as far as Lake Shetak, and, though often finding traces of where they had camped, but a day or two previous, they were always a little in advance, and the men returned to head-quarters, without having seen an Indian.

CHAPTER LVIII.

REMOVAL OF THE "GOOD INDIANS."

During the session of Congress, in the winter of 1863, a new reservation was appropriated in the vicinity of Fort Randall, in Dakota Territory, instead of Boston Common, for the occupancy of the guiltless ones, taken in charge at Camp Release, in September, 1862.

All winter, we had seen their uninviting camp, the curling smoke from the top of their tepees, and their filthy or gaily painted faces peeping from 'neath the folds of their blankets, on the flat, at Fort Snelling, where the waters of the Minnesota and Mississippi meet.

Just before their departure, a cargo of several hundred contrabands was landed and encamped near the same spot. It was a novel sight, and quite amusing to the beholder, to see them open their eyes in wild amazement, as each party gazed at the other, in mutual seeming wonder. The blacks had thought that no mortals were as degraded as themselves, but had found themselves outdone. The Indians had thought themselves the blackest of the human race, but now looked upon those of a deeper dye. And so they looked, and gazed, and talked, the few days they were privileged to remain as neighbors.

But the steamer has "rounded too," to convey away

from our sight, those government pets. Lodges are struck and packed with all their worldly goods, and with a strap passing round the forehead, slung over the backs of the squaws, as they move into their, for the present, moving quarters.

In military order, the bands were marched on board, the celebrated chief, Wabashaw, taking the lead, and counted and tallied to see that none were missing. They were followed by the bands of Good Road, Wacouta, Passing Hail, and Red Legs. The greater portion of these were women and children. Many of the trust-worthy Indians remained for scouts in Gen. Sibley's expedition, their families encamped on the prairie, in rear of the fort, and very properly provided for at public expense, and guarded, day and night, by armed men. In this company of some fifteen or twenty tepees, were some quite intelligent and cultivated women. Though most of them retained their native costume, some wore dresses and crinoline, like white women. One was pointed out to us as a teacher, acting in that capacity to the juveniles of the encampment. Industry in the domestic department prevailed, and we were struck with the evidences of improvement in personal cleanliness. But we digress.

To their shame be it said, that when the boat having the "good Indians" on board, landed at St. Paul, a crowd of soldiers, led on by one who had been wounded at Birch Coolie, commenced throwing stones and other missiles into the crowd of Indians on the boat, which it was impossible for them to avoid, as they were so closely packed on the boiler deck. Several squaws were hit upon the head, and quite severely injured. A threat by the commanding officer, who had their removal in charge, to charge bayonets on the offending crowd, soon dispersed them, and no further disturbance occurred. Such a gross outrage was strongly condemned by all good citizens, though they might have no fond partiality for the Indians. These were not the actual murderers, and hence no apology for such an act, than which nothing could have been more wanton.

While the boat "lay to," many of the Indians were engaged in prayer and singing, in which last exercise they took great delight, but whether with devout hearts, it is not ours to say.

From Hannibal, Missouri, these Indians were taken, by cars, to St. Joseph, and again embarked on the Missouri, for their new Reservation.

The new Winnebago Reservation is contiguous to the above, divided only by a small creek. Here, under the supervision of Col. Thompson, the Agent, they soon began to thrive, even in a desolated region, with scarcely a sign of cultivation.

"The Colonel's improvements," says one who writes from there so early as July 15, "are certainly a striking and cheering sight. In the foreground was a small camp of soldiers; to the right, a steam saw-mill, in full operation; to the left, a large, two story frame house, in course of erection; while temporary buildings and tents were scattered around, occupied by the workmen; and prominent in the centre, a temporary breastwork, constructed of supplies, brought for the workmen and for the Indians, in the centre of which stood a temporary building, used as an office and kitchen, the latter department presided over by "Bill," a darkey from St. Louis.

"The Colonel was pushing on the work, superintending everything himself. Buildings are rising as if by magic, and by autumn, if nothing untoward transpires, a model Agency will be nearly completed. It is laid out four hundred feet square, to be enclosed by a stockade fifteen feet high, inside of which all the buildings, of both Agencies, will be located. It will be more impregnable to Indian attacks than any I have ever seen.

"He is also making preparations for the erection of fifty houses for the Indians, to be finished before winter. For the short time the work has been in progress (only about six weeks,) it is astonishing that so much could be accomplished, and no one but a western man would believe it, if *told* the amount of work that has been done. Several of the buildings are finished and occupied. The saw mill is turning out lumber and shingles daily. The Indians are killing both deer and buffalo only a few miles away."

A company of captive Sioux from White Lodge's band were sometime confined at Fort Randall; with them was a man sent there by Col. Thompson for cutting and abusing his wife, who afterward hung herself in retaliation of the abuse. He made his way to the Agency, and was informed on by an Indian, and again sent back to prison. Two weeks later he was given over to the Indians, as the offense was against one of their own people, when a council was called and resulted in a decision for death. The uncle of his in-injured wife was appointed his executioner. The prisoner, unaware of his fate, went forth to the execution, of which he was informed on the way. He was cool and collected, and evinced no alarm. His hands were left unbound, and in the brief interim between the arrival at the ground and the fatal shot he bounded upon his executioner and stabbed him thrice before he could be interfered with. Throwing away his knife, he expressed a readiness to die, and calmly waited till the son of the man he had stabbed was sent for to shoot him, according to the custom that the nearest kin must avenge the death. The boy came, but had not the courage to do the deed, when an Indian from the crowd volunteered to do it for him.

CHAPTER LIX.

HORSE STEALING.

As the season advanced, horse stealing became the order of the day, or rather the business of the night. *Imaginary* Indians were often seen, *real* ones occasionally, and then perhaps, as they were just mounting the favorite horse of the owner, and leading another, would gallop off so rapidly that if a shot were fired, it would be without effect.

On the night of the 7th of June, a span of horses was stolen from a stable near Silver Creek, in Wright county. The following morning a party started to track the thieves, and if white or red men, regain their property. The trail led through many difficult windings in marsh and timber, giving the assurance that Indians were really the thieves. All day they wandered thus, when at night fall they saw the objects of their pursuit, not forty rods in front. Where was their courage now? where their determination to regain their stolen property? In less time than I am writing it, their horses' heads were wheeled, not so soon, however, but they heard the sharp crack of a cap and saw the emitted light. Indians and horses were left in the rear at a quick pace. Such was the dread which everywhere prevailed at the sight of one. His name even, had become a terror, and frightened men into *leaving*, sooner than by it the rollicksome pranks of boyhood were frightened into quiet. After investigation proved that the pursued had skedaddled with quite as much haste as the pursuers, leaving two packs of useful and indispensable articles on the ground, and many other things were scattered around, which nothing but fright and a desire for flight would have prevented their taking.

Emboldened by success and the probable knowledge of the fear their presence created, this increased gang of stealing, murdering desperadoes were encroaching further and still further into the settlements, threatening to overrun every part of the State.

A young man was found murdered in Pine county, under circumstances to incite suspicion against another, with whom he was in company. Nothing being known of the whereabouts of the latter, it was supposed he had made for parts unknown; and as the former was robbed of all valuables about his person, that he had appropriated it to his own personal use.

The body of the murdered man bore unmistakable evidence of severe treatment, with both club and knife. After evidence developed the fact that Indians were his murderers, and that the suspected one escaped only to share a like fate. What a theatre for tragic events had the State become! Everywhere the blood of human beings drenched the soil — everywhere decayed bodies were found — everywhere these nightly depredations were going on.

On the 14th of May, a man was killed near New

Ulm, and four horses with which he was plowing, made off with, and this, where one or two companies of troops were stationed. So sly and so hasty are their movements that they come, do whatever they list, and are gone, ere any are aware of their presence. An order embodying a bounty of twenty-five dollars, which was afterward increased to two hundred, was issued by the Adjutant General for every Sioux scalp, and otherwise high inducements offered volunteers, to scour the Big Woods, search out the lion in his lair and lay the trophy of their achievements at the feet of the Historical Society — a relic of the unparalleled tragedies to which our State has been subjected.

CHAPTER LX.

MURDER OF THE DUSTIN FAMILY.

Hennepin county, west of the Mississippi, and north of the Minnesota rivers, and lying on both, is one of the best populated in the State. Nearly every quarter section is occupied and *improved* by industrious and thriving farmers.

Minneapolis, the county seat of this county, is located on the west side of the Falls of St. Anthony, having a population of five or six thousand. Within six miles of this place the Indians came, bold in the execution of evil designs, yet cat-like in the manner. 'Tis ever so; they are always where least expected. When their presence excited no alarm, — when a score of Indians was seen to every white man, many a time has the writer been startled from a reverie by a slight rustle at her side, or a heavy breathing, to find herself in the presence of a great stalwart Indian. Once, in coming down Third street, in St. Paul, though grass-grown *then*, never dreaming of human presence, a sound somewhat like a high pressure steam engine on a Mississippi sand bar in low water, came to my ear, distant therefrom only the thickness of my bonnet, and half turning my head, I encountered a monster Indian, with gaily painted face, evidently delighted with my embarrassment, or his suggestive wit, thus to exhibit himself for approval, though "never a word he spoke," but with the usual grunt passed on.

This quality, be it what it may, is wonderfully advantageous to them in carrying out their present evil devices; and though to those far away, and unacquainted with their character and habits, it may seem strange that they should come and go and none be aware of their presence till the "fruit of their doings" is seen. Were it not so, an Indian would have lost his native character; in short, would cease to be an Indian, save in name.

Eight miles from Minneapolis, a farmer with his son was at work in the field, when a party of seven Indians came suddenly in view. As soon as they saw they were discovered, they fled to the bushes. The farmer hastened to collect his neighbors, of whom twelve or fifteen returned to the spot, found their trail which led them round Madison Lake, two miles nearer town, when they lost the trail and abandoned the search.

On Monday, the 29th of June, the day before this skulking party was seen, as above, in a more sparsely populated region, a few miles away, Mr. Amos Dustin, and his family of five persons, was passing over the prairie in an open lumber box wagon. When found on Wednesday following, Mr. Dustin was in the front of the wagon — dead. An arrow was sticking in his body, and a deep tomahawk wound was in his breast. His left hand had been cut off and carried away by the Indians.

Beneath his seat crouched a little girl of six years; her hair matted, her garments saturated, her face covered, and her shoes literally filled with the blood which had trickled from the mangled body of her father. She was the only uninjured member of the family, and in her fears thought, as she said, that "the Indians looked very sharply at her, and supposed they would kill her too," but not a hand was laid upon her.

The mother, and another child twelve years old, were alive when found, but mortally wounded. For two days and nights they had lain thus beside the dead bodies of their loved ones, unable to procure sustenance or assistance.

The mother of Mr. Dustin lay with her head hanging over the wagon, her long silvery hair matted with blood waving in the wind. An arrow in her body had done the work of death. Was there ever a picture more horrid? The horses, of course, were gone far away, conveying the perpetrators from the scene which they had enacted.

More vigorous measures for *home* defense were at once taken. Seventy stand of arms were issued to Hennepin county. No means were spared by State and military authorities to prevent future outrages.

CHAPTER LXI.

LITTLE CROW'S WHEREABOUTS.

Where now was the Commander-in-Chief of the mighty Sioux forces, whose scouting parties were doing so much evil in the land? Five hundred miles to the northwest, on the bleak shores of Devil's lake, had been their winter quarters. But he had not idled away the winter in camp life luxury. Wherever he might find a British subject, with the hope of aid from him, hither he went, setting forth his grievances in a mock pathetic manner, and begging his alliance in driving off the Americans. At Fort Garry, in British America, whither he went with sixty warriors, he made strong efforts to form a peace treaty. After impressing them with the glory of the scalp dance, Little Crow made a speech, in which he spoke of the efforts the "Big Knives" were making to catch him, in very desponding tones, though he boastfully asserted the power of his warriors, on whom he relied, and said, though "he considered himself as good as a dead man, they should fight awhile yet." He spoke of all the Government proceedings against himself and the condemned Sioux. He did "not complain that they were refused a tract of land on which to settle, which would place them under British protection," but he would "be glad of a little ammunition to kill Americans with." This, Governor

Dallas decidedly and promptly refused; to which he boastfully replied, "it made no difference, he had plenty." The people becoming tired of his insolence, begging and daring, Gov. Dallas politely ordered him and his followers to leave, and to trouble them no more with their presence.

Again, they are back to their "winter quarters," dissensions arising among themselves. Many are sick of the war — some never having been engaged in it, but having gone off with them because they were Indians, and supposed all Indians were death-doomed, if caught. Standing Buffalo had never favored the war, neither had Sweet Corn; they wanted to make peace, and were determined, any way, to deliver themselves up as soon as assured by the President that no harm should come to them.

The return of thieving parties elated Little Crow, for they had been very successful; and, failing to put a quietus to the dissatisfaction in camp, he resolved to redeem his fallen influence and fortunes in personal efforts in that direction. Ten months before, and a mighty nation bowed to his nod, he was rich in booty, and his soul feasting on the blood of the slain. Now, taking his little son, he descends to petty horse stealing, accompanied by less than twenty followers. We know naught of his wanderings, of his fastings and weariness, of his heart despondency and his howlings over his sad prospects, as his fleet foot passes over the intervening distance to the seat of his former raid! But the veritable Little Crow, who, one year before, was boasting of his prowess and might, is really and actually almost alone, a coward wanderer, avoiding the presence of those whose life he so lately sought; with retribution upon his track.

CHAPTER LXII.

THE RANSOMED.

More than two months of weary, death-inviting marches — of sleepless nights and terrible anxiety — from being constantly watched by their weasel-eyed captors, of savage abuse from which their women hearts recoiled with shuddering horror — of hunger and cold, and the wan and worn captives of Shetak memory reached the banks of the Missouri river, far to the southwest. The little girls had been allowed, sometimes, to ride on the two poles dragged behind the horse, but otherwise had received the most brutal and inhuman treatment. Little Tilla Everett, only eight years old, was one time struck on the head by a squaw with a heavy stake, from the effects of which she was for a long time insensible, and none expected or scarcely hoped her to recover, for they had then little hope of improved fortunes, or that she would ever find her father, if he still lived.

All the hellish ingenuity of their savage nature seemed taxed to invent some new phase of torture, the details of which would make the blood curdle with horror. Both the women were *enciente* when taken captives, and now were obligal to submit to the vile embraces, one of five and the other of three of these brutal monsters, till abortion followed; and even then there was scarce a suspension of suffering in this regard. Mrs. Dooley was four times sold — once for a horse, again for a blanket, and once for a bag of shot. Her little girl, six years old, was once sold for a gold watch, and again for two yards of cloth.

The most menial service was exacted, and severe abuse meted to the mothers, who endeavored to keep their helpless ones constantly beside them, and receive the blows instead of them. But there came a time when even this was forbidden. Mrs. Wright was ordered to go for water. The child of two years cried for its mother, when it was beaten by a squaw, till nearly dead, and then turned over to a male brute, who went out behind the tent and killed it, before the mother's return.

One Indian often boasted of going to a house where a woman was making bread — the mother of a small child, which lay in the cradle — that he split the woman's head open with a tomahawk, and then placed the babe in the hot oven, keeping it there till it was baked to death, when, not satisfied, he beat its brains out against the wall. This is corroborated by whites, who have been at the house where it happened, and from the appearance of the bodies, had no doubt but the "boast" was literally true.

When we reflect that these women and children fell into the hands of such monsters, we wonder at their final escape, or at their enduring powers, under such vile treatment. Thank heaven for the rescue!

On the last day of October, 1862, when love of life

had fled — their worn and emaciated bodies scarcely covered by the mere shreds of clothing left them — their first real joy since their captivity was in seeing a party of white men floating down the river. The Indians, finding they could not inveigle them on shore, commenced hostile demonstrations, when the hopes of the women sank as rapidly as they had risen. At the risk of life, however, they made themselves seen and heard enough to make known their condition. Upon this was based their final release. Major Galpin, for it was he with a small party of men, returning to his trading post, from this day devoted all the energies of his noble soul to this object, and directed, on his own responsibility, that no effort or expense should be spared for their ransom. The persons whose hearts were thus filled with gratitude to him who had secured them shelter and protection at Fort Randall, were Mrs. Wright and daughter, Mrs. Dooley and daughter, Misses Rosanna and Ellen Ireland, and Tilla Everett, the only living member of her family spared to her wounded, sorrow-stricken father. Of this, Mr. Everett remained for months in ignorance, himself suffering from wounds in the hospital at Mankato. When the public press announced the ransom of his child, he forgot the pain of his healing wounds, and started to find his lost one. At last they met. She rushed to his wide open arms, and was, in tearless silence, folded to his great throbbing heart. They who saw it wept, but the scene was too sacred for words. Like a tiny skiff and mighty ship in tempest swayed these two bodies with strong emotion, and when seemingly the heart chords must snap with the severe tension, the angel of relief came. The flood gates of the soul were opened, unsealing the surging, pent-up waters of the heart, and in the moment of almost delirious joy they half forgot what heart and flesh had suffered in the anxious past. But the billows of sorrow again swept over the soul, as the only antidote for the vacuum the lost and slain had made. May the world deal gently by all these sufferers, and as much as may be, smooth life's rugged pathway for their thorn-piereed feet and lacerated hearts.

CHAPTER LXIII.

THE INDIAN EXPEDITION.

Camp Pope, where the troops to compose the expedition under command of Brig. Gen. Sibley, were ordered to report, was at the mouth of Red Wood river, so late the theatre of the terrible massacres which inaugurated the war in Minnesota.

For weeks, activity and bustle prevailed here, in anticipation of a three months' campaign — and this was no small undertaking. The Brigade Commissary, Capt. Wm. H. Forbes, who had suffered the loss of some forty thousand dollars in the great raid, evinced his usual energy, ability and good sense in the management of this department; and that no want of calculation in him would bring failure to the expedition. Two hundred and twenty-five wagons were at last loaded with well packed provisions, and in due time, all was ready.

On the ninth day of June, the monotony of camp life was interrupted by the arrival of Gen. Sibley in a grand military reception. All were anxious to be on the move, and this argued favorably for a start. Every domestic circle in the State was more or less personally interested in the success of the expedition. Its officers, from the Lieutenants to the General commanding, were from our own hearth stones. The troops were our own,

CAPT. WM. H. FORBES.

fathers, brothers and sons of Minnesota, and were walled in by a cordon of prayer from "loved ones at home," which must secure the blessings of God upon the enterprise, whatever of danger or defeat lay in their path, and whatever doubts might arise with envious evil-thinkers and evil-speakers.

Gen. Sibley, with the great energy of purpose which had characterized his life and insured its success, now bent all these powers to this one purpose — to forever free the beautiful northwest from the assassins against whom this expedition was planned.

Scarcely had the excitement attendant on the occasion of his arrival, subsided, when the strong man "bows himself and weeps," as only a bereaved father can. The first tidings from home brings the sad message of a beloved daughter's death, smitten down by sudden disease. O, how vain seemed all earthly glory then, how brittle the cords that bind us to our dearest earthly loves! But there was no time for communion with grief. All things in camp reminded him of the responsibility of his position, and he must needs gird him for the duty.

On the 16th of June, 1863, all things being in readiness, the forward order was given, and the expedition took up the line of march for the almost unexplored region of Dakota territory. The entire force numbered about four thousand men, distributed as follows: Sixth Regiment, Col. Crooks, eight hundred and sixty men; Seventh Regiment, Col. Marshall, seven hundred and forty men; Tenth Regiment, Col. Baker, five hundred and seventy-eight men, (three companies had been detailed for special duty); Cavalry, Col. McPhail, eight hundred and six men; and Capt. Jones' Battery, one hundred and forty men and eight guns.

Gen. Sibley's Staff was organized as follows;

Capt. R. C. Olin, Acting Adjutant General.

Capt. C. B. Atchinson, Assistant Commissary of musters, and Acting Ordnance officer.

Captain Douglas Pope, Aid-de-Camp.

Captain Edward Corning, Quartermaster.

Captain Wm. H. Forbes, Commissary.

George H. Spencer, Chief Clerk of Commissary Department.

Captain Wm. H. Kimball, Quartermaster's Assistant, assigned to special duty as pioneer in charge of pontoon trains.

Lieutenant Joseph R. Putnam, Aid-de-Camp.

F. J. Holt Beever, A. St. Clair Flandrau, and Archibald Hawthorne, Aid-de-Camps, with rank of Second Lieutenant.

Seventy scouts, half of whom were volunteer Indians, and a majority of the balance half-breeds, were numbered with the expedition. These were in command of Major J. R. Brown, J. McCleod, and Wm. J. Dooley, who were to act as chief of scouts, each half to serve on alternate days, and precede the expedition in all its movements. The position of Rev. S. R. Riggs was changed from chaplain to interpreter, and yet he acted in the first with quite as much acceptance as before, and with all the temptations around him which tended to so demoralize the army, he proved his trust in that Being who alone can deliver from the evils of vice, and that his soul was safe in that fortress.

For transportation of commissary stores, there were two hundred and twenty-five wagons; for ordnance, twenty; pontoons, eleven; and battery, two;—for camp equipage of thirty-eight companies, nineteen; quartermaster's department and medical supplies, seventeen; regimental head-quarters, eight; head-quarters of the expedition, two. Surgeon Wharton received the appointment of medical director.

The sale of intoxicating liquors was prohibited by general order, to remain in force during the expedition; notwithstanding, those who so desired, by the working of some magic wand, always found their canteens re-filled whenever they had been emptied. — Strange and mysterious are the genii of this prince of evil, and the working out of his secret plottings none but his leagued hosts can fathom!

Thus the efficient and well organized force was on the move, making a train of five miles in length, formidable enough in appearance alone to awe the whole Sioux nation, and of courage and daring equal to any danger or effort.

The setting out of such an expedition was most unpropitious. Such a season of drouth was never known in all the West. The prairies were literally parched with heat, and all the sloughs and little streams dry. The fierce prairie winds were like the hot siroccos of the desert, withering every green thing. Clouds of dust, raised by this immense column, would blind the eyes, choke the throat and blacken the faces of the men, so that they looked more like colliers than soldiers. In time, serious effects began to tell upon the wagons and provision boxes, some of which fell in pieces, and much time was spent in making secure those uninjured. Both men and animals suffered for water, but the health of the men was not seriously affected, and, therefore, the spirits did not yield to circumstances. On the 19th, Mr. Riggs, writing from Camp Baker, one mile above the ruins of Hazlewood Mission Station, says:

"We have travelled three days, and have made about thirty miles from Camp Pope. The teams are all very heavily loaded, so heavy, indeed, that although we all wish for rain to make the earth rejoice, yet if that rain should come, it might very seriously affect the progress of this command at present. But the green grass is so dried up that fires run on the prairie wherever it was not burned last fall. And the streams of water too, are falling, so that we shall be obliged to keep near to the larger rivers or lakes, to obtain a supply of water for these 4,000 men, and as many animals."

"Our soldiers have marched, carrying their knapsacks, their blankets and their guns, an average of ten miles a day, which, with the immense train we have, in its present state, is thought as much as can reasonably be calculated upon. Yesterday morning, while the train was crossing the Yellow Medicine, I obtained from the General a squad of scouts and orderlies and came on to gather currants in the deserted gardens of the Missions. We found, and brought away with us a quantity of the pie-plant. These are the last remnants of civilization to be found in this direction. I gathered a few pinks and other flowers from my own garden at Hazlewood. Some of the men brought in lettuce, which they found in the gardens of the Agency.

"It is to me quite saddening to look on the desolation which the outbreak has made in the land. Seeing them again, has more deeply impressed me with the exceeding folly as well as sin of the Dakotas. By that one wicked act they have forever deprived themselves of homes in this beautiful land. But there is a Providence that shapes the destinies of people as well as individuals, brings good out of evil, and makes the wrath of man to praise HIM."

On the holy Sabbath day the standard rested from its march. This arrangement was, on the first Sabbath, made known to the campaign by the Commanding General, unless in cases of extreme and urgent necessity. Here again we endorse the sentiment of Mr. Riggs, that on the low ground of temporal economy they would find it profitable. "We shall march further," he says, "week after week, by resting on God's day, than we should by marching through the seven. But there is a higher view of this subject: If God be with us in this campaign, we shall make it a success; if God be not with us, we shall fail of accomplishing the desired objects. And one way to secure the presence and assistance of God, is to 'remember the Sabbath day, to keep it holy.'"

CHAPTER LXIV.

DEATH OF GENERAL LITTLE CROW.

On the third of July, 1863, when all the boys in the land, and many of the men were preluding the morrow with fire crackers, and preparations for big sounds and grand display of fire works, a boy and his father, "way out in Minnesota," were ignorantly performing a far more important service to their country — a service which will immortalize the name of Lampson, and render the two famous on historic page. They lived for an important end and have not lived in vain.

Mr Lampson lived at Hutchinson, a town which suffered much, you will remember, early in the troubles of 1862, since which siege everybody had been on watchful lookout for "a shot" in retaliation, and seldom went unarmed any distance from town. Mr. L. and his son Chauncey, were six miles in the country on this eventful day, when they discovered two Indians *picking berries* in an "opening" in the woods. Bushes and scattering poplars were interspersed, so that the Indians did not discover the two pair of eyes and the sure aim upon them. With commendable forethought, Mr. L. determined to make sure of his game before announcing his presence, so he crept cautiously forward among the vines and rested his gun against the tree which they climed. He fired, his shot taking effect, but not a deadly one, as evinced by the loud yell and sudden movement backward. His victim, however, fell to the ground, severely wounded. With the prudence and caution which characterized his first movement, not knowing the number of Indians, Mr. L. thought best to retreat a little, where he could obtain the shelter of some bushes.

The wounded Indian was not to be foiled in a shot at his antagonist, and so crept after him, and thus each were brought into distinct view of the other, when the two Indians they had first seen, and Chauncey Lampson who was concealed from their view, fired simultaneously. Chauncey's ball killed the wounded Indian, and the other one instantly sprang to his horse and rode away. A ball from the Indian's rifle whistled close to his cheek, while one from the other's gun struck his father on the left shoulder blade, making only a slight flesh wound.

Mr. Lampson dropped when the shot struck him, and his son, supposing him killed, and fearing a large force of Indians were near, having no more ammunition, and not daring to approach his father, who was some distance away, to obtain more, lest he should share the same fate, beat a hasty retreat for town.

He arrived home at ten o'clock in the evening, when the exciting news flew like wild fire on the prairie in a windy day. An army squad from the company stationed there, with a number of the citizens, were soon marching rapidly to the scene of conflict, while others started in other directions to warn the citizens, and others still, went to Lake Preston for a squad of cavalry, who, acting with promptness, were guided to the spot before daylight, and relieved "Mr. Injun" of his scalp, and *mark this, reader, this was the first scalp for which the twenty-five dollars reward was claimed, the first Sioux scalp taken by white man* in 1863.

When found by the company who had been first guided to the spot by young Lampson, the body of the Indian had been straightened, new moccasins put upon his feet, and his blanket carefully adjusted, as no dead "Injun" could do it. This led to the conviction that these were not alone in their evil designs and purposes.

But we will not leave the reader to suppose that the elder Lampson "laid him down to die," from the slight though unpleasant wound he had received. With the determined courage which characterized his first movement, he crawled into the bushes, reloaded his gun, drew his revolver, and waited for the re-appearance of the foe. Thus he waited, and none coming, he profited by the cover of night to come forth from his concealment. Divesting himself of his white garments, that they might not prove a fatal mark for prowling Indians, and taking a circuitous route, he reached home about two o'clock on the morning of the "FOURTH."

On the return of the military squad with the citizen's coat, moccasins, and a number of trinkets found on the person of the dead Indian, the programme of the day was changed, by sending out a detachment for the body which was brought in about three o'clock in the after noon. For two or three hours it was the common centre of attraction, and all professed to have known him well in life. The coat he wore was identified as the one taken from the man murdered some distance from there, of which mention has been heretofore made. All who beheld, declared a striking resemblance between this Indian and Little Crow, only this one a shade lighter, — the age about fifty. Both arms were withered and deformed by breaking and permanent displacement of the bones, the palpable result of rough handling in past time. A strange coincidence they thought, as this was the case with Little Crow, and so, as the body was becoming offensive, they "dumped" him into a hole and left him there, no tears of regret having fallen upon his unhonored grave; and the Lampsons little dreaming the service they had rendered the State in ridding it of one for whom a government train five miles long was in pursuit.

The press published the facts as here in substance related. In two weeks it reached the camp of General Sibley, then far on his route to catch the wily chief. The striking coincidence, the minute description of the body, its resemblance to Little Crow, attracted the attention of the Commanding General, who had known him well for years, and he declared it to be none other than the arch-enemy himself. In this opinion Major Brown and Capt. Forbes, who knew him equally well, concurred. Calling to the aid of their memories the Indian scouts and half-breeds, not one was known in the whole tribe who bore this resemblance in all the minutiæ to Little Crow. It was considered, too, a strongly corroborative circumstance, that the citizens of Hutchinson, who knew him, should detect this resemblance. This opinion was returned to the press, when investigation commenced, and every evidence adduced confirmed the fact that the *scalp of the terror-inspiring* LITTLE CROW *was a trophy at the historical rooms in the State Capital.*

A more marked instance of Providential retribution, history probably does not record. The leader of the bloody insurrection and the first Indian war which has scourged our State, in which, for the first time, white men felt the scalping-knife of the savage, now his own head, in turn, paying the forfeit, furnishing the *first* scalp which white man has ever taken!

The grave of Little Crow, which was only a hole dug for the receptacle of the offals of slaughtered cattle, being lightly covered, his head was soon exposed to view, and with a stick was sloughed from the body, where for several days it remained, the brains oozing out in the hot sun, till evidences of its identity began to accumulate, when a more critical investigation was made. The teeth were found to be double set around the mouth, which was known to be the case with Little Crow; and now the offensive, worthless thing, suddenly magnified into importance, was carefully prepared in a strong solution of lime. The putrid, decaying body, almost devoid of flesh, was exhumed, placed in a box, and sunk in the river, a cleansing preparation before passing into the anatomist's hands.

CHAPTER LXV.

CAPTURE OF WO-WI-NAP-A, SON OF LITTLE CROW.

Five hundred miles to the north-west, at Camp Atchinson, not forty miles from the shores of Devil's lake, the expedition train was divided, a portion remaining in camp, with orders to explore and root out the Indians, if any remained in that region. The other division, with General Sibley at its head, had moved in a south-western direction, for the Missouri river, where the main body of the hostile foe had fled.

Three companies, in command of Capt. Burt, went out from Camp Atchinson, on the 28th of June, to scour the region for a trail, which the scouts had reported as having seen the day before. Nearing the shores of Devil's lake, they crossed the trail, which was lost in a dried-up slough. In their search to regain the trail, the head of an Indian was discovered instead, protruding from a clump of bushes.

One of the scouts approached him and demanded his surrender. He threw down his gun, glad, in his half starved condition, of the prospect of getting something to eat on any terms. The remains of a lean wolf were beside him, which he had before killed with his last charge of ammunition, and cooked for his last rations. He very soon recognized and spoke to William Quinn, the half-breed interpreter, by whom, and several others, he was at once recognized as the son of Little Crow. He was very much emaciated by his fastings and wanderings, and was moreover in great straits, not knowing whither to go or what to do. He had expected to find his own people still there, but instead, not an Indian had he seen, and he would, doubtless, soon have starved to death. His head was full of vermin, and was at once shaven, and he was taken into camp to await the order of the Commanding General. We subjoin his own statement, rather than our own version of his story, that the reader may compare it with the afore given circumstances at Hutchinson, which this statement fully corroborates:

"I am the son of Little Crow; my name is Wo-wi-nap-a; I am sixteen years old; my father had two wives before he took my mother; the first one had one son, the second one a son and daughter. The third wife was my mother. After taking my mother, he put away the first two. He had seven children by my mother, six of whom are dead, I am the only one living now. The fourth wife had five children born; do not know whether they died or not; two were boys and three were girls. The fifth wife had five children, three of whom are dead, two are living. The sixth wife had three children, all of them are dead, the oldest was a boy, the other two were girls. The last four wives were sisters.

"Father went to St. Joseph last spring. When we were coming back, he said he could not fight the white men, but would go below and steal horses from them and give them to his children, so that they could be comfortable, and then he would go away off.

"Father also told me that he was getting old, and wanted me to go with him to carry his bundles. He left his wives and other children behind. There were sixteen men and one squaw in the party that went below with us. We had no horses, but walked all the way down to the settlement. Father and I were picking redberries near Scattered lake, at the time he was shot. It was near night. He was hit the first time in the side, just above the hip. His gun and mine were lying on the ground. He took up my gun and fired it first and then fired his own. He was shot the second time while firing his own gun. The ball struck the stock of his gun and then hit him in the side, near the shoulders. This was the shot that killed him. He told me that he was killed, and asked me for water, which I gave him. He died immediately after. When I heard the first shot fired I laid down, and the man did not see me before father was killed.

"A short time before father was killed, an Indian named Hi-a-ka, who married the daughter of my father's second wife, came to him. He had a horse with him, also a gray colored coat, that he had taken from a man whom he had killed, to the north of where father was killed. He gave the coat to father, telling him he would need it when it rained, as he had no coat with him. Hi-a-ka said he had a horse now, and was going back to the Indian country.

"The Indians who went down with us, separated.

Eight of them and the squaw went north; the other eight went further down. I have not seen any of them since. After father was killed, I took both guns and the ammunition, and started for Devil's lake, where I expected to find some of my friends. When I got to Beaver Creek, I saw the tracks of two Indians, and at Standing Buffalo's village saw where the eight Indians who had gone first had crossed.

"I carried both guns as far as Shayenne river, where I saw two men. I was scared, and threw my gun and ammunition down. After that, I travelled only in the night, and as I had no ammunition to kill anything to eat, I had not strength enough to travel fast. I went on until I arrived near Devil's lake, when I stayed in one place three days, being so weak and hungry that I could go no farther. I had picked up a cartridge near Big Stone lake, which I still had with me, and loaded father's gun with it, cutting the ball into slugs. With this charge, I shot a wolf, ate some of it, which gave me strength to travel, and I went on up the lake, until the day I was captured, which was twenty-six days from the day my father was killed."

Sixteen years before the capture of Wo-wi-nap-a, the writer had been, for many days, a guest at the house of Doctor Williamson, then, as in latter years, the Sioux missionary at Little Crow's village, before its removal up the Minnesota Valley. When the novelty of a white woman's landing from a "fire canoe" had a little subsided, this, then baby Chief, with others, was held up, that my unsophisticated admiration might be sealed with a kiss, an accorded honor with which I feared not to comply — the same pappoose which I sometimes saw affectionately caressed by his father, but a weakness on his part, which he would prefer should have passed unnoticed. Like Joseph, he was the favorite son of his father, because his mother was loved more than all his wives. Wo-wi-nap-a returned with the expedition, and has since been in the guard house, awaiting military disposal.

CHAPTER LXVI.

TWO CAPTIVE BOYS.

In the month of June, 1863, considerable sympathy was elicited in St. Paul, by the arrival of two little ransomed boys, who had been, since the outbreak, in savages' hands. Their ages were six and nine years, and to the good Catholic priest of St. Joe, they owed their release from captivity. He had parted with all his worldly goods to effect this, and then even robbed himself of his own needful apparel, to clothe them decently and comfortably for their journey.

George Ingalls, the eldest of these boys, was, when the trouble commenced, living near Yellow Medicine. Like others, the family fled for the fort, but before reaching there, were seized upon by Indians, who sprang from a hole in the earth. Mr. Ingalls was killed, and the rest of his family made prisoners. His three daughters, sisters of young George, were carried off to the plains, suffering incredible hardships, till finally ransomed at the Agency, on the Missouri river.

George was sometimes at Big Stone lake, and in the same camp with a boy who forms the subject of another chapter. Finally, they moved on to the north-west, towards Devil's lake, where the main Indian forces were to concentrate for the winter.

My reader will recollect the little Jimmy Scott, of Old Crossing, who submitted to go with his captors, as his grandmother bade him, whom we now again introduce as the veritable boy, but having passed through such suffering and hardship as to remember little else, and having even forgotten the name of his grandmother. The poor child would cry most piteously, when questioned relative to his adventures. Both physical and mental powers seemed seriously affected by the terrible ordeal through which he had passed, for a child of such tender years.

The boys say they never suffered for food in quantity, but the quality, with little variation, was not the most desirable, much of the time having only buffalo meat. They suffered much from intense cold during the long tedious winter, in the bleak winds from the lake which visited them very roughly, and there was much of human misery in the severe drudgery put upon boys so young. What mother's heart but bleeds at their woes and rejoices in their release! The Indian women who had played mother to them, were sad to part with them, and seemed unwilling to do so, until plead with most earnestly in the eloquence of tears by the boys themselves. Little Jimmy cried bitterly on the neck of his Indian mother, when he "kissed her good-bye."

May friends be so kind,—the healing balm be so gently applied to childhood's bitter memories, that this eventful experience be no serious drawback on their future lives, whose history will be marked with intense interest by those who have sympathized with them in these dark hours.

CHAPTER LXVII.

THRILLING ADVENTURES OF MR. BRACKETT AND DEATH OF LIEUTENANT FREEMAN.

The monotony of Camp Atchinson was interrupted on the evening of August 2d, by the appearance on the outskirts, of an emaciated human figure, who at once fell to the ground, in sheer weakness and exhaustion. He was picked up and carried into a tent, and was at once recognized as George E. Brackett, of Minneapolis, beef contractor of the expedition, who had gone with the main body, and was now nearly dead from hunger and fatigue.

He had, in company with Lieutenant Freeman, of St. Cloud, when about sixty miles out, left the main column and flanked off to the left for a day's adventure, with little thought of its sad ending. Five miles away, having met nothing worthy of note, they overlooked the country from the summit of a range of hills, when they saw several of the scouts not very far away. Passing a fairy-like lake, three graceful antelopes tempted a shot, one only was wounded, which Lieut. Freeman followed, giving his horse in charge of Mr. Brackett. This drew them from their course, though the train was in sight several miles distant. Seeing the scouts on the other side of the lake, curiosity led them on, through fresh evidences of Indians near.

These dangers passed, they shaped their course towards the train, or to strike its trail. On the lookout for the enemy, they discovered three objects between themselves and the train, who they soon decide to be *real* Indians, following up the train. Each made preparations to meet the other, and with all the caution at command, crept forward around the bluff. A mutual surprise ensues, when they recognize in each other friends of the same party. One of these scouts was Chaska, who is already well known.

Just at this time a large squad of men were noticed on the bluff, nearly three miles away, at the same time a squad of cavalry, as they supposed, started toward them. The scouts turned off to the lake to water their horses, and the cavalry and themselves in motion, perceptibly lessened the distance between them, and no doubt existed but that Gen. Sibley's full command was on the other side of the hill, and so sure, that while they almost counted the horses, they gave no heed to the men. But suddenly they disappeared, they could not have sunk into the earth, and, therefore, must have turned back. So said these men as they rode carelessly along.

Judge of the surprise when, instead of their own cavalry, fifteen Indians, deceptively bearing a flag of truce, suddenly charged upon them. They yelled to the scouts and rode toward them, but before they reached them, Lieut. Freeman was shot, with an arrow, through the back, and at the same time, another Indian fired at Mr. Brackett, who escaped the ball by clinging to the neck of his horse, and at the same time Chaska, from the top of a knoll, let fly at the Indians. Lieut. Freeman sat on his horse till they had passed in the rear of the scouts, when he remarked, "I am gone," and fell. He asked for the string to be cut from his neck, to which was attached a piece of the slain antelope, for water which was given, then slightly changed his position, and was gone.

The Indians were now all around them, but were held in check by an invisible power, and fell back as the daring scouts rode rapidly toward them, ready to fire. This brief respite gave Mr. Brackett a chance to get the Lieutenant's rifle and revolver before he followed the scouts, and to overtake them while his pursuers waited to catch the horse from which his comrade had just fallen. This done, with loud and triumphant yells, they start on again, and after a race of four miles, the fleeing party are completely surrounded. All jumped from their horses, and the faithful Chaska, more intent on the safety of his friend than his own, first saw him safely hid in the bushes, and then went forward to meet his red brethren. This was the last Mr. Brackett saw of the scouts, but lay in his concealment with his rifle cocked, while the Indians quarreled which should have his horse. But for this they would doubtless have searched out his hiding place.

The afternoon was now far spent, and in a half hour after the Indians had left in a circuitous course round a marsh, probably to avoid pursuit by Gen. Sibley's forces. Mr. Brackett crawled out from the rushes, and with the sun to his back, travelled for two hours, and thus he did for two days, and when the sun had set, hid in a marsh, where he slept at night. After the third day he began diligent search for the trail, which he struck on the afternoon of the fifth day, about twelve miles from where they encamped the night before he left the train, and about seventy miles from Camp Atchinson. So little advance had been made, that a man of ordinary caliber would have yielded to despondency, and there have died. Not so with the hero of this adventure.— Though subsisting on frogs, birds and cherries, and these in limited quantities, for five days, his feet worn and blistered with constant travel, his forehead blistered by the scorching sun, and sleeping every night with only the upper region of his nether garment for a covering, his indomitable energy enabled him to go on, though when he reached the camp, he could not have held out another day. The remainder of this perilous adventure we give in Mr. Brackett's own words:

"About ten miles before reaching Camp A, I sat down to rest, and had such difficulty in getting under weigh again, that I determined to stop no more, feeling sure that once again down, I should never be able to regain my feet unaided. I entered the camp near the camp fire of a detachment of the "Pioneers," (Capt. Chase's Company of the Ninth Minnesota Infantry,) and fell to the ground, unable to raise again. But, thank God! around that fire were sitting some St. Anthony friends, among whom were Messrs. McMullen and Whittier, attached to that company, who kindly picked me up, and carried me to my tent.

"I lost my coat, hat and knife in the fight on the first day. I took Lieut. F.'s knife, and with it made moccasins of my boot-legs, my boots so chafing my feet in walking that I could not wear them. These moccasins were constantly getting out of repair, and my knife was as much needed to keep them in order for use, as to make them in the first place. But just before reaching the trail of the expedition on the fifth day, I lost Lieut. F.'s knife. This loss I felt at the time decided my fate, if I had much farther to go, but kind Providence was in my favor, for almost the first object that greeted my eyes upon reaching the trail, was a knife, old and worn to be sure, but priceless to me. This incident some may deem a mere accident, but let such an one be placed in my situation at that time, and he would feel with me, that it was a boon granted by the Great Giver of good. On the third day, about ten miles from the river spoken of, I left Lieut. F.'s rifle on the prairie, becoming too weak to carry it longer, besides it had already been so damaged by rain that I could not use it. I wrote upon it that Lieut. F. had been killed, and named the course I was then pursuing. I brought the pistol into Camp Atchinson.

"While wandering, I lived on cherries, roots, birds

eggs, young birds and frogs, caught by hand, all my ammunition but one cartridge having been spoiled by the rain on the first day. That cartridge was one for Smith's breech loading carbine, and had a gutta percha case. I had also some waterproof percussion caps in my portmonaie. I took one-half the powder in the cartridge, and a percussion cap, and with the pistol and some dry grass, started a nice fire, at which I cooked a young bird, something like a loon, and about the size. This was on the second night. On the fourth, I used the remainder of the cartridge in the same way, and for a like purpose. The rest of the time I ate my food uncooked, except some hard bread (found at the fourth camp mentioned above,) which had been fried and then thrown into the ashes. I have forgotten one sweet morsel, (and all were sweet and very palatable to me,) viz: some sinews spared by the wolves from a buffalo carcass. As near as I am able to judge, I travelled in seven days at least two hundred miles. I had ample means for a like journey in civilized localities, but for the first time in my life, found gold and silver coin a useless thing. My bootleg moccasins saved me; for a walk of ten miles upon such a prairie, barefooted, would stop all further progress of any person accustomed to wear covering upon the feet. The exposure at night, caused, more particularly, by lying in low and wet places in order to hide myself, was more prostrating to me than scarcity of food. The loneliness of the prairies, would have been terrible in itself, without the drove of wolves that, after the first day, hovered, in the day-time, at a respectable distance, and in the night time howled closely around me, seemingly sure that my failing strength would soon render me an easy prey. But a merciful Providence has spared my life, by what seems now, even to myself, almost a miracle."

Mr. Brackett speaks in the highest terms of Chaska, his courage and devotion to the cause in which he was enlisted being unsurpassed in Indian life. He feels that he owes his life to him, by his firing in the first encounter, and rushing toward him in the second, which enabled him to hide as he suggested.

Lieutenant Ambrose Freeman, who fell as above related, was a native of Virginia, and for seven years a a resident of St. Cloud, Minnesota, where his wife and five children waited his return, when he should recount to them the adventures and perils of the way. He bore an unblemished character, and was best loved and respected where best and longest known. His character in civil, accompanied him in military life, and no man in the expedition could have been more generally regretted. He enlisted for frontier defense of our Minnesota homes. His body was promptly recovered and buried with honors due, at Camp Sibly, near the Big Mound, where a great battle with the Indians was fought soon after his fall.

The scouts came safely into camp, minus horses.

CHAPTER LXVIII.

THE CAPTIVE JOHN JULIEN.

The subject of this chapter was one of the three boys who were ransomed by the kind-hearted Catholic priest at St. Joe. His captivity was of ten months' duration, but there is less of real bitter misery in it than of the other boys. John Julien was cook for the government laborers at Big Stone lake at the time of the savage onset there. He escaped and hid in the woods until he supposed the danger passed, and then thought he would return to the tent and find out if possible the fate of his employers, when he was made prisoner by an Indian who lived near, with the humane intent of protecting till he could set him at liberty. His name, which deserves historic record, is Eu-kosh-nu, meaning the "man with short hair." He took no part in the massacres, and taking the boy across the lake, with some valuable suggestions to guide him, sent him off alone. No sooner had he turned back, than he found the enemy were on his track, and running after, brought him back, and for several days kept him concealed at his own lodge.

Then he allowed him to go with his own son to the lake, but no sooner was he seen, than a vicious Indian, one who had deeply drank of the extermination spirit, and vowed that no white blood should be left unspilled, took aim at his heart, and then ran off, not waiting to know the result, but supposing his pistol had performed its intent.

His little Indian companion ran and told his father of the cruel act, who came at once, took him kindly in his arms, carried him to his house, washed and dressed his wounds, and made him as comfortable as he could in his comfortless tepee. Then he took down his gun, his eye flashing vengeance, declaring he would shoot Hut-te-ste-mi, who had shot the white boy. This, John, in his forgiving spirit, overruled; so he put up his gun and went forth, hatchet in hand, to avenge the deed by a demand of the pistol, which he smashed upon a stone, thus inciting the anger of the would-be boy murderer, and endangering his own life.

Eu-kosh-nu dare not be found at his own house, and to protect his captive, whose life was now more than before in danger, had him taken to his cousin's, about half a mile distant. Good care was given to his wound during the five days he remained there, and the ball extracted from his side.

One month later, thirty lodges of the vicinity were struck, and the occupants fell in with Little Crow's party, who having been ousted in battles, had started for Devil's lake, in the north of Dakota Territory, where it was their intent to mass their forces, after receiving all the pledges of assistance from other tribes they could get.

The wounded, suffering captive must go with them on this long, wearisome journey. He walked the first day, as his captor had no way for him to ride, who seeing he could not hold out thus another day, gave him to his relative, who protected him at Big Stone lake. He rode in the wagon of his new owner the rest of the way, and was with him during the remainder of his captivity.

Instead of remaining at Devil's lake, a portion of this party passed on to the Missouri river, among whom was John Julien. The cold had now become intense, and the snow was deep; still these savage wanderers continue to move on, following up the windings of the river, till, after an abundance of sameness in experience, an encampment of Yanktons, five hundred lodges strong, falls in their way. Here they rested and feasted on buffalo meat for five days, when they were joined by Little Crow with sixty lodges, with whom they remained during the rest of the winter.

None of these were stationary. The Yanktons broke camp and went in one direction, Little Crow's camp in another. The latter was very desirous to make peace with the Arickarees, (commonly known as the Rees,) and obtain their assistance in his anticipated campaign against the whites in the spring. Little Crow compelled the captive boy to go in front, when his delegation went forward to meet the delegation of Rees, that if trouble ensued he might be first to suffer. The object of the embassy being known, there followed an assent, a shaking of hands, and the smoking of pipes. But scarcely had the Rees reached the protection of their own people, when they commenced firing. There was among them a peace and an anti-peace party, the latter the strongest, and of course overruling the former. Our little hero was again wounded in the fleshy part of his leg. Eight Sioux were killed and one squaw, during the battle, which lasted from noon till sundown. Little Crow was completely routed, and retreated for the camp where he had wintered, forty miles distant. This was the last of April.

The wounded boy tried hard to keep up with the retreating party, and after running five miles, his leg became too painful to proceed, and he hid himself to avoid the enemy in pursuit. At dark, however, he followed in their trail, and after travelling all night and the following day, reached the Sioux camp, where they were safe from their pursuers.

Little Crow again bends his steps towards Devil's lake, and for the first five days they are entirely destitute of food. Fifty miles above Devil's lake, ——— the trader from St. Joseph, met them with a parley for their furs, for which they received provisions and blankets. We mention this because it is an important link in the chain of circumstances which led to the boy's release. This trader carried the tidings of this boy's captivity, as also, the two others then at other points, to St. Joe, when the kind hearted priest arranged for him to buy them.

The owner of the boy was reluctant to sell him, he preferred rather to take him to the settlement and deliver him up, in proof of his friendship for the whites, combined with the testimony of the treatment he had received while in his care. He had exacted nothing unreasonable, had not required him to work, and when he sold a pony for a cap, coat, vest, pants, three shirts, a pair of stockings aud a blanket, he clothed his captive with them instead of himself. The other Indians would not accede to his wish to go to the settlement, and thinking that Gen. Sibley, to whom he had hoped to deliver him, would not come into the neighborhood, he finally consented to sell him; and on the 13th of June he reached St. Joseph, where he was received by the priest and kindly cared for while he remained, and was sent to St. Paul, where he arrived the 17th of September, glad to be once more in civilized life, with the hope of a speedy reunion with the remnant of his father's family.

CHAPTER LXIX.

PROGRESS OF THE EXPEDITION.

Slowly, but surely, plodded on the gigantic train, with all the drawbacks which beset its course. Little or no rain had visited them, and there fell scarcely a drop of dew to relieve the aridity of the earth, while the heat was much of the time one hundred degrees or more, and the hot sirocco air, when filled with dust, was almost unendurable. The true man may die, but he never fails. Whatever the discouragements, he is true to his purpose, and if he dies, it is with the harness on, and his mantle falls on another, as true as himself. Clouds may be around him, but, eagle-like, he soars above them, and heeds not the muttering thunders, or the tongue of calumny. The same rear fire which followed the expedition now, was kept up all through the campaign of the previous fall. It is an easy matter to find fault, while reclining at ease in one's office or home; but not so easy to perform, successfully, a great and important work, and meet, at the same time, the impatient demand of the public.

The objects of the expedition were kept constantly in view, from the first. The release of the prisoners was successfully accomplished. The punishment of guilty parties followed, so far as the action of the General commanding was concerned, and over three hun-

COL. WM. R. MARSHALL.

dred guilty warriors and murderers were condemned to death. That they were not executed, was no fault of his. *The supreme law of the army forbids the execution of any sentence of court martial, without the sanction of the President of the United States.* Where, then, rests the blame?

Still, unmoved by the clamor of fault-finders, the expedition was pushing on to the desired end, though never an Indian had they seen. At last they come upon their trail — tent poles and camp fire remains, where game had been cooked, and other signs evince their nearness — as they advance toward the Missouri.

Days — weeks had passed, and no tidings came from the main column to the anxious outer world; and nothing was known of them at Camp Atchinson. But they were far from being idlers or laggards in the field, and were far in the heart of the enemy's country, away from civilization and refinement, amid scenery though beautiful to the eye, devoid of all other attractions — the country poor, in the extreme — fully determined to mete to the foe the justice they merited. Nor was it a boy's play to bring about this grand result. Every man felt the responsibility of his position, and worked as if success depended alone on him. Time was flying fast and events were hastening to their final issue.

At last it is known, for Col. Marshall brings the tidings that three several engagements have taken place, in which the enemy, more than two thousand strong, the largest Indian force ever giving battle, had been completely routed, with heavy loss, and driven in terror and confusion across the Missouri river.

Col. Marshall left the expedition after one day on the return march, and performed the hazardous trip of nearly four hundred miles in seven days, and much of the way without an escort and only two scouts. The main features of the battles we leave the reader to get from the official report of the commanding officer. Some items, however, not therein mentioned, may not be uninteresting.

The great Sioux camp, when discovered by our forces, were in consultation for proposing terms of peace, instigated to this by Standing Buffalo, who had long since declared his intention to deliver himself up, whenever opportunity offered to do so. To this proposition all but eight daring, reckless young braves consented, who mounted their horses and rode swiftly away. A party followed to bring them in, and had just come up with them on the hill overlooking the camp of white men. The scouts went up to parley, and several messages were returned from them to individuals, among which was a special request from Standing Buffalo to George Spencer, to "come over and see him." George lacked no confidence in the friendly chief, but something whispered him, "go not up," and fortunately he obeyed the monitory voice. Several of the men followed the scouts, and even shook hands with several Indian acquaintances. — Among these was Doct. Weiser, from Shakopee, Surgeon of the Mounted Rangers; but scarcely had he spoken to one, when one of the determined eight came

STANDING BUFFALO.
(The Friendly Chief.)

behind and shot him through the heart. He fell from his horse and never spoke again. The scouts returned the fire, when the Indians fell back behind the ridge, firing as they went. One of them was slightly wounded by a spent ball, which had passed through a rubber blanket rolled up on his saddle. All peace overtures were now at an end. Those who had encouraged a surrender "fell in" to save themselves from their own people. Standing Buffalo, still persistent in his peace principles, ran away to the north, where he remained many weeks afterwards.

The fighting propensities of the savages were roused to their full tension, and their awful war-whoop rang through all the prairie air. It was three o'clock in the afternoon of July 24th, 1863, when Gen. Sibley ordered his troops forward to meet the foe. Then arose a terrible thunder storm, which shook the earth, and sent a bolt of lightning into their midst, killing one man and his horse instantly. For three full hours the contest raged, when the savages fled in wild confusion. The mounted regiment of Col. McPhail pressed on in pursuit, while the main body of the infantry, having marched from early morn till three o'clock before engaging the enemy, went into camp.

An unhappy mistake, (for such will occur in military circles as well as in well regulated families,) occurring at this time, has furnished food for the the capacious, craving stomach of calumny. But we think it due to the General commanding, to set the facts before the world in their true light, and as we obtained them from one who *heard* the order, and received and executed an auxiliary — whose statements are above suspicion of cavil, we vouch for their correctness.

Why was not the advantage gained at the first battle followed up, and the Indians more severely punished? is the query of dissatisfaction. We reply, such was the design. We have seen Col. McPhail's cavalry, supported by the Seventh of infantry, under Lieut. Col. Marshall, in pursuit of the fleeing foe, to be followed by the main column. But no man or body of men can accomplish impossibilities. It will be recollected that they had marched that day forty miles, before engaging the enemy. The advance scouts had just reported at head-quarters, the finding of the enemy's trail, when Captain Forbes, of the Commissary Department, rode to the front to say that the teams were giving out, and they were near the only water reported for several miles. Accordingly they went into camp.

"You ride to Col. McPhail — tell him not to pursue the enemy after dark, but to act discretionary as to a bivouac on the prairie," was the verbal and definite order given by Gen. Sibley to Lieut. Beever, who volunteered to deliver it. This was followed by another to the Chief Clerk of the Commissary Department "to start three days' rations to reach the advancing force early in the morning. Promptly the last order was executed, and five loaded teams were on the way by eleven o'clock that night, but when one mile out stragglers were met, and finally the entire pursuing force. The order had been strangely misunderstood, and its most important phraseology delivered in a positive "re-

COL. WM. CROOKS.

turn to camp." The regret of its bearer was too poignant for censure when he awoke to this serious blunder. But his was too noble a nature not to acquit the innocent of all blame, even though his own name would be branded on historic page, and he frankly admitted the mistake to his comrades, and awaited his opportunity to do so before the world. He sleeps in the shadow of the woods in which he met his untimely fate, and his living testimony cannot exonerate the man on whom an envious world throws the blame, and who nobly suffers the tongue of calumny to declare his unfitness for the command, rather than cast it on a worthy, defenseless dead man. And thus it rests.

At last they have repulsed the enemy in three successive battles, killing a large number, and driving him, in large force, across the Missouri river, between which and the expedition's encampment, was a mile of dense forest, interspersed with a heavy growth of prickly ash, the most impenetrable of all northern undergrowth. Imperfect Indian trails ran through them to the river, but, forbidding as were the circumstances, Col. Crooks, as valorous a man as ever led a regiment, called for volunteers to follow him there. After thoroughly shelling the woods, and scouring the "bottom," they drew rein at its shore, and drank themselves and their horses from the sweet though turbid stream, which was truly refreshing, after having drank naught, for many days, but brackish water. While here, they were fired on from the opposite shore, but the balls fell harmlessly into the river, a warning, however, for them to make quick time in return to camp.

Again it is inquired, why this last engagement was not the finale of the Indian war, and why they were not followed across the river?

We have shown the nature of the ground between them and the river. In the language of another, "white men cannot fight naked, and draw their subsistence from the lakes, woods and prairies, as the Indians can." They must have their baggage wagon and provision train, otherwise they cannot carry on an offensive war. Men and animals were well nigh exhausted when they reached the Missouri: besides the commissary stores were scarcely sufficient for return rations. They would have had great difficulty in getting the teams through the dense forest, and then three days' time would have been consumed in crossing, which would have given the enemy three days' start, else they would have been all this time exposed to their fire.

"White people," says Mr. Riggs, "are superior to an Indian in a thousand things, but fighting is not one of them. Our big guns, and our long range muskets and our better drills, give us an advantage over them. But in fleeing and fighting, fighting and fleeing, they are our superiors. Moreover; they cover a retreat most beautifully. If any one supposes it is an easy matter to annihilate these Arabs of the desert, let him try it. Perhaps he will come back a wise man." Some ask, he says, "why Gen. Sibley did not kill more Indians? We reply, "they would not stay to be killed." He might have disgraced his humanity and killed the Teton boy — he might have killed an old woman brought in by the scouts, and in one or two other instances he might have performed like humane acts, had he been a brute, but manhood triumphed, and aside from these, not an Indian escaped that could be reached by hand or bullet.

Every man, whether he has been in a campaign or not, claims the privilege of deciding how a campaign should be conducted, and the qualification of its General. A free country guarantees to them this right, however great the injustice of that decision.

If we look to historic facts, we find no more successful campaigns against the Indians, than have been those of Gen. Sibley; and all in it, with whom we have conversed, agree that all was done which human wisdom and human energy could do. Let us not forget the vast army power, and the forty millions of money expended in unsuccessful attempts to drive the Seminoles from their swamp retreats, in Florida. A fish, thrown from its native element, will flounce about for a little while, and die of itself. So with the envious tongue. As sure as water finds its level, time and an overruling Providence will work all right. The name of Henry H. Sibley will live on history's unsullied page. Posterity will laud him, when those of his calumniators will be lost in the great whirlpool of oblivion.

We ignore any claim, in the military line, from political preference. The right man in the right place, is our motto. Gen. Sibley is a Democrat — a loyal, conscientious one, we have no doubt; while the writer is a wool-dyed Republican, (if expression on this point is admissible,) and when WOMAN'S RIGHTS (?) prevail, shall vote that ticket, *strong*, but, then, as now, will accord to every man his due.

CHAPTER LXX.

THE CAPTURE OF A TETON.

On the morning of the 28th of July, just as Gen. Sibley's command was breaking camp at Stony lake, they were attacked by Indians, in full force, and after three hours of sharp fighting, repulsed the foe, who fled toward the Missouri, and moved on in pursuit. Mr. Spencer, under the escort of scouts, full of the spirit of adventure, left the main column in the dim distance, and discovered a solitary pony, quietly grazing, about a mile to the left. Putting spurs to their horses, they started for its capture. As they approached it, a dark, motionless object was seen lying upon the ground. Coming nearer, some one cried out, "It's an old buffalo robe;" but as one stooped to pick it up, it sprang from the earth, and bounded off like a deer, being extended to full size, and flying swiftly, in a zigzag manner. It was a broad mark for the carbines, but where in it was the motive power? It was impossible to tell. Some thirty shots were fired, all hitting the robe, but still he kept on with the same zigzag course, and a constant motion, from side to side, of the robe, so that it seemed impossible to hit him.

At last, Bottineau, the chief guide, reined up to him, put a revolver to his head, and fired, but he dodged the ball. He now stopped, dropped the robe, and threw up both hands, in token of surrender. The robe was literally riddled with balls, but not a scratch was on his person, and he had enlisted the sympathy and admiration of his captors, for his brave and gallant bearing. He was unarmed, save with a knife, stuck in his belt, which he silently threw away, on being ordered to do so. He was placed behind one of the scouts, and brought before General Sibley, to whom he extended his hand in friendly salute, which was not taken; but with stern eye upon him, the General questioned him closely, till well satisfied with the truth of his statement, when they shook hands, and were friends. He belonged to the Teton band, one of the largest divisions of the Dakota nation, living west of the Missouri river, taking no part in the war. His father was one of the head chiefs, and the son had come out on a visit to the Yanktonians, and learning they were soon to have a fight with the "Long Knives," curiosity led him on to see it. He retired with the repulsed Indians, but coming to a little valley of good grass, stopped to let his pony graze, and, wrapping himself in his robe, laid down to rest, and was fast asleep, before he knew it, and thus the scouts had come upon him.

For the five days that he remained prisoner, General Sibley caused him to be treated according to the dignity of his rank, as heir-apparent to the chieftainship. He became strongly attached to Mr. Riggs, and seldom left his side. Mr. Spencer says, "he was not more than twenty years old, and his was as fine a specimen of the human form, as he ever beheld."

When the return order was given, General Sibley wrote a letter to his father, commending the wisdom of his course, in refusing to take up the tomahawk against the whites, saying he wished them to know that the whites were a merciful people, and though his son had been captured among the hostile Indians, he had spared his life, and permitted him to return to his own people. This was, no doubt, a stroke of good policy, as the death of this young Teton would have exasperated his tribe, and rendered the Indian war much more formidable than otherwise.

A few days after the dismissal of the young Teton, a party of miners, rich in gold dust, washed from the deposits of Idaho, were descending the Missouri, at the very spot where our men went down to drink. Indians were all around, ready to spring from the weeds and bushes, and the young Tenton, desiring peace, rushed toward them, holding the letter to his father, over his head. But they understood not the signal, and shot him dead, when they were at once surrounded, and, though fighting desperately, and killing more than twice their number, every man of them was killed, and all the rich avails of toil fell into the spoiler's hands.

CHAPTER LXXI.

DEATH OF LIEUT. BEEVER.

While Col. Crooks and his regiment were at the river, General Sibley, becoming aware of the proximity of Indians, and the dangers which surrounded them, executed an order for their return to camp, which the bold and daring Lieutenant Beever volunteered to deliver. He was unmolested by the way, and though desired by Col. Crooks to remain until the men should be formed, and return under their protection, he was too true a soldier to disregard the discretionary order of a superior officer. Midway in the forest, the trail forked in several directions — unfortunately, he took the wrong one, though it would just as soon have brought him into camp.

Col. Crooks returned, and though Lieut. Beever messed with him, his tent was at Gen. Sibley's headquarters, and for several hours his absence was not noticed, each party supposing him with the other. Night shadows had fallen upon the encampment before inquiry arose in relation to him, and no little alarm was created when it was known that he had not been seen since receiving the message from Col. Crooks.

The sudden disappearance of one in universal favor, cast a gloom over the camp. Thursday, July 30th, Gen. Sibley sent out a command of eleven companies under Col. Crooks, to make thorough reconnoissance of the woods, and if possible, find his body, and that of private Miller, who was missed the same day. The latter had said, before going out, that *"he wanted a shot."* He received a *shot*, but whether he gave one or not, is unknown. He was found scalped, not far from Lieut. Beever, but whether the same rencounter terminated both lives, of course will ever be unknown, unless the facts be imparted by some friendly Indian.

But a short distance from where Lieut. Beever lay, were two pools of blood, proving pretty conclusively that he had not yielded his life without a recompense. His horse had been shot through the head, and three arrows were in his back, and a ball had passed through his body, but the finale had been the blow from a tomahawk. He was a "good shot"—had with him two revolvers, carrying eleven balls, which had doubtless, found sure lodgment, the dead or wounded Indians having been carried off by their comrades.

The remains were duly prepared and deposited in as good a coffin as could be obtained, and with his body servant (between whom and himself there was a mutual attachment,) as chief mourner, followed by almost the entire command, was placed in his prairie grave, near that of Docter Weiser, there to rest till the "graves give up their dead."

This event was one of the saddest connected with the campaign. Frederick J. Holt Beever was an English gentleman of means and education, travelling for his health and improvement. His love of romance and adventure led him to embrace the opportunity offered by the expedition, for seeing the western prairies, and he was attached to General Sibley's staff, as volunteer Aid-de-camp. He was a jovial, social man, brave, energetic and reliable, and after "life's fitful fever," in his lone and lowly bed he rests well.

CHAPTER LXXII.

TERMINUS OF THE CAMPAIGN.

In obedience to the order given below, the campaign was ended, and on Saturday morning, Aug. 1st, commenced retracing their steps towards civilization and friends:

"*To the Officers and Soldiers of the Expeditionary forces in camp :*

"It is proper for the Brigadier-General commanding to announce to you that the march to the west and south is completed, and that on to-morrow the column will move homewards, to discharge such other duties connected with the objects of the expedition, on the way, as may from time to time present themselves.

"In making this announcement, Gen. Sibley expresses also his high gratification that the campaign has been a complete success. The design of the Government in chastising the savages, and thereby preventing, for the future, the raids upon the frontier, has been accomplished. You have routed the miscreants who murdered our people last year, banded, as they were, with the powerful Upper Sioux, to the number of nearly 2,000 warriors, in three successful engagements, with heavy loss, and driven them, in confusion and dismay, across the Missouri river, leaving behind them all their vehicles, provisions and skins designed for clothing, which have been destroyed. Forty-four bodies of warriors have been found, and many others concealed or taken away, according to the custom of these savages, so that it is certain they lost in killed and wounded, not less than from one hundred and twenty to one hundred and fifty men. All this has been accomplished with the comparatively trifling loss on our part of three killed and as many wounded. You have marched nearly six hundred miles from St. Paul, and the powerful bands of the Dakotas, who have hitherto held undisputed possession of the great prairies, have succumbed to your valor and discipline, and sought safety in flight. The intense heat and drought have caused much suffering, which you have endured without a murmur. The companies of the 6th, 7th, 9th and 10th regiments of Minnesota Volunteers, and of the 1st regiment Minnesota Mounted Rangers, and the scouts of the battery, have amply sustained the reputation of the State by their bravery and endurance, amidst unknown dangers and great hardships. Each has had the opportunity to distinguish itself against a foe at least equal in numbers to itself.

"It would be a gratification if these remorseless savages could have been pursued and literally extirpated, for their crimes and barbarities merited such a full measure of punishment; but men and animals are alike exhausted after so long a march, and a further pursuit would only be futile and hopeless. The military results of the campaign have been completely accomplished, for the savages have not only been destroyed in great numbers, and their main strength broken, but their prospects for the future are hopeless indeed, for they can scarcely escape starvation during the approaching winter.

"It is peculiarly gratifying to the Brigadier-General commanding, to know that the tremendous fatigues and manifold dangers of the expedition thus far, have entailed so small a loss of life in his command. A less careful policy than that adopted, might have effected the destruction of more of the enemy, but that could only have been done by a proportional exposure on our part and the consequent loss of many more lives, bringing sorrow and mourning to our homes. Let us, therefore, return thanks to a merciful God for his manifest interposition in our favor, and for the success attendant upon our efforts to secure peace to the borders of our own State, and of our neighbors and friends in Dakota Territory, and as we proceed on our march toward those most near and dear to us, let us be prepared to discharge other duties which may be imposed upon us during our journey, with cheerful and willing hearts.

"To the Regimental and company officers of his command, the Brigadier-General commanding tenders his warmest thanks for their co-operation and aid on every occasion during the progress of the column through the heart of an unknown region, inhabited by a subtle and merciless foe.

"For the friends and families of our fallen comrades we have our warmest sympathies to offer in their bereavement.

"General Sibley takes this occasion to express his appreciation of the activity and zeal displayed by the members of his staff, one and all.

"By command of

"BRIGADIER-GENERAL SIBLEY."

The night previous to leaving, several shots were fired into camp by prowling Indians, who on the following morning made their appearance to the number of thirty or forty, determined to annoy where they could do nothing more.

CHAPTER LXXIII.

OFFICIAL REPORT OF BRIGADIER GENERAL HENRY H. SIBLEY TO MAJ. GEN. POPE.

MAJOR:—My last dispatch was dated 21st ultimo, from Camp Olin, in which I had the honor to inform Major General Pope, that I had left one-third of my force in an intrenched position at Camp Atchinson, and was then one day's march in advance, with 1,400 infantry and 500 cavalry, in the direction where the main body of the Indians were supposed to be. During the three following days, I pursued a course somewhat west of south, making fifty miles, having crossed the James river and the great coteau of the Missouri. On the 24th, about 1 P. M., being considerably in advance of the main column, with some of the officers of my staff, engaged in looking out for a suitable camping ground, the command having marched steadily from 5 A. M., some of my scouts came to me at full speed, and reported that a large camp of Indians had just before passed, and great numbers of warriors could be seen upon the prairie two or three miles distant. I immediately corralled my train upon the shore of a salt lake near by, and established my camp, which was rapidly intrenched by Col. Crooks, to whom was entrusted that duty, for the security of the transportation in case of attack, a precaution I had taken

whenever we encamped for many days previous.—
While the earthworks were being pushed forward, parties of Indians, more or less numerous, appeared upon the hills around us, and one of my half-breed scouts, a relative of "Red Plume," a Sissiton chief, hitherto opposed to the war, approached sufficiently near to converse with him. "Red Plume" told him to warn me that the plan was formed to invite me to a council with some of my superior officers, to shoot us without ceremony, and then attack my command in great force, trusting to destroy the whole of it.

The Indians ventured near the spot where a portion of my scouts had taken position, three or four hundred yards from our camp, and conversed with them in an apparently friendly manner, some of them professing a desire for peace. Surgeon Joseph Weiser, of the First Minnesota Mounted Rangers, incautiously joined the group of scouts, when a young savage, doubtless supposing from his uniform and horse equipments that he was an officer of rank, pretended great friendship and delight at seeing him; but when within a few feet, treacherously shot him through the heart. The scouts discharged their pieces at the murderer, but he escaped, leaving his horse behind. The body of Dr. Weiser was immediately brought into camp, unmutilated, save by the ball that killed him. Dr. Weiser was universally esteemed, being skillful in his profession, and a kind and courteous gentleman.

This outrage precipitated an immediate engagement. The savages in great numbers, concealed by the ridges, had encircled those portions of the camp not flanked by the lake referred to, and commenced an attack.

Col. McPhail, with two companies, subsequently reenforced by others as they could be spared from other points, was directed to drive the enemy from the vicinity of the hill where Dr. Weiser was shot, while those companies of the 7th Regiment under Lieut. Col. Marshall and Major Bradley, and one company of the 10th Regiment, under Capt. Edgerton, was dispatched to support them. Taking with me a six-pounder under the command of Lieut. Whipple, I ascended the hill towards "Big Mound," on the opposite side of the ravine, and opened fire with spherical case shot upon the Indians who had obtained possession of the upper part of the large ravine, and of the smaller ones tributary to it, under the protection of which they could annoy the infantry and cavalry without exposure on their part.

This flank and raking fire of artillery drove them from these hiding places into the broken prairie, where they were successively dislodged from the ridges, being utterly unable to resist the steady advance of the 7th Regiment and the Rangers, but fled before them in confusion. While these events were occurring on the right, the left of the camp was also threatened by a formidable body of warriors. Col. Crooks, whose regiment (the 6th,) was posted on that side, was ordered to deploy part of his command as skirmishers and to dislodge the enemy. This was gallantly done, the Col. directing in person the movements of one part of his detached force, and Lieut. Col. Averill of the other, Major McLaren remaining in command of that portion of the regiment required as part of the camp guard.

The savages were steadily driven from one strong position after another, under a severe fire, until, feeling their utter inability to contend longer with our soldiers in the open field, they joined their brethren in one common flight. Upon moving forward with my staff, to a commanding point which overlooked the field, I discovered the whole body of Indians, numbering from one thousand to fifteen hundred, retiring in confusion from the combat, while a dark line of moving objects on the distant hills indicated the locality of their families. I immediately dispatched orders to Col. McPhail, who had now received an accession of force from other companies of his Mounted Regiment, to press on with all expedition and fall upon the rear of the enemy, but not to continue the pursuit after nightfall, and Lieut. Col. Marshall was directed to follow and support him with the companies of the 7th, and Captain Edgerton's company of the 10th, accompanied by one six-pounder, and one section of Minnesota howitzers under Captain Jones.

At the same time, all the companies of the 6th and 10th regiments, except two from each which were left as a camp guard, were ordered to rendezvous, and to proceed in the same direction, but they had so far to march from their respective posts, before arriving at the point occupied by myself and staff, that I felt convinced of the uselessness of their proceeding farther, the other portions of the pursuing force being some miles in the advance, and I accordingly directed their return to camp.

The cavalry gallantly followed the Indians, and kept up a running fight until nearly dark, killing and wounding many of their warriors, the infantry under Lieut. Col. Marshall being kept at a double quick in their rear. The order to Col. McPhail was improperly delivered, as requiring him to return to camp, instead of leaving it discretionary with him to bivouac in the prairie. Consequently he retraced his way with his weary men and horses, followed by the still more wearied infantry, and arrived at the camp early the next morning, as I was about to move forward with the main column. Thus ended the battle of the Big Mound.

The severity of the labor of the entire command may be appreciated, when it is considered that the engagement only commenced after the day's march was nearly completed, and that the Indians were chased at least twelve miles, making altogether full forty miles performed without rest.

The march of the cavalry, of the 7th regiment, and of "B" company of the 10th regiment, in returning to camp after the tremendous efforts of the day, is almost unparalleled, and it told so fearfully upon men and animals that a forward movement could not take place until the 26th, when I marched, at an early hour. Colonel Baker had been left in command of the camp (named by the officers Camp Sibley,) during the engagement of the previous day, and all the arrangements for its security were actively and judiciously made, aided as he was by that excellent officer, Lieut. Colonel Jennison, of the same regiment.

Upon arriving at the camp from which the Indians had been driven in such hot haste, vast quantities of dried meat, tallow and buffalo robes, cooking utensils, and other indispensable articles were found concealed in the long reeds around the lake, all of which were, by my direction, collected and destroyed. For miles along the route, the prairie was strewn with like evidences of a hasty flight. Col. McPhail had previously advised me that beyond Dead Buffalo lake, as far as the pursuit of the Indians had continued, I would find neither wood nor water. I consequently established my camp on the border of that lake, and very soon afterwards parties of Indians made their appearance, threatening an attack. I directed Capt. Jones to repair with his section of six-pounders, supported by Capt. Chase, with his company of pioneers, to a commanding point, about six hundred yards in advance, and I proceeded there in person. I found that Col. Crooks had taken position with two companies of his regiment, commanded by Captain and Lieut. Grant, to check the advance of the Indians in that quarter. An engagement ensued at long range, the Indians being too wary to attempt to close, although greatly superior in numbers. The spherical case from the six-pounders soon caused a hasty retreat from that locality, but perceiving it to be their intention to make a flank movement on the left of the camp, in force, Capt. Taylor, with his company of Mounted Rangers, was dispatched to retard their progress in that quarter. He was attacked by the enemy in large numbers, but manfully held his ground until recalled, and ordered to support Lieut. Colonel Averill, who, with two companies of the 6th regiment, deployed as skirmishers, had been ordered to hold the savages in check.

The whole affair was ably conducted by these officers, but the increasing numbers of the Indians, who were well mounted, enabled them, by a circuitous route, to dash towards the extreme left of the camp, evidently with a view to stampede the mules herded on the shore of the lake.

This daring attempt was frustrated by the rapid motions of the companies of Mounted Rangers, commanded by Captains Wilson and Davy, who met the enemy and repulsed them with loss, while Maj. McLaren, with equal promptitude, threw out along an extended line, the six companies of the 6th regiment, under his immediate command, thus entirely securing that flank of the camp from further attacks. The savages, again foiled in their designs, fled with precipitation, leaving a number of their dead upon the prairie — and the battle of Dead Buffalo lake was ended.

On the 27th, I resumed the march, following the trail of the retreating Indians until I reached Stony lake, where the exhaustion of the animals required me to encamp, although grass was very scarce.

The next day, the 28th, took place the greatest conflict between our troops and the Indians, so far as numbers were concerned, which I have named the battle of "Stony Lake." Regularly alternating each day, the 10th regiment, under Col. Baker, was in the advance and leading the column, as the train toiled up the long hill. As I passed Col. Baker, I directed him to deploy two companies of the 10th as skirmishers. Part of the wagons were still in the camp under the guard of the 7th regiment, when, as I reached the top of the ridge in advance of the 10th regiment, I perceived a large force of mounted Indians moving rapidly upon us. I immediately sent orders to the several commands promptly to assume their positions, in accordance with the programme of the line of march; but this was done, and the whole long train, completely guarded at every point, by the vigilant and able commanders of the regiments, and of corps, before the order reached them. The 10th gallantly checked the advance of the enemy in front, the 6th and cavalry on the right, and the 7th and cavalry on the left, while the six-pounders and two sections of mountain howitzers, under the efficient direction of their respective chiefs, poured as rapid and destructive fire from as many different points. The vast number of Indians enabled them to form two-thirds of a circle, five or six miles in extent, along the whole line of which they were seeking for some weak point upon which to precipitate themselves. The firing was incessant and rapid from each side, but so soon as I had completed the details of the designated order of march, and closed up the train, the column issued in line of battle upon the prairie, in the face of the immense force opposed to it, and I resumed my march without any delay. This proof of confidence in our own strength completely destroyed the hopes of the savages and completed their discomfiture. With yells of disappointment and rage, they fired a few parting volleys, and then retreated with all expedition. It was not possible, with our jaded horses, to overtake their fleet and comparatively fresh ponies.

This was the last desperate effort of the combined Dakota bands, to prevent a farther advance, on our part, towards their families. It would be difficult to estimate the number of warriors, but no cool and dispassionate observer would probably have placed it at a less figure than from 2,200 to 2,500. No such concentration of force has, so far as my information extends, ever been made by the savages of the American Continent.

It is rendered certain, from information received from various sources, (including that obtained from the savages themselves, in their conversations with our half-breed scouts,) that the remnant of the bands who escaped with Little Crow, had successively joined the Sissitons, the Cut Heads, and finally the "Yank-tonais," the most powerful single band of the Dakotas, and together with all these, had formed one enormous camp, of nearly, or quite, ten thousand souls.

To assert that the courage and discipline displayed by officers and men, in the successive engagements with this formidable and hitherto untried enemy, were signally displayed, would but ill express the admiration I feel for the perfect steadiness and the alacrity with which they courted an encounter with the savage foe. No one, for a moment, seemed to doubt the result, however great the preponderance against us in numerical force. These wild warriors of the plain had never been met in battle, by American troops, and they have ever boasted that no hostile army, however numerous, would dare to set foot upon the soil of which they claim to be the undisputed masters. Now that they have been thus met, and their utmost force defied, resisted, and utterly broken and routed, the lesson will be a valuable one, not only in its effect upon these particular bands, but upon all the tribes of the Northwest.

When we went into camp, on the banks of Apple river, a few mounted Indians could alone be seen. Early next morning, I dispatched Col. McPhail with the companies of the Mounted Rangers, and the two six-pounders, to harass and retard the retreat of the Indians across the Missouri river, and followed with the main column, as rapidly as possible; we reached the woods, on the border of that stream, shortly after noon, on the 28th; but the Indians had crossed their families, during the preceding night, and it took but a short time for the men to follow them, on their ponies. The hills, on the opposite side, were covered with the men, and they had probably formed the determination to oppose our passage of the river, both sides of which were here covered with a dense growth of underbrush and timber, for a space of more than a mile.

I dispatched Col. Crooks, with his regiment, which was, in turn, in the advance, to clear the river of Indians, which he successfully accomplished, without loss, although fired upon, fiercely, from the opposite side. He reported to me that a large quantity of transportation, including carts, wagons, and other vehicles, had been left behind in the woods.

I transmitted, through Mr. Beever, a volunteer Aid on my Staff, an order to Col. Crooks, to return to the main column, with his regiment, the object I had in view, in detaching him, being fully attained. The order was received, and Mr. Beever was entrusted with a message, in return, containing information desired by me, when, on his way to headquarters, he unfortunately took the wrong trail, and was, the next day, found where he had been set upon and killed by an outlaying party of the enemy. His death occasioned much regret to the command, for he was esteemed by all for his devotion to duty, and for his modest and gentlemanly deportment.

A private of the 6th regiment, who had taken the same trail, was also shot to death with arrows, probably by the same party.

There being no water to be found on the prairie, I proceeded down the Missouri to the nearest point on Apple river, opposite Burnt Boat Island, and made my camp. The following day, Col. Crooks, with a strong detachment of eleven companies of infantry and dismounted cavalry, and three guns, under the command of Capt. Jones, was dispatched to destroy the property left in the woods, which was thoroughly performed, with the aid of Lieut. Jones, and a portion of the Pioneer Corps. From one hundred and twenty to one hundred and fifty wagons and carts were thus disposed of. During this time, the savages lay concealed in the grass, on the opposite side of the river, exchanging occasional volleys with our men. Some execution was done upon them, by the long range arms of the infantry and cavalry, without injury to any one of my command.

I waited two days in camp, hoping to open communication with General Sully, who, with his comparatively fresh mounted force, could easily have followed up and destroyed the enemy we had so persistently hunted.

The long and rapid marches had very much debilitated the infantry, and as for the horses of the cavalry, and the mules employed in the transportation, they were utterly exhausted.

Under the circumstances, I felt that this column had done everything possible, within the limits of human and animal endurance, and that a further pursuit would not only be useless, as the Indians could cross and recross the river in much less time than could my command, and thus evade me, but would necessarily be attended with the loss of many valuable lives.

For three successive evenings, I caused the cannon to be fired, and signal rockets sent up, but all these elicited no reply from General Sully, and I am apprehensive he has been detained by insurmountable obstacles.* The point struck by me on the Missouri, is about forty miles, by land, below Fort Clark, in latitude forty-six degrees forty-two minutes — longitude, one hundred degrees thirty-five minutes.

The military results of the expedition have been highly satisfactory. A march of nearly six hundred miles from St. Paul has been made, in a season of fierce heats and unprecedented drouth, when even the most experienced voyageurs predicted the impossibility of such a movement; a vigilant and powerful, as well as confident, enemy was found, successively routed in three different engagements, with a loss of at least one hundred and fifty killed and wounded of his best and bravest warriors, and his beaten forces driven in confusion and dismay, with the sacrifice of vast quantities of subsistence, clothing, and means of transportation, across the Missouri river, many, perhaps most of them, to perish miserably in their utter destitution, during the coming fall and winter.

These fierce warriors of the prairie have been taught by dear bought experience, that the long arm of the government can reach them in their most distant haunts, and punish them for their misdeeds; that they are utterly powerless to resist the attacks of a disci-

---

*While Gen. Sibley was pushing his forces to the South-west, General Sully was moving up the Missouri, in the opposite direction, to cut off the retreat of the fleeing foe; and on the 4th of September, surprised four hundred of their lodges, fought and dispersed them with a loss of fifty men, and killing more than twice that number of the enemy, — capturing provisions, furs, horses, and ammunition, and regaining a large amount of property, taken in the raid of the previous year.

plined force, and that but for the interposition of a mighty stream between us and them, the utter destruction of the great camp containing all their strength was certain. It would have been gratifying to us all, if the murdering remnant of the Meda-wakanton and Wak-paton bands could have been extirpated, root and branch, but as it is, the bodies of many of the most guilty have been left on the prairie, to be devoured by wolves and foxes.

I am gratified to be able to state that the loss sustained by my column in actual combat was very small. Four men of the cavalry were killed, and four wounded, one, I fear, fatally. One private of the same regiment was killed by lightning, during the first engagement, and Lieut Freeman of company "D" also of the Mounted Rangers, a valuable officer, was pierced to death by arrows, on the same day, by a party of hostile Indians, while, without my knowledge, he was engaged in hunting at a distance from the main column. The bodies of the dead were interred with funeral honors, and the graves secured from desecration by making them in the semblance of ordinary rifle pits.

It would give me pleasure to designate by name all those of the splendid regiments and corps of my command who have signalized themselves by their gallant conduct, but as that would really embrace officers and men, I must content myself by bringing to the notice of the Major General commanding, such as came immediately under my observation.

I cannot speak too highly of Colonels Crooks and Baker, and Lieut. Colonel Marshall, commanding respectively the 6th, 10th and 7th regiments, Minnesota Volunteers, and of Lieut. Colonels Averill and Jennison, and Majors McLaren and Bradley, and of the line officers and men of these regiments. They have deserved well of their country and of their State. They were ever on hand to assist me in my labors, and active, zealous, and brave in the performance of duty.

Of Col. McPhail, commanding the Mounted Rangers, and of Majors Parker and Hayes, and the company officers and men generally, I have the honor to state, that as the cavalry was necessarily more exposed and nearer the enemy than the other portions of the command, so they alike distinguished themselves by unwavering courage and splendid fighting qualities.

The great destruction dealt out to the Indians is mostly attributable to this branch of the service, although many were killed or disabled by the Artillery and Infantry also.

Captain Jones and his officers and men were ever at their posts, and their pieces were served with much skill and effect.

To Captain Chase of the Pioneers and his invaluable company, the expedition has been greatly indebted for service in the peculiar line for which they were detailed.

Captain Baxter's company H, of the 9th regiment, having been attached to the 10th regiment, as a part of its organization temporarily, upheld its high reputation for efficiency, being the equal in that regard of any other company.

The Surgical Department of the expedition was placed by me in charge of Surgeon Wharton, as Medical Director, who has devoted himself zealously and efficiently to his duties.

In his official report to these head-quarters, he accords due credit to the Surgeons and Assistants of the several regiments present with them. Of the members of my own staff I can affirm that they have been equal to the discharge of the arduous duties imposed upon them.

Captain Olin, my Assistant Adjutant General, has afforded me great assistance, and for their equal gallantry and zeal may be mentioned Captains Pope and Atchinson, Lieutenants Pratt and Hawthorn, and Captain Fox, temporarily attached to my staff, his company having been left at Camp Atchinson.

The Quartermaster of the expedition, Captain Corning, and Captain Kimball, Assistant Quartermaster, in charge of the pontoon train, have discharged their laborious duties faithfully and satisfactorily; and for Captain Forbes, Commissary of Subsistence, I can bear witness that but for his activity, attention, and business capacity, the interests of the Government would have suffered much more than they did, by the miserable state in which many of the packages containing subsistence stores, were found.

Chief Guides, Major J. R. Brown and Pierre Bottineau, have been of the greatest service by their experience and knowledge of the country; and the Interpreter, Rev. Mr. Riggs, has also rendered much assistance in the management of the scouts. The scouts generally, including the Chiefs McLeod and Duly, have made themselves very useful to the expedition, and have proved themselves faithful, intrepid and intelligent.

I have the honor to transmit herewith the reports of Colonels Crooks, Baker, and Lieut. Colonel Marshall, commanding respectively the 6th, 10th and 7th regiments of Minnesota Volunteers, and of Colonel McPhail, commanding 1st regiment Minnesota Mounted Rangers.

I am, Major, very respectfully,
Your obedient servant,
H. H. SIBLEY,
Brig. General Commanding.

CHAPTER LXXIV.

OFFICIAL REPORT OF BRIGADIER GENERAL ALFRED SULLY.

> HEAD-QUARTERS INDIAN EXPEDITION, CAMP AT
> MOUTH OF LITTLE SHEYENNE RIVER,
> Sept. 11th, 1863.

MAJOR: The last report I had the honor to send you was from the mouth of the Little Sheyenne river, bearing date August 16, 1863; since which time my movements have been too rapid and the danger of sending any communication such that it has been impossible for me to do so. I therefore have the honor to report my movements from last report up to date.

On the morning of the 19th, the steamer I was waiting for with supplies finally arrived. She was immediately unloaded, and all the baggage of the officers and men of the command was sent down by her to the depot at Ft. Pierre, together with every man who was in the least sick or not well mounted. By this I reduced my force considerably, and was enabled to transport, with the wretched mule that had been furnished me, about three days' rations and forage enough to keep these transportation animals alive, depending on grass I might find, to feed the cavalry and artillery horses. Luckily for me, I found the grazing north much better than I had dared to hope for.

On the 20th, were visited by one of the most terrific rain and hail storms I have seen. This stampeded some of my animals and a few were lost — they swam across the Missouri — and it also destroyed a quantity of my rations in the wagons, thereby causing me some delay in the march; but I succeeded in getting off the afternoon of the 21st, and marched up the Little Sheyenne about eleven miles, the road being very heavy. The next day we marched only seven miles, camping on a slough on the prairie without wood. The next day we marched in a north-westerly direction to the outlet of Swan lake. On the 24th, we marched due north, eighteen miles, and encamped on a small creek, called Bois Cache. Here we came into the buffalo country, and I formed a hunting party for the command, which I had soon to disband, as they disabled more horses than buffalo. We continued our march north about twenty-two miles and reached a small stream called Bird Archie creek. This day the hunters succeeded in killing many buffalo, and reported that they saw Indians near the Missouri.

Early on the morning of the 28th, I sent out a small scouting party, who captured two squaws and some children and brought them into me. These Indians reported that Gen. Sibley had had a fight near the head of Long lake, and that they were on their way to the Agency at Crow creek, but were lost, and were alone; but the scouts found tracks of lodges going up the Missouri. I therefore immediately detailed companaies F and K of the 2d Nebraska cavalry, under command of Captain La Boo, ordering them to go to the Missouri, and follow up the trail, with orders to capture some Indians if possible and bring them in, so that I might get information; if they could not do that, to kill them and destroy the camps. I continued the march with the rest of the command that day, passing through large herds of buffalo, and was obliged to make a march of thirty-five miles before I could reach water. The weather was very hot, and it was night before we reached camp on the Beaver river.

On the 27th, I started late, having had some difficulty in crossing the river, making a march of five miles still in a northerly direction, and encamped on another branch of the same river. Company K of the 2d Nebraska joined me this day, having been separated from the other company. The next day we had to make some deviations to the west, on account of hills and sloughs, and made the outlet of Long lake, a march of about twenty miles. On the way we saw numerous signs of Indians in large numbers having been recently there, and found an old lame Indian concealed in the bushes, who was well known by many of the men of the command as having for some years resided near Sioux city. He had the reputation of being what is called a "good Indian." He stated that "his horse had been taken away from him and that he had been left there." He looked almost starved to death. He gave me the following details, which have since mostly turned out to be correct: he stated "Gen. Sibley had fought the Indians at the head of Long lake, fifty miles north-east from me, some weeks ago; that he followed them down to the mouth of Apple creek; that the Indians attacked him on the way, and that there was some skirmishing.

"At Apple creek, Sibley had another fight, and that in all the fights, about fifty-eight Indians were killed; that Gen. Sibley fortified his camp at Apple creek, and after a while returned to James river; that a few days after Gen. Sibley left, the Indians, who had their scouts out watching, recrossed the Missouri, and while doing so, discovered a Mackinaw boat on its way down. They attacked the boat, fought the entire day until sundown, sunk her, and killed all on board — twenty-one men, three women and some children; that before she was sunk, the fire from the boat killed ninety-one Indians, and wounded many more; that a small war party followed Sibley some days, returned with the report that he had crossed the James river; then some of the Indians went north; the larger portion, however, went towards the head of Long lake; and that he thought a portion of them were encamped on the Missouri river west of me."

The report was so much in keeping with the Indian mode of warfare, that though it came from an Indian, I was led to give it some consideration, particularly the part that stated the Indians, after watching Sibley's return, recrossed, when all danger was over, and went back to their old hunting grounds. Besides, the guides who were acquainted with the country, stated that "a large body of Indians could not live on the other side long, without going a great distance west; that always at this season of the year the Indians camped on the Octeau, near the tributaries of the James, where the numerous lakes or springs kept the grass fresh; here the buffalo were plenty, and the lakes and streams full of fish; and that here they prepared their meat for the winter, moving to the Missouri where the fuel was plenty to winter." I therefore determined to change my course towards the east, to move rapidly, and go as far as my rations would allow.

I felt serious alarm for the safety of Capt. LaBoo, who had but fifty men with him, and who had already been out over two days without rations. I encamped here for the next day, and sent out four companies of the 2d Nebraska and of the 6th Iowa, under command of Major Pearman, 2d Nebraska, to hunt him up, and see if there were any Indians on the Missouri. The next day, however, Capt. LaBoo's company returned, having made a march of one hundred and eighty-seven miles, living upon what buffalo and game they could kill, scouring the country to my left, overtaking the camp of ten lodges he was sent after, destroying them, but seeing no Indians.

This same day, (29th,) I sent two companies of the 6th Iowa to the mouth of Apple creek. They reported, on their return, that they found the fortified camp of Gen. Sibley, his trail, and his return trail towards the east; that they could see no signs of there having been any fight there, nor could they see the Mackinaw boat reported by the old Indian. This detachment was under command of Captain Cram, 6th Iowa. The battalion of Major Pearman joined me before starting, having seen nothing, and, after a march of above ninety miles, through a country with no wood whatever, but with good grass and plenty of lakes, of the most abominable water. On the 3d of September, we reached a lake, where, on the plains near by, were the remains of a very large number of buffalo killed, some quite recently. Here I encamped, to wait the reports of the commands I had out, during the march, who, every day, discovered fresh signs of Indians, their lodge trails spread over the country, but all moving towards a point known to be a favorite haunt of the Indians. I had this day detailed one battalion of the 6th Iowa, Maj. House commanding, and Mr. F. La Framboise, as guide, to keep ahead of me five miles, and, in case they saw a small band of Indians, to attack them, or take them prisoners. If they should find a large band, too large to successfully cope with, to watch the camp at a distance, and send back word to me, my intention being to leave my train under charge of a heavy guard, move up in the night time, so as to surround them, and attack them at daybreak. But, for some reason, satisfactory to the guide, he bore off much to my left, and came upon the Indians, in an encampment of over four hundred lodges, some say six hundred, in ravines, where they felt perfectly secure, being fully persuaded that I was still on my way up the Missouri. This is what the Indian prisoners say. They also state that a war party followed me on my way up, in hopes of stampeding me; but this they could not do. I marched with great care, with an advance guard and flankers; the train in two lines, sixty paces apart; the troops on each side; in front and centre, myself, with one company and the battery; all the loose stock was kept between the lines of wagons. In this way, I lost no animals on the campaign, except some few, about a dozen, that got out of camp at night. Nor did the Indians, during all the trip, ever attack me, or try to stampede me.

Major House, according to my instructions, endeavored to surround and keep in the Indians until word could be sent me; but this was an impossibility with his 300 men, as the encampment was very large, mustering at least 1,200 warriors. This is what the Indians say they had; but I, as well as everybody in the command, say over 1,500. These Indians were partly Santees from Minnesota, Cut-heads from the Coteau, Yanktonais and Blackfeet, who belong on the other side of the Missouri; and, as I have since learned, Unkapapas, the same party who fought General Sibley, and destroyed the Mackinaw boat. Of this I have unmistakable proof, from letters and papers found in camp, and on the persons of some of the Indians, besides relics of the Minnesota massacre; also from the fact that they told Mr. La Framboise, the guide, when he was surrounded by about 200 of them, that "they had fought Gen. Sibley, and they did not see why the whites wanted to come and fight them, unless they were tired of living, and wanted to die." Mr. La Framboise succeeded in getting away from them, after some difficulty, and ran his horse a distance of more than ten miles, to give me information, Major House, with his command, still remaining there. He reached me a little after four o'clock. I immediately turned out my command. The horses, at the time, were out grazing. At the sound of the bugle, the men rushed, with a cheer, and in a very few minutes, saddled up and were in line. I left four companies, and all the men who were poorly mounted, in the camp, with orders to strike the tents and corral the wagons, and starting off with the 2d Nebraska on the right, the 6th Iowa on the left, one company of the 7th Iowa, and the battery in the centre, at a full gallop, we made the distance of over ten miles in much less than an hour.

On reaching near the ground, I found that the enemy were leaving and carrying off what plunder they could. Many lodges, however, were still standing. I ordered Col. Furnas, 2d Nebraska, to push his horses to the utmost, so as to reach the camp, and assist Major House in keeping the Indians corraled. This order was obeyed with great alacrity, the regiment going over the plains at a full run. I was close upon the rear of the regiment with the 6th Iowa. The 2d Nebraska took the right of the camp, and was soon lost in a cloud of dust, over the hills. I ordered Col. Wilson, 6th Iowa, to take the left, while I, with the battery, one company of the 7th Iowa, Capt. Millard, and two companies of the 6th Iowa, Major Ten Broeck commanding, charged through the centre of the encampment. I here found an Indian chief, by the name of Little Soldier, with some few of his people. This Indian has always had the reputation of being a "good Indian," and friendly. I placed them under guard, and moved on. Shortly after, I met with the notorious chief, Big Head, and some of his men. They were dressed for a fight, but my men cut them off. These Indians, together with some of their warriors, mustering about thirty, together with squaws, children, ponies and dogs, gave themselves up, numbering over 120 human beings. About the same time, firing began, about a half a mile from me, ahead, and was kept up, becoming more and more brisk, until it was quite a respectable engagement. A report was brought to me, (which proved to be false,) that the Indians were driving back some of my command. I immediately took possession of the hillocks near by, forming line, and placing the battery in the centre, on a high knoll. At this time, night had about set in, but still the engagement was briskly kept up, and in the melee it was hard to distinguish my line from that of the enemy. The Indians made a very desperate resistance, but finally broke and fled, pursued in every direction by bodies of my troops. I would here state, that the troops, though mounted, were armed with rifles, and, according to my orders, most of them dismounted and fought afoot, until the enemy broke, when they re-mounted and went in pursuit. It is to be regretted that I could not have had an hour or two more of daylight, for I feel sure, if I had, I could have annihilated the enemy. As it was, I believe I can safely say, I gave them one of the most severe punishments that the Indians have ever received. After night set in, the engagement was of such a promiscuous nature, that it was hard to tell what results would happen; I therefore ordered all the buglers to sound the "rally," and building large fires, remained under arms, during night, collecting together my troops.

The next morning, early, (the 4th,) I established my camp on the battle field, the wagon train, under charge of Major Pearman, 2d Nebraska, having, in the night, been ordered to join me, and sent out strong scouting parties, in different directions, to scour the country, to overtake what Indians they could; but in this they were not very successful, though some of them had some little skirmishes. They found the dead and wounded in all directions, some of them miles from the battle field; also immense quantities of provisions, baggage, &c., where they had apparently cut loose their ponies from "travailles," and got off on them; also numbers of ponies and dogs, harnessed to "travailles," running all over the prairie. One party that I sent out, went near to the James river, and found there, eleven dead Indians. The deserted camp of the Indians, together with the country all around, was covered with their plunder. I devoted this day, together with the following, (the 5th,) to destroying all this property, still scouring the country. I do not think I exaggerate in the least, when I say that I burned up over four or five hundred thousand pounds of dried buffalo meat, as one item, besides three hundred lodges and a very large quantity of property, of great value to the Indians. A very large number of ponies were found dead and wounded on the field; besides a large number were captured. The prisoners (some 130) I take with me below, and shall report to you more specially in regard to them.

The surgeon of the 2d Nebraska regiment, Dr. Bowen, who has shown a great energy and desire to attend to his duties during the campaign, started out during the night of the engagement with a party of fifteen men, to go back to the old camp to procure ambulances. But as they did not return on the morning of the second day, I knew he was either lost or captured. (He returned about noon of the second day.) I therefore sent out small scouting parties in every direction to hunt them up. One of these fell into an ambuscade, by which four of the party were killed and the rest driven in. I immediately sent out five companies of the 2d Nebraska regiment, Colonel Furnas in command, who, after a long march, found the Indians had fled. They succeeded, however, in overtaking three concealed in some tall grass, whom they killed. The fight has been so scattered, the dead Indians have been found in so many different places, that it is impossible for me to give an accurate report of the number killed of the enemy. I, however, think I am safe in reporting it at 100. (I report those that were left on the field and that my scouting parties found.)

During the engagement, for some time, the 2d Nebraska, afoot and armed with rifles, and there are among them probably some of the best shots in the world, were engaged with the enemy at a distance not over sixty paces, pouring on them a murderous fire in a ravine where the enemy were posted. The slaughter, therefore, was immense. My officers and the guides I have with me think one hundred and fifty will not cover their loss. The Indian reports make it two hundred. That the General may know the exact locality of the battle-field, I would state that it was, as near as I could judge, fifteen miles west of James river, and about half way between the latitudes of Bonebut and headwaters of Elm river, as laid down on the government map. The fight took place near a hill called by the Indians White Stone Hill.

In conclusion, I would state that the troops of my command conducted themselves well; and though it was the first that nearly all of them had ever been in, they showed that they are of the right material, and that in time, with discipline, they will make worthy soldiers. It is to be regretted that we lost so many valuable lives as we did, but this could not be helped; the Indians had formed a line of battle with good judgment, from which they could only be dislodged by a charge. I could not use my artillery without greatly endangering the lives of my own men; if I could, I could have slaughtered them.

I send you, accompanying, the reports of Colonel Wilson, 6th Iowa, and Colonel Furnas, 2d Nebraska, also official reports of killed and wounded, and take this occasion to thank both those officers for their good conduct and the cheerfulness with which they obeyed my orders on the occasion. Both of them had their horses shot in the action. I would also request permission to state that the several members of my staff rendered me every possible assistance.

On the morning of the 6th, I took up my line of march for Fort Pierre. If I could have remained in that section of country some two or three weeks, I might have accomplished more; but I was satisfied by the reports of my scouts that the Indians had scattered in all directions; some toward the James river; some, probably the Blackfeet, to recross the Missouri, and a part of them went north, where they say they have friends among the half-breeds of the north. My rations were barely sufficient with rapid marches to enable me to reach Fort Pierre. The animals, not only the *teams* I have already reported to you as worthless, but also the cavalry horses, showed the effect of rapid marching and being entirely without grain.

I brought with me all the prisoners I had, and tried to question them to gain some information. The men refused to say much, except that they are all "good Indians," and the other bad ones joined their camp without their will.

Their squaws, however, corroborate the report I have already given you in regard to the destruction of the people on board the Mackinaw boat and the fights with General Sibley, in which these Indians had a part. They also state that the Indians, after recrossing to this side of the Missouri, sent a party to follow Sibley until he went to the James river, then returned to their camp on Long lake to procure a large quantity of provisions and other articles they had "cached" there, and then came to the camp where I met them.

After marching about one hundred and thirty miles we reached the mouth of the Little Sheyenne on the 11th, where I found the steamboat I had ordered to be there on the 8th instant. It was lucky she was there, for without the grain she brought up I could not have brought my empty wagons back. For some miles north of Sheyenne and Pierre, the grass is about all gone. I placed my wounded on the boat, and as many empty wagons as she could carry. I am afraid the loss of horses and mules will be considered very great, but it could not be helped. When I found it *impossible* for the rear guard to get an animal along, I had it killed, to prevent its falling into the hands of the enemy.

Very respectfully, your ob't serv't,
ALF. SULLY,
Brigadier General Commanding.

P. S.—By actual count, the number of my prisoners is one hundred and fifty-six — men thirty-two, women and children one hundred and twenty-four. I would also beg leave to say that in the action, I had of my command between six hundred and seven hundred men actually engaged. My killed number, as far as ascertained, twenty; wounded, thirty-eight.

Very respectfully, your ob't serv't,
ALF. SULLY,
Brigadier General Commanding.

CHAPTER LXXV.

THE TIE OF COMRADESHIP — THE DEATH OF CHASKA.

"Among most of the Indian tribes of the North-west there exists a tie or degree of relationship, when entered into by two or more persons in good faith, which is more binding than any other known to the savage race. It is considered by them far more sacred than the matrimonial tie. It is the tie of comradeship! A man may, on any pretext whatever, throw away his wife and take another, if he chooses, but to his comrade he is firmly bound until death separates them. Nothing is considered more base or cowardly than to desert one's comrade in the hour of danger.

"Most white persons residing in the Indian country endeavor to select some Indian who is possessed of courage, intelligence and a good hunter, and who also can exert some influence over the band to which he belongs, for a comrade; knowing that in whatever situation he may be placed, it is in the power of his Indian friend to materially assist him.

"All Indian traders have comrades upon whom they rely to exert their influence to prevent the other Indians from trading their furs and skins with any one else, and to come up and pay their debts, which, as a general thing, they are not very prompt in doing. The Indian who stands in this relation to a trader, expects some valuable present from his 'ko-da' or friend, for his valuable service, and not unfrequently does he give in return the best he can afford — such as a horse, or his money when he receives his annuities, &c. But the circumstances of the two being taken into consideration, the Indian generally has the best of the bargain, for he is poor, and though he returns present for present, his offerings of friendship are of so little value, generally, that at the end of the year he is greatly your debtor. This tie involves the most implicit confidence in each other, and the idea of deceiving one's friend in any respect whatever, is held most dishonorable."

A compact like the foregoing had long existed between Wa-kin-yan-ta-wa, (which means in English His Thunder,) or Chaska, as more familiarly known to the whites, and George H. Spencer; and very valuable has the reader seen the practical workings of this tie to have been. The compact was formed in 1851 at Little Crow's Village, then located six miles below St. Paul, soon after their acquaintance commenced. Though an uncultivated Indian, he possessed much general intelligence, and was a young man of pleasing manners and address, rather good looking, with great energy and activity of mind. In 1857 he accompanied Little Crow and several of the Chiefs to Washington, to see their Great Father, relative to making a treaty for a portion of their Reservation. He was distinguished for bravery on the war path against the hereditary enemies of his tribe, and had taken the scalps of seven Chippewas, and also killed one of his own tribe, in revenge for the death of a brother. For several years previous to the late outbreak, he had held the dignified position of "Head Soldier" to Little Crow. But when he refused to act in that capacity, or to join in the war against the whites, then the ire of his chief was raised against him. The tie of comradeship was stronger than the tie of chieftainship. He could break the tie of the latter but not of the former.

When in 1860 his comrade built his trading house on the shores of Big Stone lake, Chaska, true to the existing relation, insisted on going with him, for, said he, "though you may risk yourself there, I will not risk you alone with those wild, strange Indians." So with wife and children he went, and remained till he deemed it safe to leave him. From such rare specimens of manhood have the noble attributes ascribed to the Indian character been drawn. But such are isolated exceptions. The general rule — the standard of estimate, appears in bloody boldness all through these pages. We love to present a contrast. Like a bright star in the rift of tempest-driven clouds, seems such an one amid the dark, evil plottings and evil workings of his own people. Though their lightnings should smite him, he was alike unmindful of persuasion or threats, when, in 1862, the horrid massacres commenced. We will not say that there was no leavening influence, which produced this pacific state, nor will we say it was wholly unmixed with selfishness — but we aver it was not the predominating idea.

When his comrade was shot, we have seen how Chaska, at the risk of his own life, true to the existing relation, saved him, taking him to his own lodge, washing and dressing his wounds, and caring for him, with all the watchful love of a tender brother. We have seen him active in forming the friendly camp, and getting the prisoners into it. We have seen him surrendering himself to General Sibley, for the crime of being an Indian, with a desire of being acquitted, before the world, of any complicity in the horrid massacres and war which followed. We have seen him avowing a readiness to comply with any terms which should elevate him to the dignity of the white man's standard of man.

"I am not pleased to see you in your blanket," said Gen. Sibley.

"Then I will wear it no more," was the prompt reply.

From that day, save in name and skin, Chaska was, to all intents and purposes, a white man. In the expedition he was very valuable as a scout, and was a universal favorite. We have seen him, just before the first battle with the Sioux, saving the life of Mr. Brackett, and in the fight conducting himself with great bravery. At the Missouri river, we hear him trying to persuade his friend to return to camp, urging, as a reason, I "do not like the way things look here, " a prophetic suggestion, for while they were yet speaking, came a shower of bullets from the woods and bushes of the opposite shore. Even then, Lieut. Beever had received the fatal arrow shot, and the woods must have been full of the foe.

The journey westward was completed. The order

for return had been read, and on the first of August, faces were turned homeward. Mr. Spencer says of it, "on the second, we rode along, talking pleasantly of the future, he telling me how he would like to be situated on a small piece of land near me, and congratulating himself that his trouble was over, and that he would soon be restored to the bosom of his family. Alas, for my friend! he now sleeps tranquilly near the turbid waters of the Missouri, under the shadows of our intrenchments. Savage though he was, he was a noble man!"

On the evening of the second day after camp was formed, he went round to his friend's tent, where he knew he was always welcome, and supped with him. He spoke of having captured a pack of furs from the enemy, which he desired to have taken home in a wagon of the Commissary Department; and for this purpose returned to the tent about nine o'clock in the evening, and then, in apparent health, went to his own quarters for the night. Immediately after he was taken ill, and sent for his comrade, who hastened to his bedside, to find him senseless—dying. He talked wildly, and predicted a thunder storm, such as should shake the earth, and blind the people with its light, the day he should be put into the ground, and it was as he predicted. He never once recognized the friend whose life he had saved, and who, with weeping heart, stood by him till the last, and closed his eyes at 11 o'clock the same evening, at the age of thirty-two. There were strong suspicions that poison, administered by some secret foe, was the cause of his death, but there was no time for investigation, and the following morning, August 3d, Mr. Spencer says, "we laid his body in a rifle pit, concealing it, as best we could, to prevent the enemy from finding it, and opening the grave. He leaves a wife and two interesting children, to mourn his untimely end," whom his friends and his country will not forget, for he was faithful among the faithless.

Rt

CHAPTER LXXVI.

HOME AGAIN.

Joy, such as only home lovers know, animated the hearts and enlivened the steps of the men. Their long, weary out-marches were ended, and all had left loved ones at home, whose hearts beat in unison with theirs to the return music. Every man in that long column had acted well his part, without which its history would be incomplete. Henceforth, more emphatically than ever, they are the sons of the State. A cautious and wise policy had been pursued, when a daring, dashing, reckless leadership would have brought irretrievable disaster to the expedition. Comparatively few casualties had occurred. God had evidently been with them, and nearly all were returning healthier, stronger, and wiser men than when they left. From nearly all hearts, devout thanksgiving arose, as the distance lessened between them and all held most dear. They had left their homes when June's fresh roses shed fragrance on their way, — through summer's intensest heat had wandered through dry and parched regions, — had met and driven the enemy, and now on the first flush of autumn's golden tints, return; making it, if not a complete, *a great success.* A halo of glory enshrouds these weary veterans of the prairies. The loud booming cannon announces their approach, and glad hearts bound with joy as they go forth to meet and welcome their return. A larger column of mothers, wives and children wait with open arms and hearts to receive them. Only a few look in vain for those who had gone forth, in the full flush of manhood, so full of life, of courage, and hope!* Hearts big with sympathy bid them be comforted with the hope of reunion in immortal life.

A halo of glory encircles the brow of the General commanding the expedition. High in the confidence of the nation, and better fitted for the work assigned him than any other man, — erect in manhood's glory, he stands. Human greatness has been thrust upon Nature's nobleman, and fittingly he has worn it all.

When a few hundred citizens around the region of St Anthony's Falls desired to be recognized as the Territory of Minnesota, no so fitting a person was found to represent their interests in Congress as Henry H. Sibley. When this vast territory emerged from its minority and took upon itself the privilege of State rights, its first elected Governor was Henry H. Sibley. Retiring to private life, as a true citizen, he always served its interests; and when called by executive power to this most important military post, he accepted the honor and girded on the armor. Promotion followed till he ranked among the higher military powers of the nation. Surrounded by all this halo of earthly glory, he draws near the spot where, in absence, memory has delighted to linger. But he is a man,

---

*The entire column was decreased but seven.

with the heart of a man, which has been sorely afflicted since his presence was missed from the home circle. How freshly, now he nears that spot, now that the responsibilities and excitement of the campaign are over, come up the forms of those there left. And how, like a surging billow, sweeps over the soul the reminder of the fact that two of those forms will not bound to meet him; two of those faces he will see no more there! The tramp of the "pale horse" has been heard in his dwelling, and has carried away his angel Mary and his only son Frank of eleven years, to a land where brighter and perpetual sunshine falls, and where shadows will not come. And here, at his own domestic hearth-stone, — here, grateful for its remaining blessings; — here, listening to the love notes of those left to breathe them — here, while he plans in more public capacity, for the finale of the war — till the last echo of the Dakotas' war-whoop shall have died on the ear, — here, with the heart-mellowing influences of home loves, we leave him; with the prayer that he may receive the full fruition of the promise that "*all things shall work together for good.*"

CONCLUSION.

Worth and merit form the only true basis for preferment in political, military or civic life. It is a pleasure to record the names of those whose laurels worn, were *won*, as of one and another conspicuous in this book.

When the war-clouds rose on our national horizon, the first tender of troops was made by Governor Ramsey, and as by a stamp of the foot arose the MINNESOTA FIRST, led on to a world-wide renown by Colonel Gorman* and Stephen Miller, second in command. With tear-full hearts we pause to lay the wreath we have wrought on the honored graves of the immortal slain, and crave a benison on its remnant of veteran heroes.

In response to the 300,000 call, Lieut. Col. Stephen Miller was placed in command of the SEVENTH, and in the home field, as on the Potomac, was deservedly popular. In October, 1863, Col. Stephen Miller was promoted to BRIGADIER GENERAL of volunteers, and the following month Brigadier General Stephen Miller was, by an overwhelming majority, elected GOVERNOR OF MINNESOTA.

---
* Since Brigadier General.

For Product Safety Concerns and Information please contact our EU
representative GPSR@taylorandfrancis.com
Taylor & Francis Verlag GmbH, Kaufingerstraße 24, 80331 München, Germany

www.ingramcontent.com/pod-product-compliance
Lightning Source LLC
Chambersburg PA
CBHW071235300426
44116CB00008B/1044